CHURCHES AND COMMUNITIES

Churches
and Communities

An approach to development in the local church

George Lovell and
Catherine Widdicombe

Search Press

First published in Great Britain in 1978
by Search Press Limited

Reprinted 1986

Printed and bound in Great Britain by
A. Wheaton & Co. Ltd, Exeter, Devon

Set IBM by ⫟\Tek-Art, Croydon, Surrey

ISBN 0 85532 387 6

Contents

This report of Project 70-75 has been prepared by the two full-time members of the project team (the Revd Dr George Lovell and Miss Catherine Widdicombe) with the help of their consultant (Dr T.R. Batten) and endorsed by the part-time members of the team (the Revd John V. Budd and Patrick Fitzgerald) and the recorder (Miss Elizabeth Rownan). It is, however, essentially the report of the two full-time workers and, whilst George Lovell has done most of the writing, it represents their joint views. They are equally committed to the ideas and conclusions it contains and together accept responsibility for them and the report.

Acknowledgments

We make our acknowledgments with deep gratitude: to the Grail who made the project possible by acting as sponsoring agency when the team's ideas were being considered by charitable trusts and when work had to be started without guarantees that adequate finance would be forthcoming – without their support it is highly doubtful if the project would have got off the ground; to the Methodist church, the Grail, the parishes of Hatfield and Little Amwell, and to the White Fathers, who all gave permission for people to serve the project; to the Calouste Gulbenkian Foundation, the Edward Cadbury Charitable Trust, the Nicholas Coote Trust, Caldey Abbey and anonymous donors who between them funded the project; to Mr Richard Mills of the Calouste Gulbenkian Foundation and to the secretary of another trust who contributed greatly to overcoming major difficulties through their understanding, concern and advice; to the Southwark Diocesan Housing Association Ltd for making one of their houses available to a member of the team and especially to Mr Laing who was so understanding; to the consultative groups, and advisers and church leaders for the time and trouble they took to consider our work, to discuss it with us and to raise critical issues; to Mr Ron Press for all that was involved in helping to make the most of the money available; to Molly Lovell who committed herself to the project when its financial viability was far from certain; to John Budd, Patrick Fitzgerald and Elizabeth Rownan for their colleagueship; to Reg Batten who opened our eyes to new ways of working with people, helped us to resolve innumerable problems, surmount daunting obstacles and who has made major contributions to the writing of this report and who, with his wife Madge, has encouraged and supported us as we have worked through the project – without their help and backing and the great amount of thought, time and energy they have contributed the project would have been a much poorer affair; to the clergy and church leaders in Ronsey for granting us the privilege of working and worshipping with them and for all that they contributed to this project; and to the late Dorothy Household for the practical and personal support that could only come from a person who had profound insights and deep concern about people.

Preface

The project described in this report was designed to test whether the ideas and methods associated with community development are as appropriate to the work of the churches as they are to the work of secular agencies engaged in various forms of neighbourhood and community work.

Such a project is particularly relevant at the present time. There is not much experience written up in such a way that church leaders, administrators and local clergy can make up their own minds about its value. Whilst George Lovell was the minister of the Parchmore Church Youth and Community Centre in South London, he tested the applicability of the non-directive approach to community development to the work in which he was engaged. He showed how the use of this approach brought new life to a local church and enabled it to help an increasing number of its neighbours meet their own needs. He concluded that it was applicable to work in the Methodist church and that it seemed likely that it would also be applicable to local church work of other denominations. He described the rewards and returns of working in this way and the many demands it makes upon ministers who really do adopt it. The Parchmore experience was thoroughly documented and written up as a PhD thesis but, as it has not been published, it is not generally available.

In fact, leaders, administrators, clergy and laity need to have much more precise information in order to assess for themselves whether or not they think that the values and methods associated with community development are entirely consonant with the beliefs, purposes and work of the Church; and in order to assess realistically what kinds of church work it is most appropriate for, and how practicable it may be for the churches to adopt it in view of its potential work implications for the rank and file of local clergy and church workers. For example, would clergy and church workers need to learn new skills? If so, just what skills and how could they acquire them?

Project 70-75 was planned to assist the churches to consider such questions by providing them with a detailed and objective record of experience gained while working with sixteen churches of seven different denominations in one typical 'Council of Churches' area. It was specifically designed to provide a rigorous test of the relevance of the non-directive community development approach in local church and neighbourhood work. It was an 'action-research' project in which the work done was carefully recorded and its results evaluated both by the project workers and by the clergy and the people with whom they worked. This report is based on those records and the conclusions finally reached are firmly grounded in what was learnt by all concerned from the work done. It describes the application of the action-research concept rather than the underlying ideas, since a description of the application of the concept is often the best way of explaining what it really means.

Project 70-75 concentrated on working with clergy and laity in ordinary church situations and this is reflected in this report which gives relatively little space to discussing the theory and theology of development. This emphasis is deliberate. The theory underlying the non-directive approach to community development is relatively easy to grasp, but it is much more difficult to comprehend its practical implications unless it is seen in action or, better still, experienced in action. And the theological implications can be determined only by reflecting upon the practical application of the non-directive approach to church and community work as well as upon the theory underlying it.

The project team consisted of one Roman Catholic laywoman (Catherine Widdicombe) and three clergy (John Budd, Anglican; Patrick Fitzgerald, Roman Catholic; and George Lovell, Methodist). They were assisted for three years by Elizabeth Rownan acting as recorder. All had independently recognized their need for new skills in order to become more effective in achieving their aims as church workers, and each had separately found them in the non-directive approach to working with people developed by Dr Batten on his Community Development and Extension Work Courses at the University of London Institute of Education. All had attended one of these courses, but it was Catherine Widdicombe of the Grail with whom the idea of the project originated and it was on her initiative that the four of them met in July 1970 for discussions which led to the inauguration of Project 70-75. They constituted themselves as the project team and asked Dr Batten to act as their consultant.

They initially envisaged a five-year project and hence its name, but it was later extended for a further year. The first two years were spent in negotiating with trusts, in preliminary planning and in searching for a suitably typical local area in which to work. During this period Catherine Widdicombe was full-time and the others very much part-time. George Lovell became a full-time worker in 1972 and with Catherine Widdicombe did the greater part of the field work during the third and fourth years. During the final two years George Lovell and Catherine Widdicombe conducted the overall evaluation of the work done and wrote the report.

Pseudonyms are used for the project area and for the churches within it partly because this makes it easier to write openly and partly because it safeguards the local area from becoming a church and community development 'gold fish bowl'.

Introduction

This report describes what the team and the churches discovered about the usefulness of a particular way of promoting development in the local church. Essentially this approach involves working with the individual churches as institutions, starting where they are and working *with* rather than *for* them. It is based upon ideas, practices and methods which have become an established part of *the non-directive approach to community development work*. This approach is based upon the fact that personal and religious betterment occur when people themselves are engaged in promoting both their own inner growth and the improvement of their physical and social environment. It is therefore about self-development, self-help, self-determination and self-direction. It is about what one person (a 'worker') can do to help others to help themselves: that is, what he can do to stimulate and help people to think freely about themselves (their beliefs, purposes and needs) and about others and their needs; to discuss their thoughts and feelings openly and objectively; to decide what they are going to do and how they are going to do it; to reflect critically on what happened; and in the light of their conclusions to decide what to do next.

Prior to Project 70-75 each member of the team had independently learnt from experience that this approach could revitalize people. They had seen people in the church and in the community brought to life as they really thought for themselves, discussed openly and objectively, decided freely and, in the light of all the available information, planned thoroughly and realistically, organized themselves in their own way and acted together as best suited them to achieve what they believed to be important. Those who previously had accepted passively what had been done for them became actively involved in working with others. 'We' feelings emerged. People gained new dignity, greater self-confidence and self-respect; and they grew in mutual concern and responsibility. These experiences helped members of the team to understand those aspects of the living process of development which cannot easily be described. As they saw in reality, rather than in theory, what constitutes development and how to promote it, they were reminded of Jesus: of his claim that he had 'come that men may have life, and may have it in all its fulness' and of the way in which he had brought people to life by getting them to think, to discuss, to decide and to choose.

Intuitively they knew, and all subsequent experience has proved this intuition correct, that this approach is consistent with the ministry of Jesus and New Testament Christianity, in that it enables them to minister more purposefully and effectively to people in the church and in the community. Here were ways of translating Christian ideology into practice; of working for a better Church and a better world populated by better people; of helping people themselves to create the kind of environment in which their material and non-material needs could be met; of helping people to make their community a more satisfying place in which to worship, work and relax; of helping people to make that contribution towards their own development and to their own salvation that they alone can make; and of helping people to do all these things and more without invading their privacy or compromising their autonomy. Here indeed was an approach which emphasized what people can do for themselves without denying what God and people are doing and will continue to do for them; and which showed the team how to work for the inter-related development of people and their environment, of church and community, and to give positive expression to those beliefs and experiences of God which motivated them. New possibilities opened before them as they began to see how the resources of Christianity and the Church could be used for the development of church and community. And this for them was Christian mission.

It was these things that led them to learn how to use this approach; to try it out in their own work; to begin to see its potential relevance to clergy and laity of different denominations trying to help church and non-church people to find deeper satisfaction for their personal, social and spiritual needs in urban or rural, in stable or transitory communities and which later led them to commit themselves to Project 70-75.

Just what the non-directive approach to church and community work means in practice becomes clear in this report but in general it involved the team:

– *asking unloaded questions designed to get the people they worked with seriously to think about their beliefs and purposes, and the problems they had in trying to promote them;* (these questions were variously designed to get people to decide just what it was they wished to consider; to base their thinking on facts rather than opinions; to consider the pros and cons of every alternative open to them; and to avoid unproductive argument. In tackling problems for example, this meant asking questions such as: What is the problem? What makes it a problem for you? Do you want to discuss it? Why does the problem occur? Why has it arisen? What can we do about it? How?)

– *stimulating people to explore the relationship between their beliefs, purposes and approaches to working with people;*

– *providing information;*

– *introducing structure into the processes of discussion and decision making,* (that is, working to get people to systematize their thinking in relation to all the available information);

– *creating an atmosphere in which people felt free to say openly what they really felt.*

'Non-directive' is a very negative-sounding word to denote work of such a positive and demanding kind but whereas the English language is full of words such as lead, guide, tell, advise, instruct, teach, cajole, manipulate, force or threaten — all of which suggest action to direct people towards some pre-determined end — there is not even one word which suggests a role in which one concentrates on encouraging and assisting people to think realistically and responsibly in order to arrive at their own considered decisions for themselves, that is, in which one acts as a non-directive worker. Thus in this report it is frequently necessary for lack of anything better, to say that the team 'stimulated', 'encouraged', or 'enabled' or 'helped' people to think, decide and act, or 'supported' them as they did so, although none of these words is really indicative of what the team did and all of them, unfortunately, can suggest condescension. Again it is often necessary to refer to the team 'getting people to do such and such'. Generally this means that someone decides just what they want others to do and 'gets' them to do it whereas, in fact, the team was concerned to 'get' people to do whatever they themselves wanted to do. These words are used in this report to indicate that a member of the team was carrying out one or other of the functions of a non-directive 'worker'.

PART ONE:
SETTING UP THE PROJECT

NOTE Should you prefer first to get to grips with the work done on schemes, start at Part Three and then read Parts One and Two which describe how Project 70-75 was set up and how the work programme evolved.

1 The project

WHAT THE TEAM SET OUT TO ACHIEVE

Project 70-75 was designed to provide as many people as possible in the Christian churches with an objective record of the work done and the results obtained through the use of the non-directive approach in a group of typical local churches of several denominations so that they would then be able:

1. to assess for themselves the potential value in local church work of using the non-directive approach as a means of promoting their Christian purposes both in their relationships with each other and with people outside the churches; and

2. to think realistically about whether or not they would adopt the same approach themselves in local church work.

This was the team's overall purpose and throughout the project it gave direction to their work.

The area in which this group of local churches is situated is referred to either as 'the project area' or 'the local area' or 'Ronsey'. Members of the team had not previously worked in it.

HOW THE TEAM SET OUT TO ACHIEVE IT

Two of the principal difficulties members of the team foresaw in achieving their purpose affected the overall design of the project.

First, they were acutely aware of the difficulty of getting people to understand just what using the non-directive approach implied in terms of actual work. They aimed to overcome this difficulty by consistently using the non-directive approach themselves; and by providing key people at all levels in the churches with down-to-earth progress reports about how the approach was actually applied in conducting the project in the field.

Second, they foresaw great difficulties in stimulating sufficient interest in people in the churches to ensure that they thoroughly considered the results of the project and followed this up with appropriate action. They realized it would be difficult to get them to consider the results of the project if, prior to the publication of the final report, they had known little or nothing of the work. In fact, the chances of such a report being considered were slight as the churches would see it as a report about field work in a local area conducted by a small group of comparatively unknown people who had acted on their own. The team aimed to overcome this difficulty by trying to involve key people and groups in the churches from the beginning and especially those who, when the report was published, would be in a position to promote discussions about it.

21

Project 70-75 was what is commonly known as an action-research programme. This means in effect that the work done was continuously assessed for what could be learnt from it, and that whatever was learnt was ploughed back into the project to inform future decisions and future action. Thus members of the team kept full and complete records of everything they did, why they did it and with what observable results — including what the people they worked with said and did both as the work proceeded and after it had been completed. Wherever possible, these records were checked with those involved.

This interplay between experience and reflection, between doing and learning and between action and research was maintained throughout.

AROUSING INTEREST AND GAINING SUPPORT

Once members of the team had decided to put their idea into practice they identified four immediate objectives: to establish agreed purposes for the project and how they planned to achieve them; to attract finance; to obtain permission to work on Project 70-75; and to stimulate interest in the project and seek commitment to its purposes among people in the churches and other agencies.

Establishing agreed purposes for the project and how to achieve them

In order to do this they had to share and discuss their beliefs, ideas, experiences and concerns about church and community work. It was these discussions over several months which, more than anything else, established the clarity of purpose and mutual understanding which enabled them to work through the problems they subsequently encountered. Indeed they worked together so closely that people later asked how they could do this in spite of their very different denominational backgrounds to which they were so obviously faithful. A major part of the answer lies in the trouble they took, urged and helped by their consultant, to establish their aims, to state them unambiguously and to understand each other's motivation.

During these discussions they produced a short booklet to help them to explain their ideas to the wide variety of people they would meet as they pursued the other three objectives. It set out what they felt about community development and the mission of the church and described their purposes for the project.

Achieving this objective formed the members into a team.

Attracting finance

Mr Ronald Press A.C.C.A. acted as honorary accountant to the project. He budgetted the cost of the project as £38,867 but this was reduced to £33,142 through the Grail waiving the whole of Catherine Widdicombe's salary for the first year and £1,000 for each of four subsequent years. The remaining cost was met by the Calouste Gulbenkian Foundation, Lisbon (£15,000); the Edward Cadbury Charitable Trust (£1,000); the Nicholas Coote Trust (£100); and the balance was raised through various private donations.

Two of the trust secretaries also drew on their wide experience of other projects to alert the team members to some of the problems they were later to face.

Obtaining permission to work on Project 70-75

John Budd had permission from his parish to work one day a week and Patrick Fitzgerald from the White Fathers to work on the project part-time for two years. Catherine Widdicombe had permission from the Grail to serve the project full-time. The need for a second full-time worker was met by the Methodist church agreeing to George Lovell working on the project full-time from September 1972.

Stimulating interest and seeking commitment

In pursuit of this objective members of the team consulted some seventy people in positions of authority or influence in the churches or with specialist knowledge of community work. They had interviews with sixty-eight of these people and corresponded with the others. (See Appendix I)

All those consulted felt that it was important that local churches should strengthen community both among their own members and in their neighbourhoods, but they felt equally strongly that churches should obtain more of the kind of information and experience the project could provide before committing themselves and their resources to church and community development programmes. Therefore, they were in favour of the project taking place and wanted to be kept in touch with developments.

Some of the people consulted, however, doubted whether the project would succeed. They said that the members of the team would be seen by people in the local area as 'outsiders' and that they would find it very hard to get people to understand just what they meant by 'community development', or to get them to consider the validity of using the non-directive approach in church and community work and to use this approach themselves in churches with an authoritarian structure, or to deal with tension and conflict, or to find and train people as voluntary community development workers, or to get groups to share church premises and other resources with non-church groups. Subsequently the team did, in one way or another, face each of these difficulties.

23

Consulting so many people and recording, analysing and working out the implications of what they had said was time-consuming but also extremely profitable. It was profitable not only because many people thereby became interested in the project, but also because in the process many of them had become more aware of the relevance of community development to the work of the churches. It also produced much constructive criticism and helpful advice, some of which led directly to the team setting up a panel of advisers and a panel of consultative groups to receive and pass to others information about the project; to comment from their particular viewpoints on the project as it proceeded; to draw out the implications for the churches of working in this way; and to advise on specific issues or problems. (The members of panels are listed in Appendix I.)

Members of the team kept their advisers and consultative groups informed of developments by means of progress reports, newsletters and other memoranda and from time to time sought their advice on specific points.

THE PROJECT STRUCTURE

Thus, the final project structure evolved through members of the team discussing amongst themselves and with a wide range of people how best they could achieve their purposes. This structure is represented diagramatically on p. 25.

DIARY OF EVENTS

July 1970	Project team formed
	Dr T.R. Batten agreed to act as consultant to the project
January 1971	*Project booklet* produced
	Mr R. Press agreed to act as honorary accountant
	Consultations with some seventy people in positions of authority or influence in churches or with specialist knowledge of community work
	Consultations ended in December 1971
April 1971	The Methodist church agreed to release George Lovell from September 1972 to August 1975 to be a full-time worker to the project
May 1971	Negotiations for funds started with secular and denominational trusts. Donations received from two trusts and private sources and a promise of support from another trust
June 1971	Panel of advisers and consultative groups formed

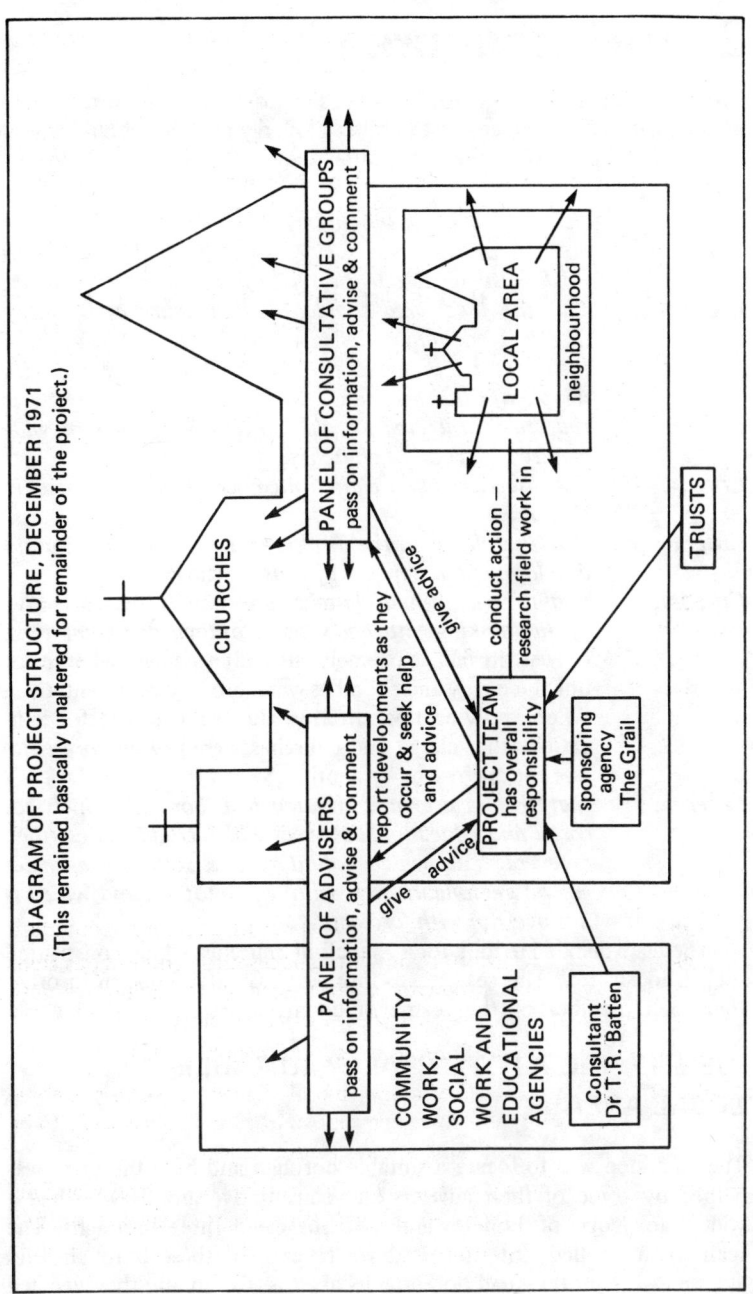

DIAGRAM OF PROJECT STRUCTURE, DECEMBER 1971
(This remained basically unaltered for remainder of the project.)

PANEL OF CONSULTATIVE GROUPS
pass on information, advise & comment

LOCAL AREA

neighbourhood

CHURCHES

give advice

conduct action —
research field work in

PROJECT TEAM
has overall
responsibility

sponsoring
agency
The Grail

TRUSTS

report developments as they
occur & seek help
and advice

give advice

PANEL OF ADVISERS
pass on information, advise & comment

COMMUNITY
WORK, SOCIAL
WORK AND
EDUCATIONAL
AGENCIES

Consultant
Dr T.R. Batten

2 The local area

The team felt that it was crucial to the success of the project to choose an area with which the greatest number of clergy and laity would find it easy to identify. After much discussion they decided on the following criteria:

Criterion 1:   *that the local area should be reasonably representative of contemporary urban society so that the lessons learnt might also be felt to be relevant to many other areas.*

Criterion 2:   *that the local area should contain churches of many different denominations whose clergy and church members are prepared to work both together and with people of other agencies.*

Criterion 3:   *that the local area should contain a reasonably wide variety of 'types' of churches.*

Criterion 4:   *that the clergy and church members want the project in their area.*

Criterion 5:   *that the clergy in the local area do not see community development as a means of proselytizing.*

Criterion 6:   *that the clergy and churches are broadly representative of the thinking, faith and worship of their denominations;* (it was, in fact, extremely difficult to assess whether or not the clergy and churches were 'broadly representative'. When applying this criterion the team looked for indications that clergy and churches were *not unrepresentative* for one reason or another.)

Criterion 7:   *that the local area is situated in a borough which has social and educational services which could be described as average; in which voluntary and statutory agencies get on reasonably well with one another; and which is not overrun with 'projects'.*

The team decided to look for a council of churches which constituted such a local area. The search was limited to Greater London in order that each member of the team could participate in the field work.

IDENTIFYING A POTENTIALLY SUITABLE LOCAL AREA

The first step was to locate a suitable borough and here the team was helped by some of their advisers and consultative groups who had a wide knowledge of London and who suggested three boroughs. The team then applied criterion 7 above to each of these boroughs and assessed whether they had potential local areas. Eventually they decided in favour of an outer London borough which met criterion 7, had five councils of churches and therefore five potential local areas, and was more easily accessible to members of the team than the other two. Of these it appeared that the Ronsey Council of Churches was the one most likely to be suitable. It contained sixteen churches of seven different denominations and a local Y.M.C.A. centre. *(See Appendix II)*

The report of a recent sociological survey and the team's own observations indicated that Ronsey was reasonably representative of contemporary urban society, and therefore would meet criterion 1. It also seemed likely that the churches in Ronsey would probably fit criteria 2, 3, 5 and 6, although this and criterion 4, could only finally be tested on the spot in discussions with the local people.

NEGOTIATIONS IN RONSEY

The team foresaw many difficulties in getting to know just what the clergy and laity in Ronsey thought about the idea of locating the project in their area because all too often views are expressed and decisions taken by only a few people who claim to speak on behalf of others but who, in practice, rarely consult them first. Tackling these difficulties involved deciding just who to approach first, and in what way. Eventually the team decided to start by approaching local churches rather than the borough authorities; to approach the churches through the clergy since they were the key people through whom to approach the laity; to contact the clergy through their fraternal so that they would all hear about the project at the same time and react to it as a group; and, if they reacted favourably, to work out with them how churches should be involved in subsequent discussions.

The clergy reach their decision

The 'fraternal', an informal monthly meeting for local clergy of different denominations in the area covered by the Ronsey Council of Churches, was well supported by clergy of seven denominations (Anglican, Baptist, Congregationalist, Methodist, Moravian, Roman Catholic and Church of Christ). Its members varied enormously in their theological outloook, their churchmanship and their understanding of community work, and, as their ages ranged from early twenties to late sixties, they represented different stages in the working lives of clergy.

The first meeting

The team attended two meetings of the fraternal. At the first meeting the team explained how non-directive workers promote community development processes; the developments that can occur in people and their communities through these processes; how the concept is applicable to work both in the church and its neighbourhood; and how projects can become interrelated developments in a church and the community of which it is a part. Each aspect was illustrated by diagrams and examples.

The clergy said they were engaged in community work but that these ideas were new to them and that *the non-directive community development approach was not their accustomed way of working*. They said it would 'change our whole way of working in the churches', 'cause us to reassess what we are doing', 'involve us in a great deal of hard work' but also 'help our people to work out why they are doing what they are doing'. They appeared to have gained some understanding of the general principles and expressed a strong desire to consider the underlying theological ideas.

Further discussion, however, showed that the clergy found it difficult to grasp just what the project would mean for them in terms of work. They wanted 'concrete examples'. They asked whether playgroups were a form of community development work. The team tried to answer this question by describing two ways in which churches could get a play-group established: they could provide and run it for mothers and their children, or they could help the mothers to organize it for themselves. It was the second way, they said, which illustrated the community development approach. The team members, using diagrams, got the clergy discussing the differences between the two ways of working. This helped some, but not all, to see that whatever the group activity might be, it is the way things get done that distinguishes community develop-ment. During this discussion the team, again by way of illustration, said that some churches might wish to form a local task force to tackle some community problems. The clergy responded to this idea with enthusiasm.

The team members again with the help of diagrams, explained what they were trying to achieve through the project and how they aimed to do it. The 'how', they said, involved the team members and those with whom they worked, taking carefully planned action, evaluating what happened and, in the light of what was learnt, deciding what to do next. This they described as a systematic 'doing-learning-doing' process. Only when the clergy got hold of this concept did the team say that this was known as 'action-research'. It was clearly understood by the clergy that what was learnt, in addition to guiding future action in the area, would also be made available to people outside the local area. The clergy agreed with the team's ideas about how they intended to work and the use to which they would put what was learnt.

The second meeting
One of the fraternal opened the discussion by saying that he thought the clergy ought to decide for or against the project at once and, if they decided for it, they should then talk about it to their churches. (He 'could guarantee his church would approve'). Others spoke in much the

same vein: 'I can easily sell the project to my people'; 'I always soft-pedal any scheme I want my people to accept' and *'L'état c'est moi'*. The team was unhappy about this because it implied that the clergy had already made up their minds to have the project in their area before they had even told their church members about it: whereas the team wanted lay people to be equally involved. The team members therefore suggested that the clergy might alternatively get their people to discuss the project thoroughly and make up their minds for themselves. Then they got the clergy to consider what effect using either approach was likely to have. (By using the first approach the clergy might gain the apparent support of people but not necessarily their commitment; by using the second they would know whether the people really were for or against the project.) In the end they agreed to let their people decide for themselves, although they said that they felt worried because they wanted the project and were afraid that their people might not!

The clergy felt that their next step should be to involve the Ronsey Council of Churches. The council was modelled on the pattern reco-mmended by the British Council of Churches. It had a chairman (clerical or lay), and an executive of fourteen members. Each member church was entitled to be represented at council meetings by its clergy and four lay representatives.

Suggestions about how to involve the council proliferated, only to be dropped when points against them were made. This made a team member think that the members of the fraternal were unclear about their relationship to the executive and the council. He therefore used information provided by the clergy to construct a simple diagram of the relationship between them. After studying the diagram, the clergy said that they had not previously conceptualized these relationships and now realized how ill-defined they were. Much too much, they said, depended on informal contacts. Also there were serious organi-zational gaps. The team member then asked them, in the light of their situation as they now saw it, to reconsider the approaches they had already suggested with a view to choosing the best. Now the discussion became specific and constructive. Each suggestion was related to the actual situation by reference to the diagram, and each contribution added to or complemented some previous point. Thus in a comparatively short time, and taking account of all the points made previously, they decided that:

1. they were unanimously in favour of having the project in Ronsey;

2. they would supply the team with information about their churches by filling in questionnaires; (the significance of this unsolicited offer and the fact that all of them completed the questionnaires, is enhanced by the negative way in which they had recently responded to a questionnaire from the local authority asking them about the use to

which their church buildings were put;

3.   the final decision must be made by clergy and church people together;

4.   the council, because it represented churches of different denominations which might be involved separately or together had an important role to play in initiating discussions;

5.   they would ask the executive to introduce the project and the team to the council, and through them to the local church people;

6.   a working party should be set up to recommend to the fraternal and the executive how best to get the project considered by as many people as possible.

These decisions were not taken lightly for they represented a very different approach from that normally adopted and the clergy were apprehensive about committing themselves to discuss with their people something they still felt they did not fully understand.

The churches and the council reach their decision

In due course the working party produced a plan but stressed that it should not be treated as a blueprint to be rubber stamped. One of their number introduced the plan to both the fraternal and the executive by building up a diagram stage by stage and asking for comments and suggestions. (He had not previously used diagrams but he used one now because he found those used by the team extremely beneficial.) In the event, the plan was adopted by both the fraternal and the executive with one important modification, and it was implemented in five main steps.

Step one: Lent house groups

A local clergyman described the project briefly at the introductory session of the inter-church Lent house groups. Because of the project the executive had decided that their theme for 1972 should be 'The biblical concepts of community'.

Step two: Distribution of leaflets

The secretaries of the executive and the fraternal, with help from the team, wrote a leaflet briefly describing the project. Over eight hundred copies were distributed during March and April 1972.

Step three: The open council meeting

In April 1972 a special open council meeting attended by one hundred and fifty people from sixteen churches considered a report from the Lent groups which said that the project would enable the council to work towards the concept of community life they had found described in the Bible. The team described community development, the project and the task force suggestion with the help of flannelgraphs. They did this to avoid the kind of difficulties they had experienced in explaining community development and the project to the clergy. They encouraged people to ask questions, especially those related to any reservations they might have. Their aim was to assist people to understand the project and its implications and to leave them to decide on the next steps. The council made arrangements for each individual church to be consulted and deferred making its decision until it knew what their views were.

Step four: Meetings held by individual churches
The flannelgraphs were used by some of the clergy at a number of local church meetings which meant that the people who attended them heard very much the same story about the project as those who had attended the open council meeting. All sixteen churches decided to associate themselves with the project.

Step five: Decision by the council
The council at its annual general meeting held in May 1972 considered the decisions made by the churches and said it wished to be associated with the project.

The sequence of events in this decision-making process is set out in the diagram on p. 32.

THE TEAM'S RESPONSE

Discussing the project with clergy and church members in Ronsey provided the team with the information needed in order to decide whether or not it was a suitable local area.

The team had found that the churches did in fact represent a wide variety of denominations, theological emphases, schools of churchmanship, forms of worship and patterns of church work. The approaches used in Christian education varied from direct biblical teaching to experiential methods. Most of the clergy and people expressed their faith traditionally and conducted their worship in ways typical of their denominations. Some used experimental forms of worship and a small minority tended to be radical. The churches in varying degrees ministered both to 'working' class and 'middle' class people: the Roman Catholic to more working-class than middle-class people, and the others to more middle-class than working-class people. The team also found that the churches in Ronsey and their clergy were working together in many ways and some were co-operating with other agencies.

The decisions made by the clergy, the churches, the fraternal, the executive and the council, and the way they were made, seemed to the team to show beyond doubt that the great majority of the people involved wished the project to be located in Ronsey and desired to be associated with it. They said they wanted the team to help them solve

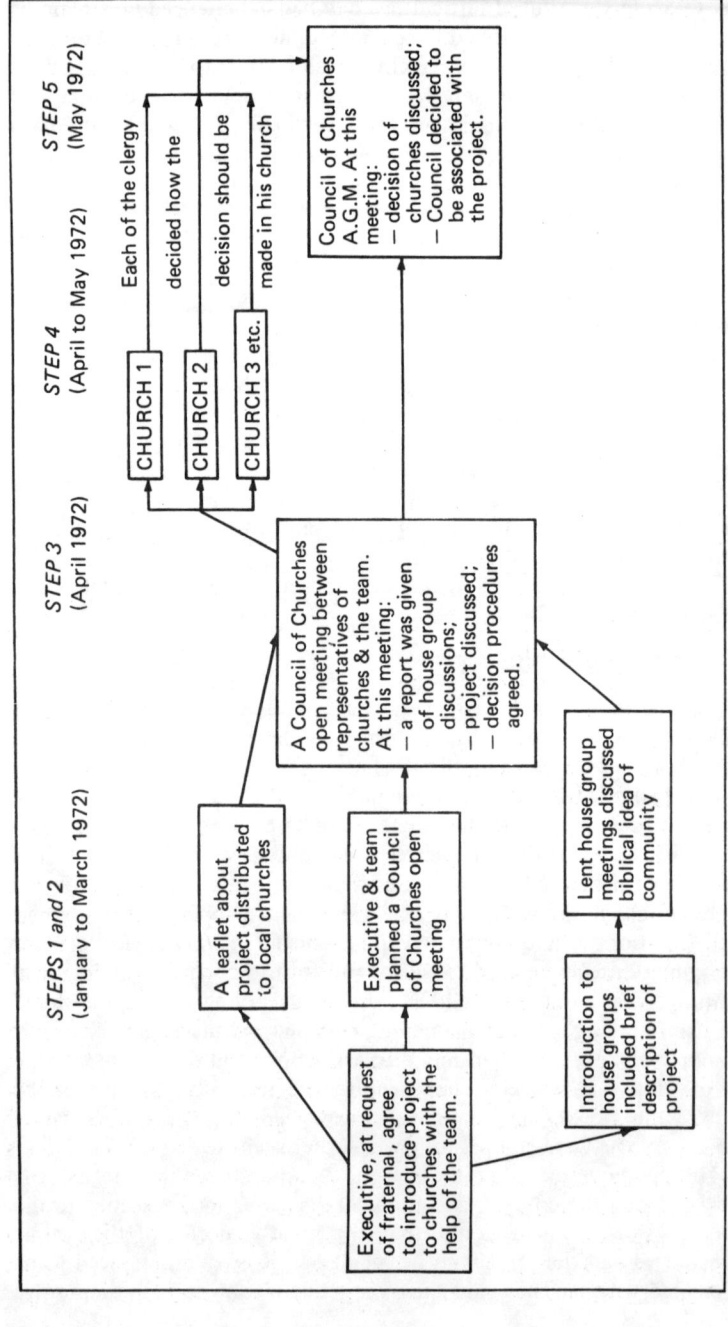

DIAGRAM SHOWING THE STEPS BY WHICH THE PROJECT WAS PRESENTED TO THE CHURCHES

their church and community problems; to encourage them to work together; to help them to do more effective work with their neighbours; to give new momentum to the work of the churches and the council; and to explore the relevance of community development to the work and mission of the Church. The decisions were made in an atmosphere of real acceptance. Therefore, the team felt that they would be able to establish the mutual trust and understanding needed in a successful action-research partnership.

All the evidence suggested that clergy and people saw community development as a way of achieving their Christian purposes for a better world populated by better people and not as a means of proselytizing.

Therefore the team welcomed the offer the people had made and accepted it so that Ronsey became the local area for Project 70-75.

ASSESSMENT AFTER THE TEAM WITHDREW

(After the team had withdrawn from the local area those with whom they had worked evaluated what had occurred. How they did this and the overall results are described in Part Four chapters 1 and 2. What people said about the discussions which led to the project being located in Ronsey are summarized here.)

The assessment showed that some people felt the decision-making process to be ideal. One said, 'The discussions were full and frank, and gave people ample time to consider and understand'. Others felt that it had been too long drawn out and that too much time had been spent on 'useless detail'. Yet others felt that insufficient time had been given to the discussions: 'Initially the team should have moved at a much slower pace because clergy and church leaders were being asked to change from their traditional ways of working'.

There was general agreement that the visual aids had been helpful.

The assessment also showed that the discussions had helped some people to understand the ideas and the implications of the project but had perplexed others. One person said, 'The discussions, at first mystifying, were satisfactory. We were clearly told that the team was not proposing to tell us what to do, but to guide us in developing community in the area according to the needs as we saw them'.

The fraternal felt that the team members would have got through to the people more effectively had they talked (or preached) about their beliefs before describing church and community development work.

The initial responses to the team varied greatly. Some who wanted help were 'dubious about what the team could do from outside'. Others were initially rather cynical about the proposed activities and thought 'Here we go with another lot of do-gooders who will divert people's attention from existing projects', but, they said, 'we soon realized how wrong we were'. One person said, 'It would have been easier if emphasis had been at first on internal church situations rather than the community at large.'

COMMENTS BY A CONSULTATIVE GROUP

A consultative group commended the way decisions were made. One of its members who had been employed by a Council of Churches as a community development worker said, 'In my case the people did not feel involved because they had not made the initial decision that I should be employed by their council'. This, he said, did not impair his ability to work in the community but it made it very difficult for him to involve the churches in community work.

PART TWO:
HOW THE WORK
PROGRAMME EVOLVED

Introduction

During the discussions about locating the project in Ronsey the local people said they were prepared to be partners in an action research project but did not want to become 'guinea pigs'. The team sympathized with these feelings. This concern led to a discussion about the nature of the work involved in the project. The team explained that it would consist of the schemes the clergy and local people themselves decided on and assured them that clergy and local churches would retain control throughout. It was then agreed that *'the work programme would be of value only if it was done for its own sake and for its learning potential'*. This allayed their fears.

Since the team's work programme was designed to assist the clergy and laity in Ronsey in relation to *their* work programme the term 'work programme' can refer either to the team's work or to that of the clergy and the laity. For example, a parish visiting scheme would be first and foremost the responsibility of the clergy and laity who had decided on it, but the team also had a part to play and that part was an aspect of the team's work programme. To minimize confusion, 'project work' is used to denote the team's work and 'schemes' to denote the work of the clergy and laity.

All the work the team did in Ronsey was of the non-directive kind.[1] This particularly needs to be borne in mind while reading the next few chapters. Words such as 'help', 'assist', 'enable', 'encourage', 'stimulate' and 'support' are used to indicate non-directive action except where otherwise stated. (cf. p. 14) Further, references to the team 'helping' or 'assisting' people may convey the idea that the team members took over some of the duties or responsibilities of the people with whom they were working. The team did not 'take over' anyone's work nor did they do it for them. Again, there are many references to the team 'getting people to do something'. In general usage this means that someone decides just what they want others to do and 'gets' them to do it whereas, in fact, the team was concerned to 'get' people to do what they themselves wanted to do. In spite of this problem of double meanings the writers have had to use these and similar words since no satisfactory alternatives are available to indicate that team members were carrying out the functions of a non-directive worker.

---

[1] This is true even though at times it was necessary to act directively in order to create situations in which to work non-directively with people (see p. 70) and at other times the team did so by mistake (see pp. 68-69).

1 Working with churches as institutions

During the discussions which preceded the decision to locate the project in Ronsey the team had given prominence to the idea of setting up a task force — volunteers from various churches to undertake community development schemes in Ronsey. This idea had appealed to members of the team. They felt that as the task force got to work it could provide the churches with a demonstration of the community development process which would stimulate the individual churches to adopt this approach to their work with their members and neighbours. Clergy and church people in Ronsey had been attracted by the idea and some had volunteered their services.

However, when team members mentioned this to their consultant he expressed doubts. Were they sure that this was the right approach? Or might the balance of advantage, after all, be in favour of each individual church evolving its own programme of community development work?

These questions led to some heart searching. It became clear that the task force would actually involve a relatively small number of volunteers working for betterment in the community. It would not, therefore, give clergy and lay workers direct experience of promoting development in their own churches. It could, in fact, make it more difficult for churches themselves to promote development because it would deprive them of the services of the very people able to undertake the necessary work.

Basing the work on individual churches, on the other hand, would mean that each church would be free to evolve its own development programme tailored to its own needs and those of its immediate neighbourhood. It would give clergy and church workers experience of adopting the community development approach in their own churches before trying to use it in the community; and it would give them greater freedom to decide what they wanted to do. Therefore, through this option, the clergy and churches would be more likely to become initiators of community development processes. And this in turn would make it more likely that the work would continue after the team had withdrawn.

For these reasons members of the team decided that in the work they did in Ronsey they should *aim to involve as many individual churches as possible in promoting development amongst their own members and their neighbours*.

In order to determine what this would imply for the work programme they listed all the possible openings which had emerged during the discussions about locating the project in Ronsey. These included opportunities for working on two church community centre schemes and a good neighbour scheme, and of discussing church and community development work with the fraternal and church committees. These opportunities related directly to the second option – a fact obscured by the previous emphasis on 'task force'. Team members based their suggestions for the initial work programme on all these possible openings and the proposals they eventually made to the executive came under four heads: work with clergy; work with individual churches: work with ecumenical groups; and work with ecumenical organizations.

The team discussed all this with the executive in June 1972. At first the members of the executive were bewildered and found it difficult to grasp what the team was talking about. When they did understand they felt very concerned about the possible adverse effects of introducing at such a late stage a change of emphasis which they thought amounted to a change of policy. But once they had really grasped the options and their implications, they fully agreed with the team that the change should be made, they accepted the work proposals and wanted work to start as soon as possible. However, they now thought it advisable to consult the council before asking the team to start work. The council, and subsequently the fraternal, agreed with the executive and thus the team was given the go-ahead. The council also decided to hold an open meeting in October 1972 to consider developments.

(Some of the team's advisers were critical of these developments. Their criticisms are considered in Part Three chapter 6.)

THE INITIAL WORK PROGRAMME

Work with clergy

The team members discussed their work proposals with the fraternal and they were asked to conduct the training course described in Part Two chapter 3.

Work with individual churches

During September and October 1972, the team members, after consultation with the fraternal and the executive, visited thirteen church committees (five Anglican, two Baptist, one Congregational and Church of Christ, three Methodist, one Roman Catholic and one United Reformed Church) and five church groups (one Moravian, three Roman Catholic and an ecumenical group of young adults). They described the work proposals and the ideas on which they were based; explained the non-directive approach to community development as working *with* rather than *for* people; stated how they could help churches wishing to adopt this approach in their work and offered to work with churches on their schemes.

The team found that the church people had not realized that this approach to community development was as relevant within their churches as it was outside them. They had seen it only as a way of meeting needs of people outside their churches and as such involving more work. As the churches were already short of manpower, this had had the effect of making many church people unwilling to become involved. (The initial emphasis on a task force had undoubtedly helped to create this misconception.) Some committees, once they realized that this approach could also help them with church work, talked freely about the problems they were facing. Others insisted they had no problems. Others again now thought only in terms of how the approach might help them in their church. The team had constantly to emphasize that the non-directive approach to community development is relevant to working with people both within the churches *and* outside them.

The problems raised were collated and later, with permission of the committees, were considered at the task force and open council meetings.

Work with ecumenical groups

Two meetings were held for task force volunteers. They considered the task force idea, the emphasis now placed upon involving churches as institutions in community development work, the work proposals, the concerns discussed in church committees, the community development approach to working with people and their own concerns. They were amazed at how much they had learnt about the churches in Ronsey. They began to see that training in community development would make them more effective in the work they wanted to do. They identified with the concerns expressed by church committees and agreed with the emphasis on involving churches as institutions in community development work. They decided:

1. to ask the council to arrange a course in church and community development work for lay people and occasional meetings for those interested in church and community work,
2. to attend a training course and to promote development through local churches;
3. to disband the task force if point one above was implemented by the council.

Work with ecumenical organizations

The executive invited the team to attend the council and the two full-time members to attend the executive. Also, two good neighbour scheme organizers asked team members to help them.

Overview by the council

When the team members prepared for the open council meeting fixed for October 1972, they felt its effectiveness would depend upon the members getting an overall picture of what had happened so far.

They provided this by describing the misconceptions they had encountered in the church committees; by defining what they meant by church and community development work; and by reporting on the concerns that had been expressed. The word 'concern' was used deliberately to avoid unproductive argument about terminology: some people had reacted strongly against the use of the word 'problem' or 'difficulty'. All committees and groups had said they had 'concerns', most said they had 'problems' and faced 'difficulties' but some were adamant that they had neither 'problems' nor 'difficulties'.

To facilitate discussion of the concerns the team prepared a large wall chart (6' x 10') and a small hand-out of the same chart for each person at the meeting to complete for himself. (For a copy of the chart see pp. 42 and 43.) Each concern was listed on this chart but only after it had been thoroughly checked (Is it understood? Is it stated correctly? Is it acceptable?).

The completed chart aroused great interest. Members of the meeting said they had never previously realized how many of these concerns they had in common. They were pleased at the way in which the chart helped them to see a way forward and they made the following decisions and suggestions:

1. that meetings be arranged periodically for those interested in church and community development work;

2. that the task force be disbanded;

3. that the team arrange a training course for lay people;

4. that the concerns about manpower and training should have priority;

5. that the executive be asked to promote inter-church discussions about church buildings;

6. that some concerns could best be considered by people from two or three churches and that arrangements should be made for them to do so;

7. that the team in consultation with the executive, continue to develop a programme of work and to explore concerns.

The meeting was lively and suggestions were adopted only after a lot of constructive and thorough discussion.

THE WORK THAT EVOLVED

As a direct result of the discussions described in this chapter the team's work programme was now:

Work with clergy
A training course
Helping a clergyman to form a parish council
Exploring concerns

AREAS OF CONCERN			THOSE CHURCHE
CONCERN (as it was expressed by the churches)	RAISED BY	asked the team to work with them on this concern	indicated the may ask the team to worl with them or these concer
Shortage of leaders and manpower	Cherry Tree Road, Holy Trinity, Manor Road, Priory Chapel, Cranstead, St Giles, St Margarets, St Philips, Young Adults		
Difficulties in making contact with people in need	Furzedowne, St Giles, Task force, Wells Road		Ronsey Free Church
What to do about needs we know of but cannot meet˙	St Saviours, St Giles		St Giles
Some church workers live outside the area	Ronsey Free Church, Cherry Tree Road, Wells Road		
Want to know more about community development	Task force	Clergy, Furzedowne, Good neighbours scheme Task force	St Giles
What is the relationship between Christian mission and community development	All church committees, Task force, Young adults	Clergy	
A mental care centre	Cranstead		Cranstead
Unmet religious needs	A general concern of all church committees		
People and buildings	Holy Trinity, Manor Road, St Philips, Wells Road, Task force	Furzedown	
Parish visiting	St Saviours, Holy Trinity	St Saviours	
Mothers under stress	Ronsey Free Church, Priory Chapel, Task force	Priory Chapel	Ronsey Free Church
Hospital visiting and transport	Cranstead		
Old people and visiting	Holy Trinity, Cranstead, Cherry Tree Road		
About immigrants in the community and the church	Ronsey Free Church, Cherry Tree Road, Wells Road, Priory Chapel, St Philips		
Various difficulties in Sunday school and youth work	St Saviours, St Philips, Cherry Tree Road, Ronsey Free Church, Task Force, Wells Road	St Saviours	
Lack of communication between and within groups of people	Ronsey Free Church, Cherry Tree Road, Wells Road, St Margarets, St Philips, Task force, Young adults		

CHART OF CONCERNS RAISED BY CHURCH COMMITTEES (This chart was compiled at the open council meeting. It does not include the concerns of two churches which were visited later.)

WHICH HAVE:		
said they would be prepared to discuss the concern with other churches	Work under way related to these concerns and on which the team is engaged	Other ways in which the team, in conjunction with the executive, council and fraternal, could work on these concerns in Ronsey
	A series of meetings for ministers on church and community development work (most of the clergy in Ronsey have said they will attend))	By organizing a series of meetings for lay people about these concerns and community development
St Giles		
St Giles		
	Furzedowne church and neighbourhood community centre scheme	By working with other churches on their schemes or problems
St Saviours Priory Chapel Cherry Tree Road Wells Road Manor Road St Giles Holy Trinity	St Anselms Parish Council Good neighbour scheme	
Cherry Tree Road Priory Chapel Ronsey Free Church Wells Road		By working with ecumenical groups
Ronsey Free Church Wells Road Cherry Tree Road St Philips Priory Chapel		

Work with individual churches
A parish community centre scheme
A church neighbourhood community centre scheme
A parish visiting scheme
Exploring concerns
Work with ecumenical groups
A training course for lay people
A scheme to help mothers under stress
Exploring concerns
Work with ecumenical organizations
Attending executive and council meetings
Helping organizers of the good neighbour scheme
Exploring concerns

THE TEAM, THE COUNCIL AND THE FRATERNAL

The executive and the council were now responsible for working out with the team the implications of locating the project in Ronsey and the team was responsible for keeping the fraternal informed of developments. This working arrangement evolved from the fraternal's decision to allow church people to decide about the project for themselves and was quite acceptable to the clergy. Also the fraternal invited members of the team to attend its meetings and said that they would be free to raise project business in the same way that local clergy raised other matters and that occasional meetings could be given over entirely to the project. The team felt very happy about these arrangements.

PUTTING THE BOROUGH IN THE PICTURE

When the council and clergy had established their overall policy for church and community development work in Ronsey they decided to introduce the team to borough officials. The secretaries of the council and the fraternal arranged two meetings: one in June 1972 with the planning officer and one of his assistants and the other in September 1972 with the director of social services, the Ronsey area team of social workers and a representative of the borough medical officer of health. At each meeting the secretaries introduced the team to the borough officials and described their plans for church and community development work in Ronsey. These plans were considered in relation to the social and community work undertaken by the borough; the working links already existing between the churches and the social services; and how the churches and the borough could work together more closely and avoid unnecessary duplication of work. The team members explained that their primary function was to help the churches to carry out their own programmes of community work.

The planning officer said his department was responsible for a borough working party on community development with special reference to what is commonly referred to as the Seebohm Report. He said that they would 'welcome more open channels of communication with the churches' and that he would tell the borough working party about the church and community development work in which the Ronsey Council of Churches was engaged.

2 Training sessions for lay people

Twelve lay people (nine women and three men) from five churches and the Y.M.C.A. attended a course of eight three-hour sessions spread over a period of three months. The average attendance was nine.

During this course the team members described the non-directive approach and the worker's job. They also did all they could to help the members of the course to consider several things about which they were concerned.

The members wanted to think about the church and community groups to which they belonged. What happened in these groups was of great importance to them but it was often far from satisfying. Through the course they began to see that their groups would be more satisfying if the members had a clear picture of what they wanted from them. They said that what they wanted from these groups were opportunities both for themselves and others to grow in their understanding of other people, Christianity and God; to work with others to meet human needs; to enjoy themselves; and to build up self-confidence and personal relationships with people in the church and community.

Having thus got their aims clear they tackled some of the problems they faced in achieving them in their groups: How to involve more church members in church sponsored activities? How to recruit more voluntary workers? How best to integrate new members and voluntary workers into a group? How to get churches to allow their premises to be used for community work? How to establish better relationships between people of different races, cultures, classes, organizations and churches? How to help people in need? They were surprised at the concerns and problems they had in common despite disparity in age, work and denomination.

To help them tackle these and other problems the team introduced them to a systematic approach to problem solving. Basically this involves groups (or individuals) defining, diagnosing and deciding what to do about problems by tackling the following questions:

What is the problem?
What makes this a problem for us?
Is it relevant to us?
Can we profitably spend time discussing it?
Why does the problem occur? Why has it arisen?
What can we do about it?
How?

They all found this approach to problem solving helpful when the team used it with them and wanted to learn how to use it themselves but found it difficult to develop skills in doing so. Gradually they began to feel that by concentrating on what they themselves could do to overcome their problems they could tackle some which previously they had found almost unapproachable. They said 'it is important to look at problems from the point of view of the factor you can handle rather than those aspects over which you have no control'. Doing just this on the course had reduced their anti-feelings towards those who were having an adverse effect on their work. Tackling problems in this way, they said, could help them and others to take effective action in relation to each of the concerns expressed by the church committees. For instance, they said, 'During this course we have discovered in ourselves abilities to lead of which previously we were unaware. This helps us to accept responsibility for work and to get others to do the same. Such courses as this, therefore, could make an important contribution towards overcoming the real concern about the shortage of leaders and manpower'.

When they evaluated the course several said they had gained self-confidence because they had learnt 'a new way of working with people': 'I now realize every member has a contribution to make and the importance of enabling them to make it', 'It has taught me a dynamic and respectful way of getting the best out of people through taking every person and every contribution seriously'. Consequently, they found they were now more sensitive towards people even if they disagreed with their views.

They said that the sessions had made them listen to each other, broken down their denominational insularity and enabled them to see ways of helping each other.

They said they had seen the value of thinking systematically and using words carefully. One said 'I've never thought so much in all my life'.

The members also said that they wanted to apply what they had learnt and decided that during the next three months they would concentrate on four things and then meet to discuss their experiences. They were:

1. to try to get their groups to clarify their purposes because 'this will help them to be clearer in discussions and more realistic in planning';

2. to try to get their groups to tackle problems more systematically, i.e., to sort out exactly what their problems were and to concentrate on what *they* could do about them;

3. to try to introduce the practice of preparing records of meetings because it helps to establish continuity, to clarify what has been said and to help people to see more clearly what is happening;

4. to try to act as a 'worker' in group discussions. (They felt they could do this whether or not they were chairing a meeting and that they would write their own check list of things to do; and subsequently consider what had happened at the meeting and the implications for the future. This they said was a way of 'self-training'.)

REVIEWING EXPERIENCES

After trying out these ideas in their working situations over a period of three months they met to discuss their experiences and decide on the next steps.

One person, the president of a women's fellowship, had got her group of elderly women to talk about the difficulties the leaders were experiencing in getting outside speakers and had discovered that the women actually preferred group activities and talks given by their own leaders to outside speakers! Relationships in the fellowship improved and members came to understand each other better. She, and another member, had also found the ideas helpful in the work they were doing with the good neighbour scheme. Two people, both former leaders of a youth club, had analyzed problems which had caused their club to close; decided how to overcome them; and formed a club leadership group.

Others had been less successful. One person had tried, but failed, to stimulate people to think about adopting a non-directive approach in a neighbourhood community project. Another had tried to promote inter-group co-operation in her parish but to no avail. Three people had failed to form a Bible study group, although one of the three had, in co-operation with her curate who had attended the clergy course, been able to get members of the parish council to clarify their purposes for a project. The remaining person, the secretary of the local Y.M.C.A. had stimulated many members to produce creative ideas about ways of developing their work but he had failed to get them to commit themselves to carrying them out.

On balance, the lay people and the team felt this to be an encouraging beginning and the lay people said that they intended to continue using the approach although they now realized it would mean a 'long hard haul'.

During this session they considered two ways in which they and the team could continue to work together. First, they could meet as a group periodically to consider work problems they were facing. Second, the team could work with individuals or small groups on their work. Members of the group reached no decision at this meeting. They said they needed more time to think and they asked the team to provide them with a form on which they could indicate which alternative they wished to pursue.

LATER EVENTS

Three forms only were returned. All three suggested further meetings and one of them invited the team to work with the Y.M.C.A. Members of the team followed up the invitation but they did not take any other conscious decisions. They allowed the situation to drift. In retrospect they can discern several reasons for this: their heavy work programme; their disappointment at the small number of forms returned; and their unwillingness to try to perpetuate meetings with people who seemed not to want them. One of the things the team learnt from this was that to allow things to drift invariably has a bad effect on both work and morale, whereas to make a conscious decision even if it is to do nothing further has positive effects. Members of the team now feel that they should have found out why others had not replied: and they feel this although ten of the twelve people who attended the course subsequently became active in community development schemes.

The work that evolved directly from this course was the Y.M.C.A. community centre scheme (see pp. 115 ff).

ASSESSMENT AFTER THE TEAM WITHDREW

This assessment confirmed what members had said about the course at its conclusion. They said that 'the team created a friendly atmosphere and made conversation within groups easier because of this' and 'helped to create self-confidence in members'. What they had continued to find particularly helpful, they said, was the non-directive approach, the systematic approach to problem-solving, the listing of pros and cons of alternatives before making decisions and the way of recording meetings.

All this had helped them and others to think through things constructively, to integrate new members into groups and to get old members to participate; to promote tolerance in church groups; and to work with people both in the church and in their full-time jobs.

One of them said, 'The whole approach of the team is a real step forward in Christian caring for others, both of and outside the faith'.

Team members were still engaged in church and community development work in April 1976.

3 Training sessions for clergy

During the period October 1972 to June 1973 the team provided seventeen three-hour training sessions for clergy. In retrospect three phases can be discerned: phase one comprised eight three-hour sessions for ten clergy and one church worker (average attendance ten); phase two, five three-hour sessions for nine clergy (average attendance seven); phase three, four three-hour sessions for ten clergy (average attendance eight).

PHASE ONE: THE NON-DIRECTIVE APPROACH, THE BETTERMENT OF PEOPLE AND THE WORK OF THE CLERGY

The overall purpose of this phase was to assist clergy to study community development, to assess it in relation to their Christian philosophy and theology and to think out the practical implications. In order to do this the team members explained what they meant by community development and how it could be applied to local church and neighbourhood work; explained the functions of a non-directive worker; and instructed the clergy in the use of systematic problem-solving techniques.

Defining betterment

Then the team got the clergy to consider critically in relation to their purposes and faith what working for 'the betterment of people' implied. They felt that for them betterment meant becoming more Christlike and helping others to do the same. And becoming more Christlike, they said, involves people becoming more loving towards God and their neighbour and accepting themselves and others as they really are. It meant facing reality, promoting justice and peace, being merciful, kind, courageous and self-controlled. It meant proclaiming and trying to live 'the ideal life' and persistently pursuing Christian purposes even in the face of evil.

Discussing problems

Next, the team got the clergy to define and discuss the problems they were facing in their work.

The problem to which they gave most time was, 'How to get church and non-church people to take the clergy seriously?' When they began to diagnose this problem some thought it was created by people in high places in Church and society who, by teaching new ideas, had undermined confidence in orthodox Christianity and morals and therefore in the Church and clergy. Some had very negative feelings towards such

50

people and they did not feel they could do much to overcome the problem. It could be solved only if key figures in Church and society — 'they', 'them' — restored confidence in the Church and in the clergy.

The team then got the clergy to consider when and how *they* experienced the problem and what *they* could do about it. Gradually the clergy realized that what *they* did would either ameliorate or exacerbate the problem and this stimulated them to analyze it further. Eventually they decided that underlying the problem was what they called a 'crisis of authority'. This, they said, led to 'people and clergy being unsure about the job of the clergy and the Church'. This promoted animated but abstract discussion about 'authority' — a subject of great concern to them. Progress was made only when the team got them to consider their experience of authority and what enabled people to accept or caused them to reject it. They now began to see that they could do something about their problem and they decided to concentrate on what they could do in Ronsey.

The clergy tried applying the problem solving approach described on p. 46 to some of their problems. They concluded that the approach would help them to consider things more thoroughly. They said, 'We move from diagnosis too quickly because we are too concerned to get things done'.

The other principal problems they were facing, as they defined them, were: How to prevent people being led away from Christianity, the Church and its work? How to get through to people in worship? How to recruit immigrant leaders? How to integrate people of other races into the Church? How to get church members to make non-church people who use their premises feel at home? How to prevent people from adopting negative attitudes? How to live a Christian life in the world of today, and help others to do the same? How to get more people in the Church to accept responsibility and to be more discerning? How to get church officers to use money wisely? How to cope with resentment and jealousy in working relationships? How to help people to express what they really feel?

Studying the non-directive approach

Also, the team stimulated the clergy to consider the non-directive approach adopted by the team. Most clergy said the team had helped them to express themselves, to see things more clearly and to work together as a group. They said the team had done this by introducing structure into discussions; by helping them to find words to express their thoughts and feelings; by taking seriously what they said; by remaining neutral; by explaining what the team was doing and why; by using diagrams; by helping them to decide and to do what they wanted to do; and by giving them time to think things through and by checking for agreement. In short, by acting non-directively. But one clergyman found the team's approach painfully slow. He felt that the team's structuring of discussions often made it more difficult for him to contribute and that the nuances of his thought were lost in agreed statements. Another felt the team had not contributed sufficient technical and academic information.

The clergy felt that the non-directive approach was in many ways more appropriate than the directive approach to work aimed at promoting the betterment of people; but that the directive approach is relevant to certain situations, for example, when people are unable or unwilling to help themselves or when taking executive action to implement agreed policies.

They also concluded that it is entirely consistent with the ways in which 'Jesus thought out, prayed out and worked out his purposes'. And they felt it was applicable to most of their work but they found it easier, they said, to apply it to counselling than to group work.

Next steps

During the last session the team summarized the eight sessions and asked the clergy what they wanted to do now. Two said they did not want to continue; one because he was out of sympathy with the team's approach and one because he was not convinced of its value. Also, one did not continue because he was about to retire.

The remaining eight wished to continue and asked the team to suggest ways by which, as a group, they could learn to apply the non-directive concept to their work. The team suggested that they could:

(a) consider what they themselves could do to promote 'development';

(b) consider what they themselves could do about some of their problems;

(c) study some 'cases'; (a case describes a piece of work which the worker feels ended unsatisfactorily; when studying a case people ask themselves if the worker had contributed to the unsatisfactory result, and if so how, and then they consider just how, if he acted differently, he could have done better[1]);

(d) learn how to use the non-directive approach by practising it within the group.

The clergy decided on (a), (b) and (c) without difficulty but it was only after a tortuous discussion that they decided on (d) because they felt that practice within their own group would be too artificial. They would have much preferred, they said, to practise 'in real situations'. In the end, however, with reluctance, they realized that they needed at

[1] T.R. Batten and M. Batten, *The Human Factor in Youth Work*, London, 1970, p. 1.

least some preliminary practice under the guidance of the team. They arranged five further sessions and thereby inaugurated phase two.

PHASE TWO: THE PROBLEM OF RECRUITING AND TRAINING LEADERS

In Project 70-75 the local institutional churches and their neighbourhoods were the key work areas and therefore the key training areas. But, in preparing for phase two with their consultant, the team came to see that in phase one the emphasis had been upon the non-directive approach rather than upon the work of the clergy. That is, phase one had been more of a theoretical-method course rather than a purpose-work course. Now in phase two, the team members aimed to focus attention on the work of the clergy in their churches and neighbourhoods. They discussed these ideas with the clergy. The clergy said they definitely wanted to focus on their work and they decided to start by considering just what they and their churches were already doing. And so, at the suggestion of the team the group listed on a large map what their churches were already doing to promote betterment both separately and in co-operation with other church and secular groups. Items were listed only when each member of the group understood just what they meant, and clergy found themselves explaining to others many things that had been previously taken for granted and not understood. This list stimulated discussion about difficulties of working with others, what constitutes effective co-operation, and the advantages to be gained by concentrating their efforts. This led to such a down-to-earth discussion of the problems they were facing that at the end of the session, one member said, and others agreed enthusiastically, 'I have learned more about the work of other churches during this session than I have through working in the area over a period of six years'.

In the light of all this the clergy decided to use the remaining sessions to consider problems they were facing in trying to promote betterment and to start with: 'How to recruit and train leaders who would work with young people and old people to the satisfaction of clergy and church leaders?' Through studying this problem the clergy came to realize that they, their church officials and their potential leaders all needed to understand each others' purposes and motivation if they were to work together effectively. They considered what they could do to promote such understanding. They listed criteria which would help them and their churches to recruit suitable leaders; identified groups and organizations which might have potential recruits; and worked out how best they could induct, train and support them. Then they tried to formulate a master recruitment plan to fit each and every situation. This they found they could not do because in certain respects their situations were quite different.

The team, realizing that the discussions were becoming abstract and the clergy frustrated, recapitulated the purpose of the sessions and summarized what had been achieved so far. This enabled clergy and team to see the drift of the discussions. The clergy said they felt confused and frustrated, started to work out why they felt like this and concluded that:

(a) 'to try to find universal solutions or to make master plans to fit so many different and complex situations, complicates the issue even further, and confuses rather than helps us;

(b) further progress will be made only by considering how to tackle the specific recruitment problems we are facing;

(c) we just don't know enough about each others' situations to be able to suggest practicable recruitment plans'.

The clergy then considered whether they could effectively tackle specific recruitment problems. They thought they could, provided that each of them prepared notes on his situation for others to read prior to the meeting at which his situation was to be discussed. They wanted to express themselves freely but they were concerned about the possibility of information leaks adversely affecting their relationships with people in their churches. Eventually, each in turn undertook not to refer to the notes outside the group or to quote or reproduce them without the express permission of the author who alone could assess the effect such action could have. With this understanding they agreed that *each* person attending the sessions would write frankly about his work and they formulated the following outline to help them to do so:

Purposes
My basic purposes concerning:

(a) adherents and others who attend church or are in fellowship with the church are . . .

(b) people who are members of the church or who were once connected with the church, but who now rarely attend, are . . .

(c) people who are not connected with the fellowship of the church are . . .

(d) people who are associated with various church community organizations and activities but who are not in the fellowship of the church, are . . .

Ways of achieving my purposes
The following are possible ways in which I might initiate new work to achieve these purposes . . .

Recruiting leaders
The organizations for which leaders in church work are needed are . . .
The leaders in church work will be required to . . .
The leaders in church community work will be required to . . .

The special factors in my situation
In thinking about recruitment in my church, the special factors to be taken into consideration are . . .

Concerns
In relation to the life and work of the church I am concerned about . . .

They also decided that distribution of the notes should be strictly limited to those who produced them and to the team.

These decisions concluded phase two and inaugurated phase three.[2]

PHASE THREE: DISCUSSION OF SPECIFIC WORKING SITUATIONS

All ten of the clergy adhered so strictly to the arrangements made at the end of phase two for the circulation of the notes of their working situations that the administration went like clockwork.

They worked in two groups each comprising five clergy, one team member acting as worker and one acting as recorder. Eight situations in all were considered, that is, one situation in each group on each of four mornings. Each meeting started with a member of the team suggesting that the clergy try to 'think and feel their way into the situation'. This took a considerable amount of time but the problems — and the situations — always became much clearer in the process and it was the essential first step towards determining what to do about them. Then the whole group worked at one or more of the problems.

Although the groups initially found it difficult to concentrate on only one situation and one problem at a time, they soon got used to it and found that what they learned in this way was also relevant to other situations and problems.

The team produced a detailed record of each of these discussions in consultation with the clergyman concerned. The clergy found these records extremely useful. Never before, they said, had they had so clear an analysis of their situation and of ideas for dealing with it.

Group A considered:
— how to help a handicapped youth leader to be more effective;
— how to get members of parochial church council sub-committees to re-organize their work so that their areas of responsibility were clear to all concerned;
— how to recruit leaders for an Anglican Sunday school;
— how to set up a community workers luncheon club;

[2] Separate courses for clergy and laity evolved naturally from the discussions about the initial work programme (pp. 41 ff). The arrangements were made without considering the possibility of joint courses. Undoubtedly a joint course at a later date could have been most productive. However had lay people been present at these sessions the clergy would probably not have embarked on phase three.

-- how to overcome problems created by new forms of education and liturgy in a Roman Catholic church.

Group B considered:
- how to recruit staff and scholars for a Sunday school and members for a youth club in a Baptist church;
- how to cope with an influx of coloured immigrant children into the Sunday school and uniformed organizations of an Anglican church and especially how to recruit immigrant adults to help;
- how to promote a youth club in the neighbourhood of a Moravian church;
- how to meet the recreational needs of young people in an Anglican church.

Groups A and B considered together:
- how best the team could work with them on schemes or plans; (this discussion had implications for the project work as a whole and is therefore described below);
- the role of clergy in open youth work conducted on church premises.

WORKING ON SCHEMES

Concurrently with these sessions the team was working on some of the schemes described in Part Four and they had come up against difficulties. First, clergy and lay workers would, from time to time, take action which had implications for the team without consulting them. Second, they did not always keep the team informed of developments as they occurred. Third, clergy, lay workers and committees frequently failed to do what they had undertaken to do. Often, in such situations, team members had found it difficult to know how to react and the longer they delayed the more difficult it became to do anything.

The team raised these points with the clergy towards the end of their course when various new schemes were being discussed and the clergy accepted that if clergy, churches and members of the team were to establish an effective working partnership their respective roles and responsibilities needed to be made clearer. Such a partnership, they agreed, would be most effective if:

(a) it was designed to fit the people and their situation;

(b) the nature of the partnership was understood by all concerned; (the team would act as non-directive workers to the clergy and lay people who would retain control of their own situation);

(c) whenever possible, situations were jointly discussed before action was decided upon;

(d) the clergy and/or the church felt they could call upon the team whenever they wished on the understanding that the members of the team would respond as and how they were able;

(e) the team was kept informed of developments;

(f) the members of the team felt they could express any concerns they might have about situations or developments;

(g) arrangements were made for periodic reviews of the work.

DECISIONS ABOUT FUTURE WORK

Phase three concluded the training sessions. Thereafter five of the clergy in sub-group B, a member of the team and the recorder continued to work together on an inter-church scheme (see pp. 96 ff) and the others decided to work individually with the team on plans which they had formulated. Some said, 'the next step is to get church committees thinking about things in the way in which we have been doing in these sessions'. Thus the sessions were carried through into the work of the clergy and their churches.

ASSESSMENT BY THE CLERGY

At the request of those clergy who had attended phase three, three of their members drafted an assessment of the sessions, circulated it for the others to comment on and then, after re-editing it, forwarded copies to the fraternal and the executive. This was done in September 1973, that is, some three months after the last training session. Their assessment was:

Phase one
'It was often difficult to find the time, but worthwhile to do so; we appreciated the concentrated thinking, and though some people found the non-directive approach a little "slow" most of us came to appreciate its significance and value. In particular we found the sessions helpful because we were enabled to think more objectively than normally about our work; we were co-operating rather than competing; we had the opportunity to discuss vital issues with "outsiders" (that is, the team) when few of us have colleagues; we were able to re-examine preconceived ideas and feelings, and to share some of our anxieties. Much of the value of the course lay in the team's careful and thorough methods and approach, the visual aids, and in particular the duplicated records. We mentioned one difficulty — that of, in the early stages, understanding just which way the team was going. Since the ending of this phase, some members are actively putting the non-directive approach into practice, with satisfactory results; and there appears to be a subtle change for the better in our relationships with other clergy'.

Phase two
'It was easier to find the time, but less easy to pick up the threads, or

in retrospect, to remember much of the content of the sessions[3] —
perhaps it was too theoretical, and might have been of more use after
writing the notes on our own situations. Nevertheless we found certain
valuable aspects, not least of all the necessity to consider situations
carefully and in detail, and to be honest with each other. It was an
essential preparation for phase three'.

Phase three
'Obviously we cannot tell you how or whether we dealt with St Barth-
olomew's Boys' Brigade or Aston Park Wesleyan Women's Fellowship!
Certainly we enjoyed the work, and much of it is still going on. We
often found that the particular problem we alone had ("I, even I, only
am left") was one which was common to others, and this was a source
of encouragement. We feel it is important to stress that we found this
work — throughout the whole year — to be a valuable breakthrough in
ecumenical working relations, and a course which has not yet ended
because the ideas and problems which cropped up are still being discussed and talked about, either by a small group of clergy, or by
individual members in relation to one or more of the team'.

Those who had attended the sessions considered this assessment at a
fraternal meeting in October 1973. Apart from the exceptions already
mentioned they had all found phase one valuable because it had helped
them to think in a new way. They had found phase two less valuable
but thought phase three very helpful because it had brought home to
them that they all faced similar problems and could work on them
together. They said that the three phases had complemented each
other and had shown them how to apply the non-directive approach to
parish work.

The executive also considered this assessment in October 1973. They
were impressed by what had been achieved and one person said that in
her opinion the executive would be more effective if it worked at tasks
in the same way as the clergy had done during the training sessions.
However, this point was not followed up.

THE WORK THAT EVOLVED

The following work evolved from these training sessions:
Work with individual clergy
1. Youth work problems in a Roman Catholic church.
2. Problems with a handicapped youth leader.
3. A community workers' luncheon club.
4. Discussing ideas for development work related to Sunday schools and
church youth work and open youth work with coloured and white
people.

---

[3] Meetings in phase one were weekly, in phase two fortnightly.

Work with a group of clergy
5. A community work clergy task group.
Work with individual churches
6. A Roman Catholic parish and Vatican II.
The first of these schemes evolved from phase one, all the others from phase three.

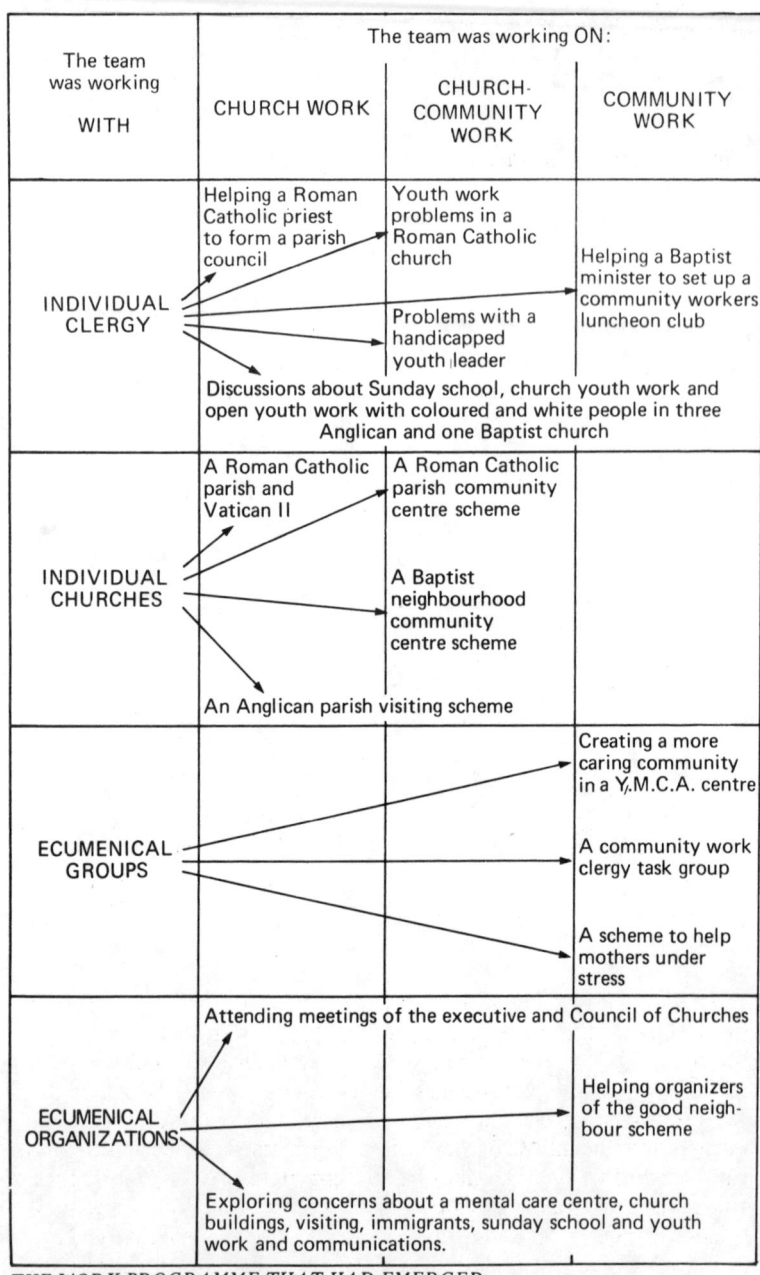

The team was working WITH	The team was working ON:		
	CHURCH WORK	CHURCH-COMMUNITY WORK	COMMUNITY WORK
INDIVIDUAL CLERGY	Helping a Roman Catholic priest to form a parish council	Youth work problems in a Roman Catholic church	Helping a Baptist minister to set up a community workers luncheon club
		Problems with a handicapped youth leader	
	Discussions about Sunday school, church youth work and open youth work with coloured and white people in three Anglican and one Baptist church		
INDIVIDUAL CHURCHES	A Roman Catholic parish and Vatican II	A Roman Catholic parish community centre scheme	
		A Baptist neighbourhood community centre scheme	
	An Anglican parish visiting scheme		
ECUMENICAL GROUPS			Creating a more caring community in a Y.M.C.A. centre
			A community work clergy task group
			A scheme to help mothers under stress
ECUMENICAL ORGANIZATIONS	Attending meetings of the executive and Council of Churches		
			Helping organizers of the good neighbour scheme
	Exploring concerns about a mental care centre, church buildings, visiting, immigrants, sunday school and youth work and communications.		

THE WORK PROGRAMME THAT HAD EMERGED

4 Classifying the work

Two principal ways of classifying the work evolved along with the work programme.

First, by reference to those with whom the team worked, that is, *individual clergy, individual churches, ecumenical groups* and *ecumenical organizations*. These working relationships derived from the decision to work with the churches as institutions.

Second, by reference to the nature of the work in which the people were engaged. During phase one of the training sessions the team referred to 'church work' and 'community work'. During phase two they tried to list under these two heads all the work in which the clergy were engaged. Eventually they found they could not do this because in fact there was a third category which the team decided to call 'church-community work'. The result was a three-fold classification: *church work, church-community work* and *community work* which helped everyone to think more clearly about the work in which local churches were engaged. It was widely used in Ronsey and was represented diagrammatically in the following way:

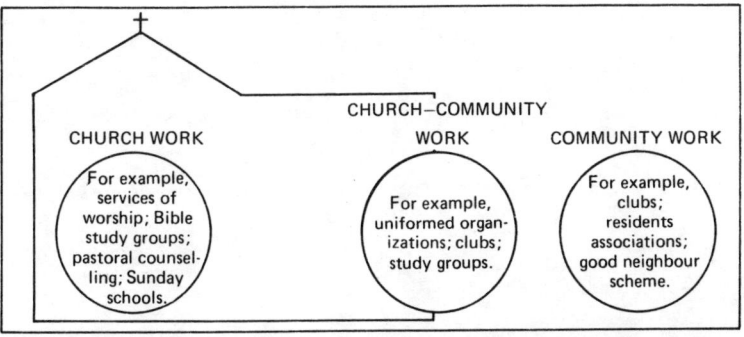

Church work refers to work undertaken primarily to meet religious needs by promoting understanding of the Christian faith and its practices. *Church-community work* refers to work undertaken on church premises to meet felt needs of church and non-church people. It is arranged around interests, tasks, concerns and activities not normally considered 'religious' and conducted with little or no religious ceremony. It is open to anyone without regard to their religious beliefs, practices or church affiliation. *Community work* refers to work undertaken by the church to promote the development and well-being of people in the community. It is carried out in groups, buildings and organizations not associated with the church.

People in Ronsey found the classification very useful. During the local assessment after the team had withdrawn one of the clergy said 'The three-fold distinction between community, church-community and church work and the idea of "cross fertilization" between Christian and non-Christian engaged together in community work are valid and useful.' Consultative groups and advisers working in Anglican, Methodist and Roman Catholic churches said that they found the classification helpful and were using a modified version.

PART THREE:
WORKING
AND WITHDRAWING

Introduction

The team members aimed to promote a process of learning by doing in the local area both for themselves and for the people with whom they worked, and at the core of this work were the training sessions and the schemes. Both the team members and the people they worked with learned from each other by assessing the work done and its implications, and at the same time many people outside the local area were involved in following the various stages of the project, assessing its progress and commenting on the work done. After the team had withdrawn from the local area there was a thorough evaluation of the work done by all those with whom the team had worked. How this was done and the overall results are described in Part Four chapters 1 and 2. What people said about the schemes is summarized in this Part at the end of the description of each of the schemes. This continuing process of interaction and evaluation gave the project its action research character.

The overall development chart on pp. 168 and 169 illustrates and gives an overview of the project work.

'Project work' is used throughout to denote the team's work and 'schemes' to denote the work of the clergy, the churches and the ecumenical groups.

Words such as 'help', 'assist', 'enable', 'encourage', 'stimulate', 'support' and 'get' are used in this Part as in the report generally to describe, except where otherwise stated, that a member of the team was carrying out the functions of a non-directive worker.

1 Working with individual clergy

This chapter is about private and confidential discussions with individual clergy.

The team members had sessions of this kind with four Anglicans, two Baptists, two Methodists and two Roman Catholics. Each of the clergy examined in some detail specific aspects of his work and, in addition, three of them reappraised their overall work programmes.

THE DISCUSSIONS

The central theme of these discussions was the work the clergy were doing and how they could do it more effectively. In each case the discussion was between one clergyman and one or two members of the team and was carried out in formal sessions (normally of one-and-a-half hours' duration) which were supplemented by telephone calls, correspondence and *ad hoc* conversations. These discussions took up a considerable amount of time — in some cases twelve or thirteen formal sessions over a period of one year — and ranged over a wide field of work.[1]

The depth of thinking in the discussions and the thoroughness with which the clergy followed them up varied enormously but in one way or another the discussions helped each of the clergy to see ways forward that he had not seen before and to feel more positive towards his work and those with whom he worked. From what the clergy said and the team observed it was one or other of the following that, to varying degrees in the different discussions, played an important part in effecting these changes.

1. Considering feelings about work

Most of the clergy said why they were worried about a situation and then directly proceeded to discuss it. They found their feelings towards their work became more positive through discussing work rather than feelings. Some, however, were distressed, saying that they were at the

---

[1] Changes in church organization; church re-building programmes and the possibility of inter-church co-operation; reviewing organizational procedures in a local church; preparing people in two churches of different denominations for the church-community work they planned to do when they had completed their re-building schemes; sharing worship and premises between a Baptist and a United Reformed church; unruly behaviour in a Sunday school; recruiting Sunday school staff; coping with an influx of immigrant children into church youth groups; meeting the diverse worship needs of members of a congregation; problems arising from unpopular mandatory changes in forms of worship; youth work problems in three churches; working with a handicapped youth leader; helping mothers of one parent families to support each other; and promoting co-operation between church people and secular community workers by means of a community workers' luncheon club.

end of their tethers, and could not discuss their work without first considering their feelings about it. During these dicussions team members acted as first-aid counsellors.[2] They helped the clergyman to work through his feelings and this enabled him to focus less emotively and more objectively on his work — the major source of his anxieties and negative feelings. This meant he was now able to concentrate on what effect he could have on his work rather than the effect it was having upon him. This had further positive effects on him and his feelings.

As they gained experience the team members became clearer about their counsellor and consultant roles and the relationship between them. Undoubtedly they made their best contribution by helping clergy become more effective in their work. Therefore they saw their role as 'counsellor' subordinate to that of 'work consultant'. The implications of this became very clear in discussions with one clergyman. For several sessions the team member failed to promote discussion about work: the clergyman could concentrate only on his feelings. The team member began to feel counselling help was required beyond what he could give and explained to the the clergyman how he saw the situation. The clergyman saw the distinction between discussion about work and discussion about feelings towards work. He recognized that he had been concentrating on feelings but said he now felt much more positive and wanted to discuss work. It was agreed that should his feelings again render him unable to think creatively about his work he would consider seeking other counselling help. The subsequent discussions helped him to become more effective in his work and consequently to feel better about it. Negative feelings did return from time to time but they were not as acute and first-aid counselling only was required. It was easier to deal with these feelings because both clergyman and team member understood the distinction between considering feelings and considering work (that is, the distinction between counselling and consulting).

2. *Establishing accurate 'pictures' of working situations*

The 'picture' consisted of statements and/or diagrams which the clergyman said accurately portrayed the essential characteristics of his working situation and which enabled the team member to conceptualize it. The picture was constructed by the clergyman and the team member: the clergyman describing his situation and the team member summarizing what the clergyman was saying and drawing a diagram of the situation as it appeared to him. Both the statement and the diagram were then adjusted until the clergyman was satisfied that it really did accurately portray his situation and the team member felt he had grasped its essential factors. (A large scribbling pad was generally used

---

[2] This is a form of non-directive counselling described by George Lovell in *The Youth Worker as a First Aid Counsellor in Impromptu Situations* (London, 1971) and 'Helping Individuals to Help Themselves' in *Working with Youth* (London, 1972).

during this exercise, the team member resting it on his knee or on a coffee table.) The team member encouraged the clergyman to make real efforts to describe his situation in a way the team member could understand — he did not allow him to resort to saying things such as, 'You know what it's like'. Doing this stimulated the clergyman to sort out and describe ideas, information and feelings in ways he did not normally do, and thereby to see things in a new light. It helped him to objectify his situation, and the diagrams and summaries contributed to this by providing a focus of attention and a common external reference point. It had a positive effect on his feelings about his work and on his ability to think rationally and creatively about it, and in most cases helped the clergyman to decide what action to take and to be more sanguine about the outcome.

3. Formulating realistic plans for action

Once a clear picture of the situation had been arrived at, the next stage was to consider what course of action the clergyman could take. Ideas for action, like the pictures of the working situation, were expressed in a series of statements and/or diagrams on a large scribbling pad. (Frequently clergy asked if they could keep them for future reference.)

Plans for action were realistic only if they fitted the clergyman's purpose, his situation and himself. Team members, by asking questions, got the clergyman to test whether in fact plans did fit.

They got him to check them in relation to his *purpose* by asking: Is this likely to help you to do what you really want to do? Can we check that it actually will? In all cases, asking questions such as these prompted the clergyman to be more specific about his purposes and gave more definite direction to his planning.

The team member then got him to check his plans in relation to his working *situation* by asking: Is this the kind of thing that can be done with your people? Will this work in your church? Will your people respond to this approach or will it put them off? Do they normally work in this way? And if the team member foresaw possible areas of difficulty he prompted discussion by asking questions such as 'If you do this with "A" what do you think "B" will say or do?'

The team member also got him to check his plans in relation to *himself* by asking questions such as: 'Is this something you think you can do? How do you feel about it? How does it fit in with the way you normally work? Can you see yourself doing it?' Considering these questions frequently showed that plans did not fit either the purpose or the situation or the man himself and led to drastic revisions.

In this way, the team members made conscious efforts to ensure that plans not only fitted the clergyman, purpose and situation, but also the man himself because they realized that at first they had been inclined to think about what they themselves would do rather than what the clergyman felt he could do. This had had the effect of deflecting some clergy from really thinking for themselves, with the result that they had 'agreed' to plans they could not subsequently carry out. *In fact, in these early sessions the team had been failing to do what they had set out to do because they had subconsciously worked directively.* When the team realized what was happening they guarded against it by asking questions similar to those described above and by getting the clergy to write up discussions and plans in their own words. This helped the clergy to work in their own way, to formulate plans themselves and, at the same time to increase their skill in working things out on paper for themselves.

This experience showed the team, not for the first time, just how difficult it is to maintain a non-directive approach. It is so easy to step into a directive approach without even realizing it.

4. Working out the initial steps in detail and considering possible developments

Initial steps were worked out in detail and their implications carefully considered before plans were implemented. If, for example, the first step involved the clergyman contacting Mr A then the team member would work out with the clergyman (in relation to purpose, situation and what he felt he could do) how he would approach Mr A (by letter? by telephone? by visiting him?); when he would approach him and what he intended to say. Clergy were concerned with such detail once they realized it could critically affect the outcome.

Further, before committing themselves to taking the initial steps, they wanted to see where they might lead, that is, to assess what they might be 'letting themselves in for'.

5. Determining priorities and ways of keeping to them

The three clergy who reappraised their overall work programme with team members were grossly overworked and none of them felt able to resist the continual pressure from church and other organizations to take on yet more work. This was a great worry to them. Fellow clergy and church officers, they said, frequently asked them in public to take on more work, and when they wished to decline because of overwork, fellow clergy and officers would refuse to take 'No' for an answer. For example, they would say that they were all overworked but that the Rev. A— was so competent that he could take this in his stride and so, more often than not, he weakened, and against his better judgment, took on the job. Again, social workers, often late on a Friday afternoon, would ring up asking if Rev. B— could arrange for someone to visit Miss C— who was housebound and desperately in need of help: and if he hesitated he was made to feel that he was denying all the Church had said about its desire to care for people. The clergy did not always know how to resist such pressures and, consequently, again accepted more work than they could possibly do.

Team members helped the clergy do something about this kind of situation in four principal ways.

First, they urged them to cut some of their activities to give them time to think. In one case, after finding that a clergyman was quite unable to do this for himself the team member told him what to cut out and how to do it and later checked that he had done so. In this instance the team member felt he had to act directively in order to help the clergyman to start to think for himself. In another situation a grossly overworked clergyman was being pressed to accept even more work and, although he was at breaking point, did not know how he could refuse. The team member, after ascertaining that he really could not cope with the additional work, typed a letter for him to sign in which he refused the work and asked that no pressure should be brought upon him to change his mind. The team member then took the clergyman to post it. The clergyman was greatly relieved and, with the help of the team member, was then able to start sorting things out. This kind of directive action, unlike that described on pp. 68-69 was an essential preliminary to helping certain clergy to help themselves.

Second, the team member got them to list their commitments and put them in order of priority.

Third, they got them to decide how much work they could reasonably undertake. One person found that classifying and charting his work in the following way (worked out during discussions) greatly helped him to review his priorities periodically and thus to control his work load.

Area of work	Aspects of work	My aim	My role	My feelings	Priority
Parish work					
Social and community work					
Youth work					

Fourth, the team members worked out with them just how they could reduce their work load and cope with the pressures put upon them to take on more work. (In one case for example, this led to a clergyman working out with a committee how he could help them without attending meetings.) As a result the clergy felt greatly relieved, much more in control of their working situation, and more capable of working purposefully. One of them illustrated the change in the following way.

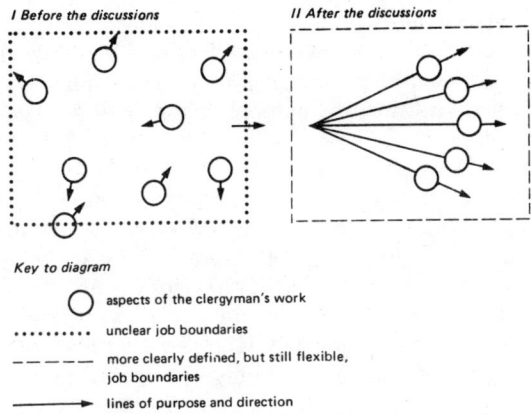

I Before the discussions

II After the discussions

Key to diagram

○   aspects of the clergyman's work

··········   unclear job boundaries

— — — —   more clearly defined, but still flexible, job boundaries

——————▶   lines of purpose and direction

6. Reviewing developments and working out their implications

In all cases the team members offered the clergy opportunities to discuss the results of whatever action they had decided to take. Most took up the offer and some arranged to meet a team member on a continuing basis. They said they appreciated the support that such an arrangement provided.

AN ASSESSMENT

After the team had withdrawn from Ronsey one of those with whom a team member worked over a period of twelve months assessed the experience in this way: 'I have learnt to function more effectively in the difficult working situation that confronts me because of the help I have received from someone experienced in working non-directively with individuals and groups. My working situation has not changed, but my mental attitude and approach have. Instead of continuing to muddle on feeling trapped, confused, and uneasy, I now apply a series of questions which sift out areas of work where I am able to exercise control from those where under present circumstances I cannot; which tease out the nature of my work in its various aspects and the roles I play; and which assess the help and support I need in carrying out my purposes and controlling the work load. The things that the team member did which I found helpful were as follows:

1. He enabled me to communicate well in a group to which he was the non-directive worker. In this group I experienced a relationship of trust and respect. The group experience enabled me privately to show distress signals. These were picked up by the worker who made a tentative offer of help with tact and courtesy that preserved my freedom to go forward or withdraw as I chose. I chose to go forward and felt that I maintained my freedom.

2. He was willing to listen very patiently and with great attention and then to reflect back in more concise language what I was trying to say.

3. He asked questions, designed to get me to picture and conceptualize my situation, clarify my purposes, and define what I can realistically hope to achieve.

4. He used diagrams as an aid to picturing situations.

5. He established an effective system of working together in concentrated work sessions of about one and a half hours alternating with intervals of several weeks for reflection and for carrying out specific tasks in preparation for the next session (for example, I would be asked to put things down in my own words, or to examine whether an idea would work out in practice, or to consider questions, or to summarize the main points of a discussion in my own words, or to review several sessions.)

The whole system was designed to establish a thought process in me which would enable me to regain control of my working situation and maintain it. There were two aspects of coming to terms with my working situation and learning to control it. First I had to regain my sense of poise. This involved *rediscovering* the still point at the heart of my life and personality, by exploring and deepening my relationship with God, until I was steadied and reassured in my willingness to accept God's will for me in Ronsey; *recognizing* and adapting to a new pattern of relationship and roles, and patiently waiting to be accepted in them; integrating the aims and purposes I am seeking to carry out in the areas of work represented by these relationships, round my understanding of ministry. Secondly, I learnt new skills in order to expand my understanding of ministry and of how to exercise it effectively in my open parish situation through learning about church and community development and especially the non-directive approach to working with individuals and groups.'

OTHER PRIVATE DISCUSSIONS

The team was engaged on other work with seven of the ten clergy referred to in this chapter. The work involved private discussions other than those referred to in this chapter. They, along with similar discussions with four other clergy, are described in the reports about schemes in Part Three chapters 2 to 4. All private discussions with clergy about work substantiate the statements made in this chapter.

SUBSEQUENT DEVELOPMENTS

The principal development that occurred as a consequence of this work was that the clergy were able to work more effectively. This of itself greatly increased the likelihood of change for the better in their working situations.

Confidentiality permits reference to only one scheme that evolved, a community workers' luncheon club. This was set up in July 1974 with an active membership of some twenty-five people from a wide range of agencies and in February 1976 was planning to review and enlarge its programme. The borough authorities thought the club was serving a useful function and arranged for the minister to talk to other groups about the club and how it was formed. This led to the establishment of similar clubs in other areas.

2 Working with individual churches

This chapter describes five schemes on which the team worked with individual churches: three on *church work* and two on *church-community work*.

AN ANGLICAN PARISH VISITING SCHEME

For fifteen months a group of twelve people led by a lay organizer had visited homes in their Anglican parish, St Saviour's. They had encountered problems which disheartened them and they did not know how to continue. They asked the team to help them to look at their problems. Between November 1972 and January 1973 two members of the team had three two-hour sessions with them.

The visitors said that they felt inadequate and each felt he lacked support from the others; they had difficulties with the people they visited, especially in multi-occupied houses; and they felt they needed help from other church members but so far had failed to get it.

They chose to concentrate on the problems they experienced with those they visited because they thought this would help them solve their other problems. Following the problem-solving approach described on p. 46 the team asked them why they found it difficult to conduct door-step interviews. But when it became clear that the ensuing discussion was not likely to prove fruitful the team suggested that the group should act out their difficulties by means of role-play.

One of them then agreed to take the part of a householder and two others (they normally visited in pairs) the part of parish visitors. The householder's part was based on people with whom they had experienced difficulties: 'non-church going people', 'lapsed communicants', 'Jesus movement people', 'those of other denominations and religions', and those 'hostile towards the Church'. The team member conducting the role-play suggested that those playing the parts of the visitors should do what they normally did, and that the 'householder' should try to think himself into the mind of the person whose part he was taking and then to act and react as he thought that person would.

The team member stopped the role-play when he thought the main learning points had emerged and then promoted discussion about what had happened during the 'interview' and about how those taking part had felt, with a view to getting members of the group to draw out the implications for future visiting. Sometimes there was a difference of opinion about how a visitor ought to have acted and when this happened the alternatives were role-played and compared.

The visitors – and this was as true of the elderly as of the young – said they learnt much of immediate practical value from this kind of role-playing, and incidentally had a lot of fun. The visitors now felt they were really achieving something when they got into a friendly and caring discussion with householders, whether or not church or Christianity was talked about, whereas previously they thought they had failed if they had not talked about these things. They now realized that if they were to achieve their dual aim — to evangelize *and* to show that the Church cares — they must first get into friendly and caring relationships with those whom they visited. And, that trying 'to get something in about the Church and Christianity' could prevent this. In fact they saw that a lot of their previous dissatisfaction resulted from thinking of success solely in terms of their desire to evangelize, which was one aspect only of their dual aim. Discovering all this had a positive effect on their approach to the householders.

Next, they discovered that they did not know what were the best times to visit. The team asked them if they could find out from people in the church. They decided to ask various groups of adults and young people in the parish when would be a good or a bad time to call. The answers helped them to determine the best times for visiting.

The team kept the vicar informed of the work being done and he attended some part of each session as an observer. The team made records of all the meetings and circulated them both to the group and to the vicar. These were found to be most useful.

By the third session the visitors said they were feeling much more adequate and ready to put what they had learnt into practice. They decided to start visiting again at the same time and in the same area. They also decided to meet for prayer before visiting and to meet afterwards with the vicar to pray, to discuss what had happened and to decide on any necessary follow-up. In this way, they felt, they would be able to support each other and to make the greatest possible impact.

Assessment after team's withdrawal

This assessment — some two years later — showed that the scheme was still working, though not without problems, and most of the visitors felt it had a future. They said they had been able to use what they had learnt to good effect. They said that the team members had helped them by listening; by showing that they understood the problems they were facing; by enabling them to discuss their problems with each other; and by making them 'think out, talk out and work out' their own solutions ('the team never provided a nice ready-made answer',); by getting them to 'appreciate the reaction of the person on the other side of the door'; and by getting them to realize the importance of listening to people. Several mentioned the value of the role-play sessions and that what they had learnt was applicable to other work.

One person felt that further meetings to consider developments and problems should have been held a year or so after the first. In fact the team had offered to attend further meetings should the group invite them, but they did not stress the point because they did not wish to impose themselves. However, they now feel that they should have been more positive.

A ROMAN CATHOLIC PARISH AND VATICAN II

Over a period of two years two members of the team had discussions with the parish priest of St Anselm's and various groups in his church about different aspects of their parish work and some of the ideas of Vatican II. The priest was trying hard to get the congregation to take a more active part in worship and in Christian education and to do more for people in need. He was also trying to engender a family spirit in the parish and to get parishioners to accept more responsibility for raising money and for administering the church. He was deeply disappointed that his efforts did not have the desired effect. Frequently, in his weekly newsletter and in his sermons, he berated his parishioners for their lack of response.

From the start he was enthusiastic about the project. He saw it as a way of getting his parishioners to do something for others and this, he thought, would have a good effect on the whole life of the parish. He was, therefore, keen on task force and got several church members to attend the meetings. Subsequently three of these people attended the training sessions for lay people and one of these became the principal worker in the scheme to help mothers under stress described on p. 107 ff. But these things did not have the effect on the life of the parish that he desired.

Prior to the advent of the project he had set up a parish council as all Catholic parishes had been told to do. The purpose was to promote consultation, co-operation, and 'co-responsibility'. But the council did not effect the kind of changes he wanted to see and eventually it ceased to meet. He then tried to form a new council by inviting all parishioners to a meeting, but this came to nothing.

It was at this stage that the team started work in Ronsey, and the priest seized the opportunity of asking a team member to help him set up a council. The team member saw a great difference between the ways in which the people and the priest lived and worked. In the main the people were Irish working-class and the priest a well-organized middle-class Englishman. Moreover the priest was trying to impose his ways on the parishioners. For example, he attached great importance to punctuality but many of his parishioners were habitually late at services. He felt this was a mark of disrespect to God, told them so, and arranged for late-comers to hear the Mass in the church hall through a relay system. This had adverse effects on his relationships with his parishioners.

The team discussed these differences with the priest with especial

reference to his attempts to form a parish council. As a result of these discussions he saw that, in trying to set up the parish council, he had not taken into account the way his Irish parishioners normally did things. He now realized, for example, that Irishmen would not distribute bazaar notices from house to house because they saw this as a woman's job. (For them, he said, a few jobs in the home are men's jobs. Others are women's jobs. Men and women do not normally interchange jobs.) The priest now realized that he needed to work with the men and women separately rather than try to get them to work together in a parish council. He did this through working with existing groups of women and through setting up a men's committee to take on some of the administrative and consultative functions of a parish council. Later on, he appointed a male parishioner who had attended the lay in-service training sessions to act as worker to the men's committee.

Concurrently the priest attended phase one of the training sessions for clergy. He began to think how he could apply in his parish what he was learning and how the team could help him, but it was not until phase three of the training sessions that things fell into place for him: when his situation was being discussed he suddenly exclaimed with excitement, 'I now know how the team can help me in my church situation and I want the team to do so'.

With the help of one member of the team he immediately started to reappraise his work in the church and the community; to state his purpose without using formal theological terminology (a difficult task); to establish his priorities and ways of keeping to them; and to reduce his work load until it was manageable.

The priest and the team member also discussed with the men's committee how to get those who attended one of the Masses to make the vocal responses and recite the prayers in the new liturgy. The men's committee suggested 'having a folk Mass and seeing what happens'. (They knew these had been successful in other parishes.) The priest, however, wanted first to discover from the people themselves why they did not respond. Initially the men's committee was strongly opposed to this idea, mainly because it could not see how it could be done without causing offence. 'It would be insulting to ask people why they do not participate in the Mass'. However, the team member got the men to think of ways in which they could, without causing offence, get the parishioners to discuss the problem openly; and to consider the relative merits and de-merits of organizing a folk Mass or exploring the problem. They were still very much for a folk Mass, but decided it 'would be simple prudence' to find out first whether or not it was likely to resolve the problem. Then they worked out a way of getting the problem discussed during a service.

At the same time, the priest, helped by two members of the team, was working at another problem. This was caused by the introduction of a new liturgy and new ways of teaching children the Christian faith. The parents preferred the old liturgy and the ways in which they had learnt their faith in Ireland before the Vatican Council of 1962-65. But their children were all for the new liturgy and responded to the new approach to Christian education. Consequently the children were confused by being told one thing at home and another at school and in the church, and their parents were distressed because they found themselves in a bewildering conflict with their children, their church and the school. The team drew the following diagram to get the problem clear.

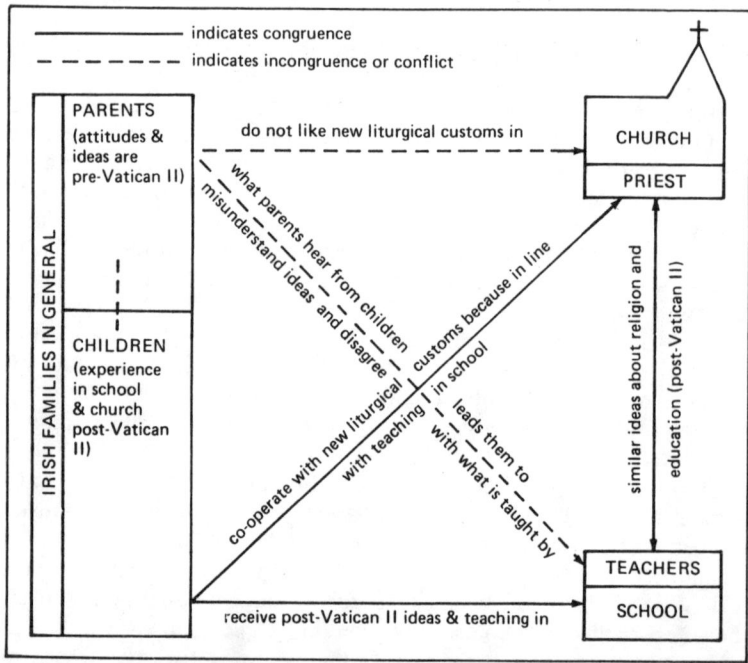

The priest saw that *either* he and the teachers could find a solution to the problem *or* he could try to get the parents involved in thinking out ways of resolving it. He decided on the latter after some hesitation because, while he could see its advantages, he had not previously been in the habit of consulting parents. He worked out a plan with the team and, in order to avoid any misunderstanding, discussed it first with the headmistress responsible for the education of infant and junior children in the parish and then with the teachers. They agreed with the approach, gave him much useful information and promised their support. He also attended a series of diocesan lectures on religious education which some of his parishioners were attending as he thought this would give a natural entry into discussions with them about the problems they were facing.

By this time one of the lay workers had seen a great difference, which she attributed to the work of the team, in the way in which priest and parishioners worked together. 'We now talk things over together in a sort of colleague relationship and a partnership. He now listens to us and takes our suggestions'. And it was at this point that the priest was unexpectedly transferred to another church and his successor did not take up these schemes and consequently both came to an end, and the potential for development inherent in them, so hard gained, was not realized in the parish. Further, whilst the priest had gained much from the work, he was deprived of the experience of working through schemes from which he would have learnt much of value about working *with* people. Whatever good reasons there were for the transfer and the way in which it was effected, it is most unfortunate that it brought to a premature conclusion schemes so full of promise.

Assessment after the team withdrew

Those with whom the team members had worked appreciated the work done and especially the way in which they had helped the men's committee to undertake the duties of a parish council. They attributed what had been achieved to the use of the non-directive approach by the team and the priest.

In December 1975 a member of the team visited the priest in his new parish to talk about Project 70-75. The priest felt that he had been transferred from St Anselm's 'at a time when I was just about to make a breakthrough'. However, he said, that as a result of Project 70-75, he now had different attitudes and approaches towards working with people. He illustrated this from the way in which he was now tackling parish problems in a non-directive way and encouraging others to do the same. Amongst other things he had made arrangements for one of his curates to attend an in-service course on church and community development work.

A COMMUNITY CENTRE SCHEME IN A ROMAN CATHOLIC PARISH

For some years the leaders of St Patrick's Roman Catholic church had felt the need for more accommodation for social activities. In 1970 their parish council set up a community centre sub-committee to find premises but they were unable to do so. However, key lay people kept on referring to the need for a centre. They said, 'The lack of community facilities is the bane of our lives'.

The need for a centre

Team members first visited the parish council in October 1972. Subsequently, by invitation, they discussed with the parish priest and curate, key lay people and the parish council, how they could help to make their parish a better community, that is, 'one in which more and more people could love and help one another'. They felt they could do it by building a community centre; by providing informal opportunities for people to discuss religious, social and personal problems and common needs; by improving communications between groups and individuals; and by establishing a parish information centre: but these things, they said, could be achieved only if priests and people found more effective ways of working together.

It became clear to the team that the people were assuming that until they had a centre they could do little to make the parish a better community, so the team got them to question whether this assumption was true. The team suggested that by starting work with people straight away needs could be met and people be prepared to run and use a centre. The clergy and lay leaders said that they had two thousand parishioners and they feared that work with groups would grow so rapidly that it would soon lead to demands for accommodation which simply could not be met. They said that what they wanted first and foremost was a community centre, and what they wanted from the team was a report which would help them decide how best they could set about getting it.

Working relationships between priests and people

Whilst preparing the report, the team became concerned about the functioning of the parish council. This had been set up to put into practice what the second Vatican Council had said about the need for consultation and co-responsibility in the church. The team found that attempts to do this had led to confusion about roles and responsibilities which in turn had generated misunderstandings between the priests and the laity and nullified some of their joint efforts. The parish priest said that he was in sympathy with the decisions made by the Vatican Council and wanted to work with the laity. But he felt that overall responsibility remained with him and that he must reserve the ultimate right to decide matters affecting the parish as a whole. The lay officers of the parish council accepted this, but they wanted to be assured that their views would be seriously considered, and they wanted to know just what kind of decisions the priest would allow them to make for themselves. It was agreed that, as a basis for further discussion, a statement describing how the priest and lay officers saw their roles and responsibilities should be included in the team's report.

The report

The report gave a resumé of the discussions. It emphasized the need for both the clergy and the parish council to be clear about each other's purposes, roles and responsibilities. It explained that the priests and lay officers saw the role of the parish council; as facilitating consultation between priests and laity; so that while the council could make recommendations and proffer advice it was the prerogative of the parish priest to make the final decisions. Thus it would be up to the priest to decide whether any proposals the parish council might make about building a centre were in his words 'realistic, feasible and likely to further the purposes for which the parish exists'.

The report also outlined ways of creating a better parish community through re-appraising the need for a community centre; promoting discussion groups; improving communications and providing an information centre. It included the following questions to help the parish council consider the report critically: 'Is the report accurate? Are the suggested ways of achieving your purposes practicable? Do you wish to pursue any of the ideas? Are you able to undertake the work involved? Do you want the help of the team?'

The report was discussed at a meeting of the parish council. The team attended to answer questions and then withdrew to allow the council members to consider the report in their own way. They did so 'paragraph by paragraph' with a priest and a lay woman who had attended the training sessions acting as workers and they adopted the report as a useful working brief. They decided to reappraise the need for a community centre in the way outlined on the chart which is reproduced on p. 82 and they asked the team to help them.

The statement about working relationships provoked a lot of discussion. The laity insisted on knowing exactly what the priests would be looking for when assessing whether or not plans for a centre were 'realistic, feasible and likely to further the purposes for which the parish exists'. Without this information they were not prepared to do any further work on the idea for a community centre because they felt that all their efforts could be negated by what could appear to be an arbitrary decision by the priests and that, they said, would make them feel bad towards the priests. Also without this information they did not see how the priests and laity could be co-responsible for the centre. Co-responsibility for them involved priests and laity — in the light of all the available information — working together towards clearly defined goals. The laity were most persistent — and they had to be to get the information. Eventually, after further discussions between priests, laity and the team, the parish priest said that he would be looking for sound evidence that the parish as a whole backed the scheme; that the premises would be used by the parishioners to help meet their needs; that the capital and running costs could be found; and that the centre would not have bad effects on the life of the parish by, for example, generating factions or cliques. Discussing all this cleared up misunderstandings and created deeper mutual understanding between priests and laity.

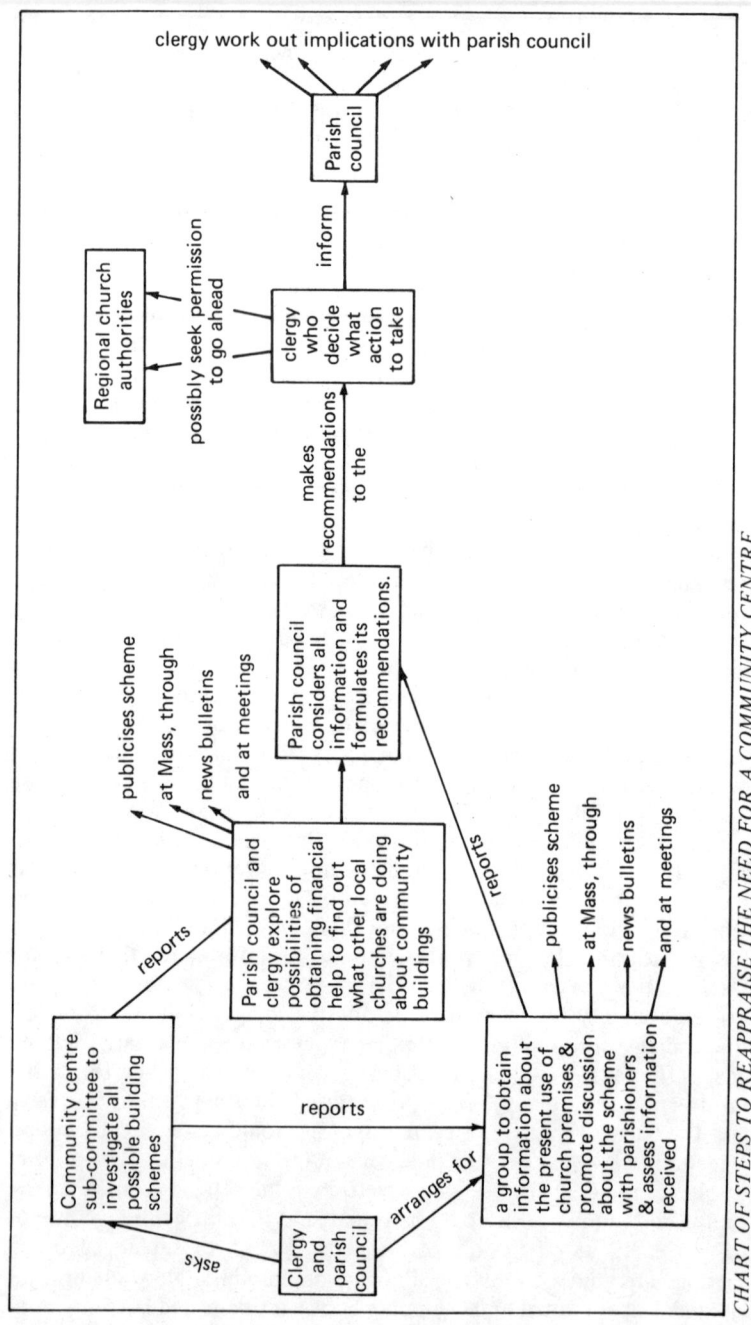

CHART OF STEPS TO REAPPRAISE THE NEED FOR A COMMUNITY CENTRE

clergy work out implications with parish council

Parish council

Regional church authorities

possibly seek permission to go ahead

clergy who decide what action to take

inform

makes recommendations to the

Parish council considers all information and formulates its recommendations.

publicises scheme at Mass, through news bulletins and at meetings

Parish council and clergy explore possibilities of obtaining financial help to find out what other local churches are doing about community buildings

reports

Community centre sub-committee to investigate all possible building schemes

reports

publicises scheme at Mass, through news bulletins and at meetings

a group to obtain information about the present use of church premises & promote discussion about the scheme with parishioners & assess information received

reports

arranges for

Clergy and parish council

asks

Reappraising, consulting and deciding

Reconsidering the community centre idea took fifteen months (March 1973 to June 1974) of hard work. The team worked closely with the parish priest, the parish council, the 'presbytery group' (so called, because of its venue) and the publicity committee. This publicity committee had been appointed by the parish council to obtain information and promote consultation about the community centre idea, and was a group of three: a curate and a lay woman, both of whom had attended training sessions, and a layman. The presbytery group – the priests and the chairmen of the parish council and the community centre sub-committee, together with members of the publicity committee – co-ordinated the work involved in the scheme.

Six major decisions were made by the priests, the presbytery group and the parish council.

Decision one: that the centre would be a community centre for the parish.
They decided initially to concentrate on working with their parishioners rather than the general public. Already, they said, they were in contact with some two thousand people through the church services and schools. The majority of these people were working class Irish people but there were also significant minority groups of working and middle class English, Polish, Asian, African and West Indian people. There was also a considerable number of English and overseas students. Through discussions with the team they saw more potential for development inherent in this large heterogeneous parish than they could cope with, and their first priority, therefore, was to help those with whom they were already in contact to form a better community. They also felt that they would be better able to work *with* others in the community when they had worked *with* their own parishioners for development.

Decision two: That the only possible way of providing a centre was through extending and modifying the presbytery next door to the church.
After thorough investigation, plans were drawn up to facilitate discussion about what would be involved in doing this and to sound out whether or not the local authority would be likely to grant outline planning permission. No difficulties were foreseen in getting planning permission.

But the decision to pursue this idea was not made lightly or easily. Some lay people were exerting considerable pressure upon the priest to agree to it, but he was most apprehensive. The team members made sure that no difficulties were glossed over and they took great pains to clarify exactly what had been decided at each stage of the discussions. This meant going over the same ground repeatedly until agreement had been reached. As the discussions proceeded attitudes changed discernibly: the parish priest became less defensive because he knew that each of his reservations and fears would be taken into account; the lay people became less aggressive because they knew their ideas were being considered seriously.

Decision three: That the parishioners should be consulted before a final decision was made.

The parish priest said that he would not make a decision for or against the centre until he knew whether or not the generality of his parishioners had any use for one, and whether or not they would help to finance, run and maintain it. He said that he 'did not want to build a "folly" or a "white elephant" '. But the problem was how to get to know just what such a vast number of parishioners thought.

The presbytery group and the publicity committee could not think of any way of doing this. The team got them to say what would not work and why. They said their congregations would not attend meetings to discuss ideas and plans even if it were possible to hold them immediately after each service. Also they would not discuss the ideas freely in the context of worship, and they would not fill in and return questionnaires because they were suspicious of them and unused to reading and writing. The team was told that fifteen hundred questionnaires had been sent out in 1970 and of these only forty had been returned.

In order to make sure that the parish priest and the presbytery group really wanted to consult the parishioners, the team members got them to see that consulting could have adverse effects if, in the end, the parishioners felt that their views and feelings had been ignored or overruled arbitrarily by the priest or the parish council. The priest and the presbytery group said that they could overcome this problem by explaining to the people their intentions and just who would play a part in making the final decision; by taking into account what the parishioners said; by keeping them informed of developments; and by explaining to them what decisions had been made, by whom and why.

Taking all this into consideration the team suggested to the presbytery group members that they might be able to get the parishioners to fill in illustrated questionnaries during the services on one particular Sunday. The presbytery group tested the idea thoroughly and thought it a good one. With the help of the team they put it into effect in the following way.

First, the parishioners were told from the pulpit and in the church newsletter over three Sundays about the idea of having a community centre and why and how they would be asked for their views before any decision was made and how a decision would be made. They were also told the kind of questions they would be asked and were invited to think about them and discuss them. Then on the fourth Sunday during each of the six services, in the time normally allocated to the sermon, the members of the congregation were asked for their views about the centre by marking a questionnaire in which the questions

ILLUSTRATED QUESTIONNAIRE USED BY ST PATRICK'S CHURCH

were illustrated by symbols (p. 85). The curate, using an enlarged version of the questionnaire, explained each symbol from the pulpit and demonstrated how their answers should be recorded by marking the symbol with a 'cross', a 'tick' or a '?'. The questions were: Do you want a community centre? For what would you use it? (symbols of various activities were used and a space for people to add suggestions); Would you help to pay for it? (a money bag symbol); Would you help to run and to organize it? (a clock as a symbol of giving time); How old are you? Are you likely to be in the parish in 1977? in 1979? (pictures of people leaving the area with the dates). All the basic information was obtained in this way. People were also given opportunities to put other ideas in writing and many did.

Some twelve hundred people attended church on that day and all of them filled in a questionnaire seriously – no papers were spoilt. Great interest was shown during and after the service and some spoke of an unusual degree of congregational participation. In their replies most people said they wanted a community centre and that they would use it and help to pay for it. A third of them said they would help to run, maintain and organize it.

From this point onwards the parishioners were kept fully informed of developments as they occurred.

Soon afterwards representatives of the church visited people living in the immediate neighbourhood, discussed the proposed centre with them and found them favourably inclined towards it.

Decision four: That people needed to be recruited and trained to manage and run the centre.

Those engaged on this scheme were already fully conversant with two aspects of the work involved – getting a centre built and finding money to pay for it. The third aspect – organizing and managing the centre and recruiting and training people to do so – would not have been considered had it not been for the members of the team. They got the key people and groups to see how these three aspects were interrelated by describing and illustrating them.

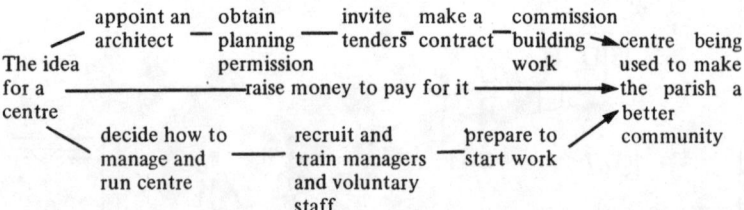

The people now saw the need for the third aspect although some thought the team overstressed its relative importance. All of them found it difficult to conceptualize just what it involved and some were quite unable to do so. The team members found it far more difficult to get people to work on this third aspect than on the other two and they had to remind them continually of it. Eventually, in April 1974, members of the publicity committee, with the help of the team undertook to work on it.

The publicity committee found the task very difficult because they just could not see what it involved. Explanations and discussions about various ways of running and managing a centre and helping people to prepare to work together did not get anywhere. Progress was made in two ways. First, the team remembered how helpful the parish council and the presbytery group had found the chart in the report and produced another chart indicating just what had to be done and in what order (p. 89). This helped all concerned to see the overall picture. Second, the publicity committee and the team decided they should take one step at a time, and that the first step should be a meeting in September 1974 for those interested in running the centre.

Decision five: That they would seek permission from their regional committee to go ahead with the scheme.

The parish council and the parish priest submitted a report to their regional committee summarizing what had occurred so far, indicating all that would be involved in building and running a centre and asking for their approval to implement the scheme. Approval in principle was given and the priest and the parish council were authorized to commission an architect to draw up detailed plans and to apply for planning planning permission.

Decision six: That they would go ahead with the scheme.

They asked the team to prepare a report for the parish council summarizing what had occurred so far, indicating what the next steps would be, and stating what the team would be prepared to do to help the publicity committee to recruit and prepare people to organize and manage the centre.

They commissioned an architect, applied for outline planning permission, set up a group to look into ways of financing the centre and accepted the team's offer to work with the publicity committee. Doing this involved the team members in working with St Patrick's after the date fixed for their withdrawal.

Assessment after the team withdrew

Those with whom the team had worked identified several changes which they attributed directly to the work of the team. *First, working relationships were greatly improved.* The clergy felt that the lay workers now had a more responsible attitude to the work of the parish and 'less wild ideas about what should or should not be done'. Also, the laity felt the clergy had 'unbent and grown in confidence' and that there had therefore been 'a lessening of the traditional arbitrary approach of the clergy'. *Second, a growing spirit of co-operation had been engendered in the parish.* The clergy felt that parishioners now understood more about the problems facing the clergy, and the key lay workers and the parishioners appreciated having been asked for their views. One person remarked that the building committee 'which had been regarded with a certain coolness' was now backed up by the parish council which felt involved in thinking about the centre. It was also noted that the team spirit, already evident at committee level, was gradually spreading to more and more people as they got caught up in the discussions. *Third, more people were now thinking for themselves.* People felt they had learnt to think logically and to co-ordinate ideas. One person said: 'The team taught us to analyze, thoroughly and methodically, our own problems and to seek our own answers'. *Fourth, the need for a community centre really had been examined in depth.* The parish council said 'The team acted as a yeast to some very long dormant dough. We now have a possibility of a viable community centre, a subject which had been bandied around for some considerable time, and whereas before the team's advent there was the will but not the way'.

People attributed these changes to the way the team had listened to both clergy and lay workers; ensured full consultation; gathered various views into simple direct propositions; clarified opinions; set out the course to be followed in charts; treated all aspects seriously; and given people time to think things out and weigh up all the points. Several people said that these approaches would help them to 'tackle all our problems'.

Subsequent developments

Unexpectedly in August 1974 outline planning permission was refused on the grounds that building the centre would result in the over-development of the site and its use would be detrimental to local residents. Members of the presbytery group found themselves more determined than ever to have a community centre but they also wanted to maintain good relationships with their neighbours. They asked for the team's help. Plans for the community centre acceptable to all parties were eventually drawn up, but only after several months of very hard work and a long series of complicated discussions and meetings — at which the team members acted as workers — between the church, the neighbours, local councillors, officers of the planning department, the planning committee and the borough community development unit. Eventually outline planning permission was granted in May 1975.

By that time, however, and to their great disappointment, costs had soared far beyond the resources of the church. They explored without success many possible ways of financing the scheme including 'The job

PHASES OF WORK

Negotiating planning permission and deciding how the people of St Patricks are going to work together on the project during the next phases	Planning and contracting the building work and deciding how and by whom the centre should be run	Building the centre and preparing and appointing people to run it	People running and using the centre
Decide who is going: – to appoint the architect and when; – to instruct him and negotiate with him and how; – to negotiate and decide about tenders and contracts; – to consider the needs of people and the building plans Initial approaches to architect(s) Deciding how money required is to be raised Deciding who is going to work with the people who have shown an interest in running, organizing and using the centre	Appointing architect Discussing and negotiating (with the architect, the builders, the chapter of the order) the plans, tenders, contracts, etc Deciding, in relation to overall purposes, how and by whom the centre should be managed and the organizations/activities led. This would involve considering – different ways of running the centre; – whether and how to involve those who have shown an interest in managing and running the centre; – ways of preparing people for the work of managing centre and running organizations Raising money	Negotiating with the architects and builders Preparing and appointing managers and leaders for organizations and activities Arranging how centre to be organized and run Arranging opening of centre Raising money	Maintaining the building Organizing and managing the work to achieve overall purposes Finding ways of overcoming problems Reviewing work periodically in light of overall purposes Raising money
Parish priests, parish council, publicity committee and building committee (with the help of the team in the earlier stages and possibly the borough community development worker) follow the progress of the work, take appropriate action and keep each other and the parishioners informed of developments			
July to September 1974?	October to January/March 1975?	February/April to December 1975 – January 1976?	January – February 1976 onwards

A POSSIBLE TIME SCALE

creation programme'. Eventually the presbytery group and the parish council decided in January 1976 that the best they could do was to re-vamp the presbytery to provide better accommodation for the priests and some large rooms for community use. Plans were drawn up for which the money was available.

In March 1976 the regional committee decided to transfer the priest and senior curate to another parish, to replace them with two other priests *and* to use some of the rooms in the presbytery to accommodate student priests. Consequently the decision to re-vamp the presbytery was put into abeyance until the new parish priest was installed.

Meanwhile the publicity committee had kept the parishioners informed of developments. They held meetings for those interested in running the centre when there was some assurance that outline planning permission would be obtained. In all they had four meetings, the first in March 1975 and the last in January 1976. The publicity committee and the presbytery group with the help of the team conducted these meetings. Many people wanted to start straight away in the premises that were already available. This again made the parish priest apprehensive that the work could get out of control. However, in November 1975, the team got the parish priest to decide just which rooms in the presbytery and schools could be used, when, and for what activities, and under what conditions. The first group to be formed was a self-help mother and baby club which was well established by May 1976.

The chairman to the parish council in a letter to the team dated May 1976 referred to a recent publication[1] and said that perhaps they ought to be thinking more of the communal use of parish schools to promote development than a community centre.

A COMMUNITY CENTRE IN A BAPTIST CHURCH

Furzedown Baptist church, now demolished, could seat over a thousand people, had extensive ancillary premises for various cultural and social activities, and had for many years attracted large congregations. In its hey-day all seats were taken half-an-hour before the evening service was due to begin. However, in recent years congregations had declined and it had become increasingly difficult to replace church workers and to maintain the premises.

During 1967 the minister and the church members gave a lot of time to thinking about what to do. They first considered their role as a church and decided that, amongst other things, they should aim at meeting the personal and social needs of the people who lived in their neighbourhood. They decided that in order to do this they would have to build new premises on the site of the old ones. They gave much

[1] *Towards a Wider Use*, the Associations of County Councils, District Councils and Metropolitan Authorities.

thought to the use of these premises and decided that they should be 'community buildings' available for worship, Christian education and community work.

Then a new minister was appointed who, through the initial discussions about locating Project 70-75 in Ronsey, saw that community development approaches were relevant to what he and his church wanted to do. On his own initiative he got the deacons and members of his church thinking about this at the beginning of 1972. The result was that in July 1972 two members of the team started to help with the community work aspects of the Furzedown re-development scheme. Doing so involved working with the minister, the church secretary, the church meeting (a monthly meeting of church members which had overall responsibility for the church), and with the deacons board (which acted as an executive committee to the church meeting).

From the outset the minister and the church found that the idea of working *with* rather than *for* people epitomized for them an approach to church and community work they had been groping after during the previous five years. Instinctively they felt it would help them to tackle two major problems they had to overcome to put their ideas into practice. First, how to get people from various church and community work organizations working together in relation to the work of Furzedown as a whole? (They felt that finding ways to do this must have high priority in their development plans.) Second, how to meet the real needs of people in their neighbourhood? (They said they found great difficulty in finding out just what these needs were.)

The team suggested how the Furzedown people could get information about the needs of people in the neighbourhood, but these suggestions were not taken up. They concentrated on the first problem. Over a period of nine months it was considered at private meetings with the minister, the church secretary, at the deacons board, at church meetings, by two working parties and finally at a half-day church conference.

At an early stage one of the team was asked how organizations had worked *with* each other in the church youth and community centre of which they knew he had been the minister. The team member felt that answering this request could lead to difficulties. In the situation to which they referred, people over a number of years had worked out for themselves how best they could work together and had ended up by organizing their own community council. He thought that if he told the Furzedown people about the council they might go for the product (that is, the council concept) and miss the significance of the process (that is, people working out their own ways of doing things). However, they kept on asking him and in the end he gave way and described the council and how it had evolved. He also explained that this particular form of council had been successful because the people themselves had shaped it to fit *their* own particular situation and ways of working. He told them how people had grown together through working out their own system and how because it was theirs, they had made it work; and he warned them of the dangers of trying to copy the *product* rather than the *process*. In spite of all this the deacons board and the church meeting decided to form a council (that is, to copy the product) since they felt it would help people from their own organizations to work *with* each other. They felt this even though some of their organizations had no apparent concern for Furzedown as a whole and were unlikely to want to attend meetings to discuss the overall Furzedown programme.

This was the situation in which the team had to try to get the minister and the Furzedown people to really think out for themselves what would fit them and those with whom they wanted to work. They tried to do this in the following ways.

First, by getting the minister and the people to define their purposes and to discuss the beliefs that motivated them. Basically, they said, they wanted to help people in the church and neighbourhood to live better and more mature lives, and to build a better sense of community by caring for others and sharing their premises with them. They said 'we hope that they will learn to feel at home with us in our premises so that they become part of a true community'. They wanted to do this to help others and to demonstrate their Christian faith by working with God in the world.

Second, by getting the minister and people to see the relationship between their beliefs, their purposes and their approach. The team members were concerned at the way in which the people at Furzedown were talking about the *'with* approach' as though it was an end in itself. By describing the relationship between belief, purpose and approach they helped them to see that the *with* approach to working with people was a means to an end and not an end in itself.

Third, by getting minister and people to picture just how Furzedown was organized and administered. A diagram showing the organizational structure of Furzedown was constructed by a working party. Copies of this enabled people who did not otherwise know the overall situation to contribute to the discussions.

Fourth, by getting minister and people to specify the difficulties they experienced in the way in which Furzedown was currently organized and administered. Community work organizations, because they were not directly represented on the governing body of the church, experienced difficulties in negotiating grants with the local authority, in raising their concerns with the church, and in seeing ways in which they could co-operate to their mutual advantage. The smooth running of Furzedown was over-dependent upon the minister and secretary negotiating between groups which used the premises but which did not normally meet each other.

Fifth, by stimulating minister and people to think of ways, other than through forming a council, of getting church and non-church people to work more effectively together for common purposes. Eventually, several ways were suggested: by organizations inviting others to their meetings; by providing opportunities for people to meet informally; by each organization sending a representative to meetings convened to discuss crises and matters of common concern as they arose; and by providing a 'communal' notice board.

After considering the advantages and disadvantages of each suggestion they reaffirmed their decision to set up a council. They also decided to provide a communal notice board.

Sixth, by getting minister and people to discover what would encourage each organization to participate in meetings about the overall work and what would discourage them from doing so. Organizations, they said, would make sure they were represented at meetings which enabled them to have a say about the design of the new premises and the way in which they were allocated *or* which enabled them to help each other with their difficulties about manpower and the use of the present buildings. However, they would be unlikely to send representatives to meetings which did not have a real job to do nor the authority to do it. They were greatly helped to see these things by a non-church person who served on one of the working parties.

Seventh, by helping minister and people at a half-day's conference to consider the implications of forming a council. A council, they realized, would bring them into closer working relationships with non-church people. They decided that they would achieve their purposes through the council only if there was mutual respect and trust between church and non-church people which led them to work in partnership and to act as 'co-workers' with other organizations concerned with the welfare of people in the community. But, they concluded, the overall responsibility for Furzedown vested in the church meeting should not — and possibly could not — be handed over to a council of church and non-church people. Therefore, they felt they could establish a partnership only if respective roles and responsibilities of the church meeting and council were clearly understood and adhered to. They decided that the church meeting should determine overall policy, for example, they said that the premises should not be used either for political or profit-making activities. They decided that the deacons board should be responsible for church work, and that the council should be responsible for church-community work. They said that the minister was a key figure and that they saw his ministry to include work with church and non-church people alike.

These discussions resulted in Furzedown concluding:

(a) that they should now implement their ideas about working with people; (this approach, they said, 'is as relevant to work being done in the

old building as it will be to that which is planned for the new premises' and that 'it could contribute to the success of the redevelopment scheme'. Some felt that this approach put the emphasis, and rightly so, on people rather than buildings.)

(b) that they could best do this by convening a meeting of represen-tatives of each organization to consider the developments that are occurring, the difficulties that could be experienced during the re-building, and the possibility of working together, say, through a council. (They felt that the policy decisions they had made provided guide lines for those who would be engaged in such discussions.)

Members of the team had prepared a report summarizing the dis-cussions up to the conference. At the request of the minister and the church secretary they now prepared a record of the conference and notes about ways of discussing people's needs (p. 91). They sent these to them together with a letter suggesting a meeting in March 1973 to discuss the next steps. Three months later, in June 1973, not having heard from either the minister or the secretary, the team asked the minister what was happening. He told them that no further action had been taken regarding the decisions reached by the conference since it had now been decided to vacate Furzedown and that currently they were busily engaged in highly confidential discussions with a church of another denomination (Priory Chapel) about the possibility of wor-shipping with them and using their premises during the time Furzedown was being re-built. He also said that he found the new situation both complex and confusing. The team helped him to analyze it and study its implications in order to help him decide what best to do about it and he said that he found this helpful. The team also reminded him that the need to find alternative accommodation would be an opportunity to put into practice the ideas they had already worked out.

The minister did not discuss the situation with the team again until October 1973, some four months later. By this time Furzedown had been closed and its congregation was worshipping with the members of Priory Chapel. Its organizations were meeting in various buildings according to arrangements made by the minister privately with each of the leaders of the organizations concerned. The minister said he had done this instead of following the approach he and his congregation had earlier decided on during the discussions with the team, because of the pressure of events associated with the closure of Furzedown. However, after discussing with the team what he had done and the subsequent developments, he realized that he had missed a valuable opportunity of bringing representatives of all the organizations together. He saw that this would have had many advantages; saved him and other people time and energy and enabled the organizations to help each other in tackling problems arising from the dispersion. And, at the same time, it would have helped to build up a sense of belonging and caring among them. He regretted not having used the approach previously decided upon and said that he now felt much more committed to working *with* people.

Therefore, two of the principal decisions which resulted from the discussions (pp. 93-94) were not implemented and Furzedown decided not to take any further steps towards forming a council until their new premises were ready.

Assessment after the team withdrew

The people with whom the team had worked said that the team had helped them to clarify their ideas and to think in a new way about community projects. Consequently, they had a better understanding of community development and its implications for churches engaged in community work. They said that they had been 'helped to face up to change' and that the full effect of the work with the team would only be felt when the new centre was open.

They felt the approaches and methods used by the team were applicable to other work in the church: preparing carefully for meetings, using a blackboard, isolating key issues, listening to problems, examining the pros and cons of alternative suggestions, describing steps to be taken, writing down decisions, producing reports. These things, they said, helped them to think and discuss.

Some said the reports had been helpful because they were so comprehensive and therefore useful as reference documents. But others felt that the reports should have been shorter and should have included summaries. One person was critical because reports told people much they already knew.

They felt that the half-day conference had been particularly helpful and some said that the development of relationships with Priory Chapel had, unfortunately, prevented the ideas worked out with the team from being put into practice.

Subsequent developments

In February 1976 the minister said that Furzedown had decided with the help of a grant from the Department of Education and Science to build on their old site premises for church, youth and community work. Priory Chapel had decided to sell their premises and continue in union with Furzedown in their new building. The new premises should be ready by June 1977.

There had been no discussions between members of the two churches about working *with* people and forming a council.

3 Working with ecumenical groups

This chapter describes three *community work* schemes on which the team worked with ecumenical groups and how one of the schemes led a member of the team to work with a non-church group.

A COMMUNITY WORK CLERGY TASK GROUP

During phase three of the training sessions for clergy, six clergymen from five churches found that generally speaking they were able to cope with Sunday schools, uniformed organizations and church youth clubs, but not with 'open' youth clubs. Each had had several regrettable experiences of the following sequence of events: successful youth club carefully and slowly opened to others – gradual growth of rowdyism and vandalism among non-church youth – withdrawal of church youth – a situation out of hand – club closed. (Diagram opposite shows an analysis they made of this sequence.) In spite of such traumatic experiences each of the clergy (three Anglicans, one Baptist, one Methodist and one Moravian) still wanted to do something to help non-church young people in their area.

During the course of these discussions it occurred to them that by organizing an open club under the aegis of all their churches they might be able to do together what they had failed to do separately. Spontaneously the group gathered round a map on the wall of the room in which they were meeting, traced out the neighbourhoods and parishes which they covered, and said that as their churches were all grouped in the same area, Victoria Park, they were ideally placed to work together. They decided to explore the possibility of co-operating in open youth work in the area served by their churches and asked a team member and the recorder to help them do so (cf. pp. 98-99).

Open youth work

The group wanted to help young people, regardless of their religious faith and without intent to proselytize, to learn to live so that their deep needs were most likely to be met. And they felt they could best do this by providing opportunities for young people to experience the kind of relationships which would enable them to understand themselves and their potential; to know they were valued for themselves by some people and by God; to understand their need to give, to love and to care for others; and to be conscious of the reality of God. (The clergy expected few, if any, to become associated with the church through this work but they did believe that young people had religious needs.)

Critical choices and decisions

The group made several *critical choices* at one or other of nine three-

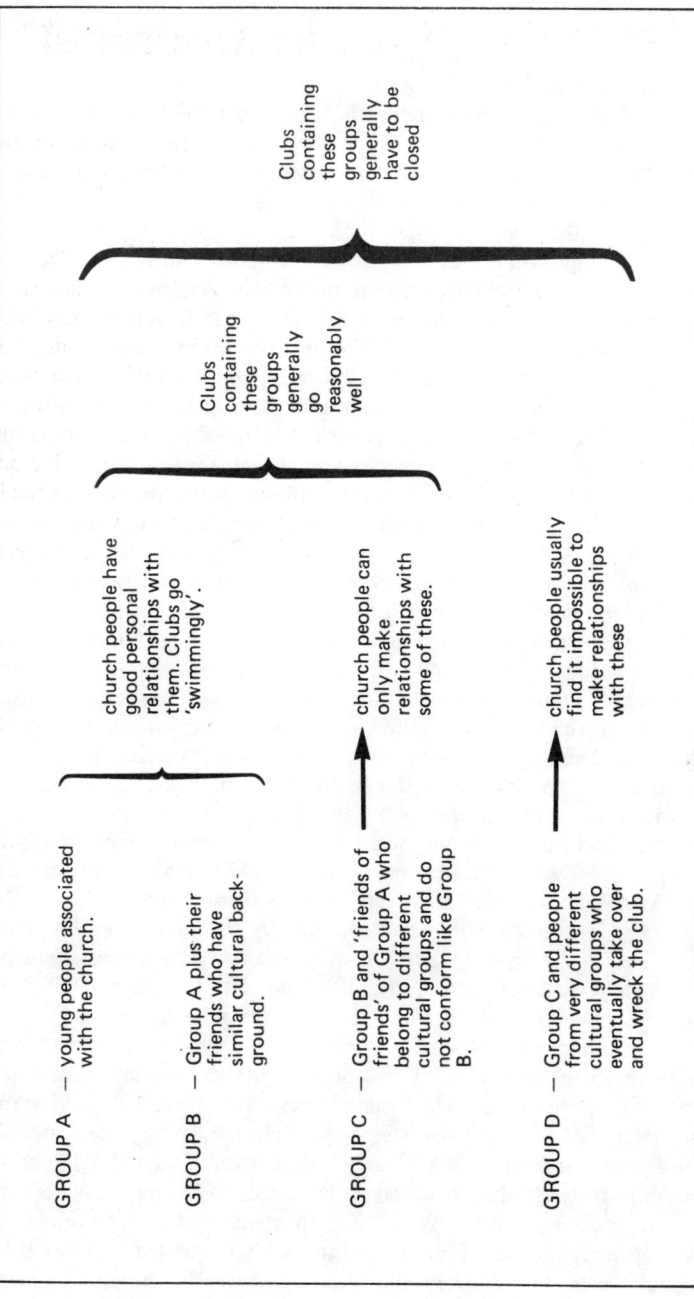

GROUP A — young people associated with the church.

GROUP B — Group A plus their friends who have similar cultural back-ground.

church people have good personal relationships with them. Clubs go 'swimmingly'.

Clubs containing these groups generally go reasonably well

GROUP C — Group B and 'friends of friends' of Group A who belong to different cultural groups and do not conform like Group B.

church people can only make relationships with some of these.

Clubs containing these groups generally have to be closed

GROUP D — Group C and people from very different cultural groups who eventually take over and wreck the club.

church people usually find it impossible to make relationships with these

ANALYSIS BY THE GROUP OF THE PRINCIPAL STAGES IN THE LIFE OF A CLUB

97

hour sessions held during July 1973 to June 1974. It was these choices which determined what the group members did and how they did it, and it was the way these choices were made and put into effect that established deep personal relationships between them. These choices led them to act in ways in which they would not normally have done.

1. They chose to think out each step thoroughly before taking action and to try to get others with whom they worked to do the same. The initial thinking and planning took a lot of time. The team member asked the clergy what they felt about this because in the past he had found that people tend to lose interest when planning is prolonged. The clergy said they had not expected this stage to take so long and that they were very conscious of the need for clubs (a group of boys regularly asked one of them when he was going to start a club). But they were quite adamant that 'the thinking and planning stages are of vital importance and should not be short circuited no matter how long they take — it would be a mistake to move forward too quickly'. Agreement on this point meant that members of the group could think things out without worrying about whether some of them were becoming impatient.

2. They chose to work through their churches rather than as an inter-church group. They felt they were more likely to achieve their purposes if their churches saw it as their project rather than one undertaken by an ecumenical group of open youth work enthusiasts. They put this choice into practice in the following way: as a group they gathered information and formulated ideas for action; as individuals each got to know just what his own church thought about their ideas; as a group they worked out the implications of what their churches had said; and as individuals each got the views of his church on what the others had said. This may seem complicated, but in fact it enabled six clergy and five churches to work together and to make more progress in one year than they had made separately in many years.

3. They chose to commend Christianity by actions rather than words, and by answering questions about their faith rather than by initiating conversations about it. They said that they often felt they were neglecting their duty when they worked with young people but did not tell them about their Christian faith and what it meant to them. The team member got them to consider the various ways in which Christians communicate what they believe to others — by speaking about it; by identifying themselves with a church; and by their actions, attitudes and insights. They decided they would be most likely to communicate what they believed through using Christian insights into life to help young people; by the way they behaved to each other and to young people; and by answering unsolicited questions about their Christian faith. And they recalled that in the early church Christians were told in some situations to let their lives speak for them and to reserve their verbal defence of their faith until questioned about it (cf. 1 Pet 3.1, 15).

Over a period of months they reconsidered this decision several times because one or two of them still had niggling feelings that they were neglecting their duty. On each occasion the decision was critically reconsidered and new points for and against it emerged. But the conclusion was always the same and gradually each member of the group became more positive towards the decision.

4. They chose to work in partnership with others rather than to 'go it alone' or act as a 'pressure group'. In making this choice they considered whether they should discuss beliefs with others before agreeing to work with them, but decided against it since they felt they should initially establish working partnerships with others solely on the basis of a common concern for young people. (This incidentally was the basis on which the members of the group had initially agreed to work together.) They said that people know what the aims of the churches are but want to know what they are prepared to do to achieve them; and that any discussion of aims and beliefs should be in the context of actual work and therefore be concrete instead of abstract and impersonal. They felt that they could be as faithful to their aims and beliefs in this way as in any other. Also, it was more likely to establish effective working relationships and it was in line with what they had already chosen to do about commending Christianity.

5. They chose to collect information about the extent of the need and ways of meeting it before making any specific plans. Initially the members were thinking about how they could get churches and other agencies to work together on a joint open youth club project, but finally decided to collect more information before deciding what to do.

They considered two possible ways of doing this. First, they could invite people such as youth officers and head teachers to a meeting, but decided against this because they felt that the people who came might not talk as freely as they would if they were on their own. Second, they could visit such people individually, collate the information obtained, and then consider it at a group meeting before deciding what action to take. They realized that this would take much more time, but decided to adopt it because they felt that in that way they would get more relevant information; and 'would not be pushed into making decisions and taking action prematurely'.

Several of the clergy and the team member made the visits. (The team member helped the clergy to prepare for the visits, took notes and prepared a record for the group.) They visited two borough youth officers, two community relations officers, four head teachers and two officers of a local tenants association. All those contacted said that there was need for open youth work in the area, were glad the churches were taking an initiative and wanted to be kept in touch.

The clergy sorted out the information and the team member listed on a black-board all the topics covered in the interviews: the size of the catchment area; the need for open youth work in the area; the kind and ages of young people in the area; the recruitment of youth workers from among teachers, the police, immigrant groups, the churches and through the local authority; financing the work; vandalism; premises, equipment and insurance; and possible approaches to open youth work. Second, under each topic heading they made notes of what had been said by the people they had seen. Third, they considered what had been said in the light of their own experience and made notes of their conclusions. The following short extract from the record of this meeting illustrates just what they did.

VANDALISM

Points made by those interviewed	*What the group thought*
Smith suggested that the way of dealing with vandalism is through establishing good relationships with the young people. This may mean getting to know them in their own neighbourhood outside the clubs.	Smith's suggestion seems reasonable.
Youth officers suggested that a group of church young people should be recruited to control vandals.	The youth officers' suggestion has not worked. No other constructive suggestions made.
The youth officer suggested (urged) the group to apply to the local authority or Urban Aid for finances.	In discussing finance the group felt that the way in which the club is financed could have an important bearing upon vandalism. If all the money is provided by the local authority, charities or churches, the young people are less likely to value the club than if they themselves have raised some of the money. Again if some of the money is raised by local people they are more likely to prevent vandalism by their own methods. (The Cranstead Tenants Association are concerned to reduce vandalism.) If the young people have some control over the finances, vandalism is likely to be less than if they have no control over them. If the whole community can be mobilized, as in Jamaica, to deal with problems of vandalism, it is more likely that they will be overcome. One difficulty is to involve immigrants. They are not involved in committees in the area.

6. They chose to discuss the scheme with their churches after they had clarified their ideas and before making specific plans. It was only after much discussion that they made this choice. Initially some of the clergy could not see their way to getting these ideas discussed in their churches. They saw advantages in churches deciding on principles before making plans but they said that people in their churches would dismiss the scheme as 'too airy fairy' if detailed information about the venue of the club, costs and names of leaders was not already available. The clergy decided to cope with requests for this kind of detail by explaining the approach they were adopting and the advantages it had over presenting schemes planned to the last detail. This enabled the clergy to get the ideas and principles discussed.

When the clergy were considering how to find out what their churches thought about the scheme, the team member suggested that they should not feel they would have succeeded if their church agreed to the ideas put forward or have failed if it did not. Such feelings could have adverse effects on the group and its work. They decided that 'the object is not to push the thing through. It is to tell people about the problem, the information and the ideas and to get their views'. Therefore, they would 'succeed' if they promoted honest discussion.

Each church was enthusiastically in favour of the five churches working together, and in partnership with such other bodies as the local authority and the tenants associations. In general they agreed with the purposes worked out by the clergy although some felt that they 'sounded very clerical and high-falutin'. They also thought that counselling young people should be an integral part of any work undertaken; that the work should start through 'street-walking leaders' contacting young people on the streets and in the parks; and that as far as possible, clubs and activities should be run by young people themselves.

7. They chose not to start on other tasks nor to invite others to join the group until they had got on top of the open youth work task and had determined just what other tasks they wanted to do as a group and how they were going to organize themselves. About half-way through the year's work three things occurred which eventually led the group to make this choice. First the group was asked by one of its members and by the co-ordinating committee of the good neighbour scheme to consider what it could do to help implement the new ideas about the scheme (see pp. 129 ff). In fact the clergy were very concerned about pastoral care and the good neighbour scheme but although they did put it on the agenda of two or three meetings each time they postponed discussing it. Second, some members suggested that others should be invited to join the group. This suggestion was turned down when the team member pointed out the possible dangers of enlarging the group at this stage in its development. Third, the clergy were finding it very difficult to decide what action to take about open youth work. True, they now had their purposes clear, the approaches they were going to adopt, the situation in which they had to work, and what their churches felt and thought, but they had not yet been able to decide what action to recommend to their churches.

The team member was concerned about the situation and eventually decided that he would summarize what had happened since they first started discussing open youth work and then ask them to say just how they felt. They did this very openly. They said that they had considered the open youth work task very carefully before accepting it and they really wanted to complete it. They said that they attached great importance to the group and its work; that changes only be made after full consideration of all the implications; and that with this understanding they were prepared to consider any suggestions about the future membership or work of the group. They decided that whatever happened about the open youth work the group ought to continue, 'it is a tremendous source of strength'. They also decided that their first priority now was to decide what action to take about open youth work; their second to consider what form the group should take in the future and what work it should do; and their third, to consider what to do about the good neighbour scheme.

8. They chose to adopt a multi-pronged approach to open youth work in place of their initial idea of inaugurating an open club. Through their discussions and the contacts the members had made they now saw several possible openings through which they could contribute to open youth work: and the team member realized that the clergy had not yet come to a decision because they were trying to decide what to do about one or other opening without seeing the overall picture. To help them do this he constructed the diagram opposite of all the various possibilities open to them.

The clergy immediately saw from this diagram that most of these openings were not mutually exclusive, and in a very short time decided just what they were going to do and who was going to do it. Between them they decided to keep people informed of developments; to continue helping and supporting members of the tenants' association in what they are doing to help working class young people, and to encourage other church people to do so; to offer to help one of the churches develop a football club; to co-operate with the headmaster and staff of a local junior school in a school-based youth programme; to stimulate young people to engage in community care; to convene consultations about open youth work when they thought the time appropriate; and to discuss with the community development and youth officers the possibility of appointing a detached worker to explore the need for, say, a shop that could be used for youth counselling.

9. They chose to form themselves into a 'community work task group'. Only when the clergy felt they had thought out a realistic

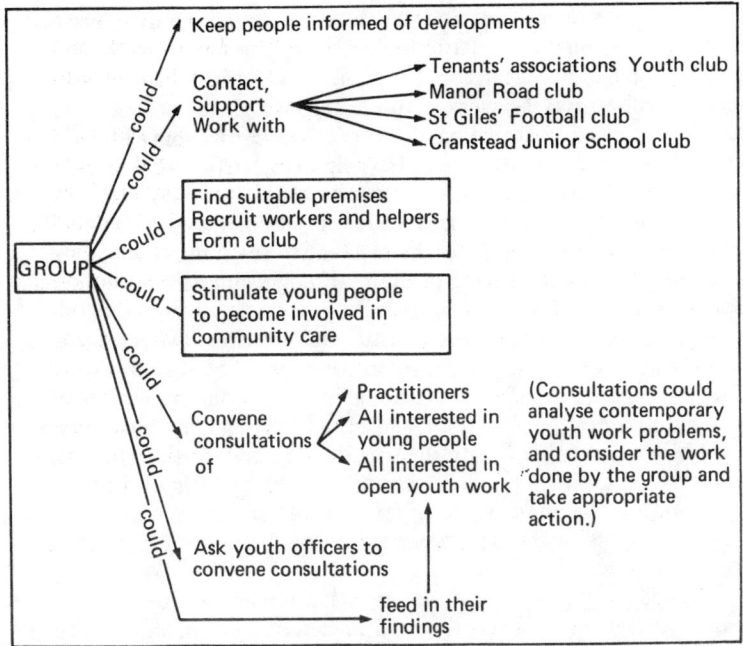

programme of youth work did they consider the future of the group. They said they had found this group different from any other they had attended. They found it satisfying because 'through working together we have grown together and achieved things'. They insisted that it must continue to be a task or working group and not be allowed to become one of those 'discussion groups which never get anywhere' – of which they said they had many unfortunate experiences.

They agreed that the tasks undertaken would be related to community work and not church and church-community work and they decided to extend their work to include the pastoral care of people in the community; and Christian, social and moral issues raised locally and nationally.

In order to consider how the group could function as a task group without the help of the team they got the team member and the recorder to describe the functions they had performed. They did this as follows:

'Before meetings The team member summarizes and considers the previous work and tries to picture the situation, to get the issues clear in his mind. He formulates questions which need to be considered and which will enable the group to explore the subject openly and constructively. He works out how to start the meeting, ways of tackling tasks or exploring subjects or examining problems. He sends information to members of the group, explains to the recorder how he proposes to start the meeting, and discusses the kind of notes that might be useful.

CHURCHES AND COMMUNITIES

During meetings The recorder takes notes and only participates verbally when matters relating to recording the meeting are discussed or when she is not clear about a point or when invited to do so. The team member acts as worker to the group. He helps the group to decided what *they* are going to do, why *they* are going to do it and how *they* are going to do it. He helps to clarify ideas, to find the relationship between them and to put them into some meaningful order, and he helps people to identify problems and tackle them systematically. Frequently he helps them to see the overall picture of what they have been saying or doing through summarizing events and discussions.

After meetings The recorder writes up the notes. The team member uses these to write a structured account or record of the meeting which clarifies the points made and sets them in order without distorting what was said or meant by the group. (This is a demanding job but one which helps him to get to grips with the situation and the issues.) The recorder reads the record to see that it represents what was said in the meeting. The team member and the recorder prepare for the next meeting. This may involve discussing with a colleague how best to act as worker in a given situation.'

The clergy studied these statements carefully. They said that the team member and the recorder had made critical contributions to the effectiveness of the group through performing the functions described. (They also said that 'the effectiveness of most church groups at local, regional and national level would be greatly increased if they were serviced by people able to perform these functions'.) *They said that the group could only continue to work effectively if they now made arrangements for someone other than the team or the recorder to perform these functions.* Eventually they decided:

(a) that no other person is likely to perform these functions in the same way as the team member and the recorder and to try to copy them slavishly would be to court folly: the group members must work out their own way of performing these functions and their own pattern of working;

(b) that different members of the group would act as worker for different subjects, (no one person felt he could or should act as worker to the group for all the subjects; two people were prepared to act as workers on open youth work and pastoral care; two others said they would probably be able to do so later if required);

(c) that the group would not undertake a task unless and until someone was able to act as worker in relation to it;

(d) that their recorder should be someone other than a group member.

In the discussions leading up to these decisions the clergy were remarkably open about what they felt they could and could not do and showed warmth of feeling to each other. They were particularly concerned when deciding who could and should take on jobs not to 'overload people or put them in embarrassing positions'. This was quite a different approach from that in other clergy meetings in Ronsey when they tended to press each other to take on jobs without respecting personal wishes. (Commenting on these developments one of the advisers said, 'If the project had only achieved this new relationship between the clergy . . . it would have been worthwhile!')

They now felt able to consider the membership of the group. They decided it should remain the same and when appropriate other people could be invited to work with the group on specific tasks.

Thus the clergy formed themselves into an autonomous community work task group and the team member and recorder withdrew in June 1974.

Assessment after the team withdrew

Many of the things the clergy felt about this scheme are reflected in their overall evaluation of the team's work (see pp. 71-72) and in what they said when planning the future of the group (see pp. 102 ff.). This assessment reports what the clergy said at an evaluation meeting with the team in February 1975.

They said that the arrangements made for people to act as workers and recorder to the group were working out very satisfactorily. Workers had been able to introduce structure into the meetings. But, they added, whilst one person accepts primary responsibility for acting as worker when a particular topic is discussed, all the members now perform worker functions at one point or another by asking questions and helping to clarify what is meant.

They said they were still a task group. After the meeting the person acting as recorder, who was not a member of a church and had joined the group after the team had withdrawn, said spontaneously, 'This group is very different from any other I go to. It does not go round and round in circles like others do, discussion is progressive. People in this group are asking questions and trying to get to the truth. They have entirely different attitudes, they are task oriented and a working group.'

Records, they said, were continuing to be useful. They were more brief than the ones produced by the team and they thought they were better for this.

They said that in relation to open youth work they had established good working relationships with the borough youth officer and the community development officers responsible for their area.

One member felt that the group had 'left too much to the team member'. He admitted that he had not always done his homework for a meeting because he knew the team would have done so! Discussing this led the clergy to see that it was only when they had experienced working through a cycle of events non-directively — that is, of determining aims, getting a clear picture, looking at alternatives and deciding what to do — that they knew what homework to do and how to do it.

The group members said that what they had found most helpful was the way in which the team member was able to help them to picture situations through diagrams which put things that appeared disconnected into 'some pattern or shape'. One person said, 'I was quite conscious of deliberately throwing things in at times which I knew didn't fit into the picture just to see what he would do with it'. Once a diagram was produced illustrating the basic shape of things, the clergy said they then saw the possibility of getting 'the picture right' and knew how to 'start to work on it'. They described this as an 'analytical approach' which they were continuing to use: 'We have the motivation to try and do it now that we have seen it is possible and have experienced its usefulness'.

They said that now they had experience of proper consultation they could not overstate its value. One person said that initially he had found the team member's approach slow. At the time he hadn't seen why it was necessary to look at all the alternatives before making choices, but in the end he saw just how effective it was to do so. He is using the non-directive approach in his church work. He said that some of his people towards whom he is adopting a non-directive approach also feel it is slow. They say 'Tell us what to do and let's get on with it'. He is trying to get them to consider the advantages as well as the disadvantages of thinking things out properly and the disadvantages as well as the advantages of short-circuiting the thinking process.

They all said that they had lost some of their suspicions of the clergy of other denominations.

Subsequent developments

By February 1976, that is, some eighteen months after the team's withdrawal, this group had established a walk-in counselling centre for young people in a shop in the centre of their area, Victoria Park. In order to do this members had got funds to run the centre; accepted responsibility for employing a full-time youth worker who was a specialist in counselling young people and who was seconded to them by the borough; appointed a part-time receptionist; recruited the part-time services of several counsellors and psychiatrists; established a network with others engaged locally in counselling and caring for young people; established steering and executive committees representative of local churches, borough authorities and the borough education service and got the people concerned working closely together. The shop, when they acquired it at a low rental, was derelict. Together with others, including some young people, they re-modelled it as an attractive counselling centre. The centre was soon used by all kinds of young people who wanted information or advice or counselling. And all this had been achieved at a time of high inflation when the borough was cutting back on its expenditure.

The members of the group felt that this counselling service would uncover other unmet needs of young people in their area and help them to decide what to do about them.

They had also become involved in the good neighbour scheme.

They said that they had continued to adopt the approach which they had learnt from the team. For instance, they now habitually arrived at decisions by assessing the alternatives open to them in relation to their purposes. They found this helped them especially when their work took unexpected turns which could have deflected them from their purposes. Also, increasingly, before entering into partnership with others they discussed openly with them whether or not there was sufficient congruence of purpose and approach to make for effective working relationships.

The clergy said they were finding the group a great source of strength and because they get on so well three of the churches of different denominations are considering other ways of co-operating and working together.

Two members of the borough authority who had worked closely with the group said that 'there is an integrity and sincerity about this group that we have not come across elsewhere. Everything is brought out into the open and discussed. No-one plays a power-game and no-one holds back information which would enable him to do something on the side to build up his own little empire'. Obviously the borough officers greatly respected the group and were pleased to work with it. These clergy had indeed got people to take them seriously (cf. p. 51).

HELPING MOTHERS UNDER STRESS

Just before the team started work in Ronsey a local case of a mother battering her baby had made Priory Chapel's Women's Council want to help young mothers likely to be driven to such violence. In October 1972 they formed an ecumenical working party to see what could be done. It consisted of four Congregationalists, an Anglican, a Roman Catholic and a person with no church affiliation. Among them were two headteachers, two playgroup leaders and a Guider. One was attending the training sessions for lay people. They invited a team member to work with them and she did so until November 1974. They had eleven meetings and did a great deal of work.

Formulating initial ideas

The working party said that they wanted to help to set up a club for mothers from the lower working class who were under stress. The team member was aware of the difficulties that the group of mainly middle and upper middle class women could have in trying to help disadvantaged working class mothers. She decided that her first task was to get them to think out what they proposed to do. She did this in three ways.

First, she got them to consider whether to provide a club for the mothers *or* whether to get the mothers themselves to say what kind of club they required and help them to provide it. They were apprehensive about the latter approach because they had no previous experience of working in that way, but in the end they chose it because it could make mothers more self-reliant.

Second, she got each member of the working party to say what she could do to help the mothers. They realized that they were at work during the day when they thought the mothers would be most in need of help. Also, they felt they might not be acceptable to the mothers because of differences in age, background and social class. (They thought that two mothers clubs had already failed in their area because they were run by middle class people.)

Third, she got them to consider finding someone who would be acceptable to the mothers and prepared to work with both them and the working party. This appealed to them and they worked out the criteria for the sort of person they were looking for: someone who lived near the mothers, was acceptable to them and accepting of them, was a good listener and a person the mothers could trust. The working party would support such a person.

The team member and the working party produced a working paper setting out the ideas for the scheme. It formed the basis for their initial work and was useful in communicating their ideas to others.

At the suggestion of the team member, they discussed their ideas with all the clergy in Ronsey, three headteachers, four play-group leaders, a health visitor, a social worker, the local N.S.P.C.C. worker, the wife of the chaplain of a women's prison, and the matron of a local hospital. All said thee were many young mothers in Ronsey in need of help and support who for one reason or another did not make use of existing facilities; but a few of them also said that only 'trained' people could help such mothers and this caused some of the working party to feel that the problem was beyond them. However, when the team member got them to reflect on their own early experiences of bringing up children, they realized that when they had felt at the end of their tether it was often the woman next door who had helped them. Their confidence restored, they decided to go ahead even if it meant starting in a small way.

Trying to get a working class mother to promote self-help in her neighbourhood

After much searching, two working class mothers interested in helping mothers under stress were found. One was particularly enthusiastic when she realized that she would have a say in making the plans and would have the support of the working party.

However — despite an agreement that they should not talk about the scheme until the time was ripe — the two mothers did talk to other women and, unfortunately put them off. This dampened their enthusiasm but they still wanted to continue and asked for a room in which mothers could meet. The working party tried, but failed, to get permission to use a room in a local church. Both mothers then lost heart and withdrew from the scheme because the negotiations with the church had taken a month.

Trying to get a group of working class mothers to promote self-help in their area

The working party said they were even more determined to find some way of helping mothers under stress. They felt that the response of the two mothers showed that it was possible to find the kind of people required. They also said that their experience over the room showed how important it was to make immediate responses to requests.

The team member suggested they might have more success if they gathered together a group of five or six working class mothers and considered with them what they could do to help mothers under stress. After much discussion the group adopted this idea and decided to try to implement it in one neighbourhood but only when they had the promise of a meeting room. They got the promise of a room and asked several people to help them to recruit a group of mothers. Two tried: a headmistress, but she was unsuccessful, and a Roman Catholic parish sister, who found two mothers.

Therefore the attempt to put this second idea into practice failed but the two mothers were prepared to help in the scheme, and a member of the working party was now prepared to work with the team member and the mothers on the scheme. She was a mother with young children, deeply committed to the aims of the scheme, got on well with working class people, and had attended the training sessions for lay people.

The Wednesday Helping Hand Club

Again, the team member got the working party to review the situation, and they decided to continue with the two mothers they had found.

The team member, the member of the working party and the two mothers decided to try to form a 'Wednesday Helping Hand Club'.

109

They composed a leaflet advertising it 'for mothers with young children who want an outlet – like to meet others – sometimes need help themselves – would like to make friends'. The working party distributed the leaflets to all local doctors, dentists, clinics, shops, libraries, churches and schools. They also gave copies to people who worked with mothers in the neighbourhood, talked to them about the idea and asked them to tell any mothers about it.

This led to the Legion of Mary (a group from St Patrick's of mostly working class women) and people from other churches offering to distribute leaflets to all the homes in the selected area. Two of the working party and the team member met them to explain the ideas underlying the scheme and to help them to work out how best to distribute the leaflets, to start off the door-step conversations; to describe the club; to explain their own involvement ('We ourselves are from the church, but we are doing this to help a community group'); to explain why St Mark's was being used ('We had to have somewhere to meet and we were offered this room – it's very central'); and to respond to people who did not seem to be interested. The Legionaries offered to put brief reminder notices on the evening before the first meeting through the letter boxes of those houses in which mothers had sounded interested. To lessen any possible adverse reactions to leaflets they put a recipe on the back, 'at least one side of the paper will be seen to be useful!' they said.

In January 1974 the club started to meet one afternoon a week. The team member and the working party member were co-workers to the club. They arranged the club affairs with those who attended: the two mothers who helped found the club came spasmodically. When the working party member had gained confidence she worked with the mothers on her own whilst the team member looked after the children with a member of the good neighbour scheme who had volunteered to help. By July 1974 over twenty mothers, some of them under severe stress, had attended at one time or another, although there had rarely been more than two or three at any one meeting. Undoubtedly some of those who had come had been considerably helped but the team member and the working party member had found the work 'an uphill struggle'. Nevertheless they still wanted to continue.

The team member got those most interested in the club to review the situation. The outcome was a decision to use the club as an informal first aid centre for people under stress; the main purpose of which would be to introduce them, as they gained confidence, to other clubs with appropriate facilities. And the two mothers who had recently become members of the club – neither of them under stress and one of whom had attended the training sessions for lay people – offered to help run the club.

This inaugurated a new phase of work. The team member no longer attended the club but she met regularly with the four helpers to prepare for club meetings, to establish links with other clubs and caring organizations in the neighbourhood and to think of ways of building up the club. The helpers decided to put a lot of effort into publicizing the club during the autumn of 1974 and in January 1975 to decide whether or not to continue.

During the autumn the attendance remained low and erratic but those who came were working class mothers of many nationalities and some were under great stress. The helpers were able to put one mother in touch with the social services and they were also able to support other mothers between meetings, but they continued to find the small response depressing.

In January 1975 when they came to decide whether or not to continue, the helpers had very mixed feelings. On the one hand, they felt they were making little headway despite all the time and energy they were expending on the club and they were disappointed that those professionally in touch with mothers in the area were not making use of their services. On the other hand they felt committed to each other and to the mothers they were trying to help.

After a great deal of discussion they decided to try to arrange a meeting of professional people in the area to tell them what they had been doing about the problem of mothers under stress and the difficulties they had met. They said they hoped that such a meeting would enable them to decide what future action they should take. They discussed their plans with the working party who said they would continue to support the club, ensure that there were supplies of leaflets at strategic places, and keep in touch with developments.

This was the point at which by agreement the team member withdrew.

Assessment after the team withdrew

All those involved were pleased at the way in which mothers coming to the club had formed good relationships and found relief from strain through talking about their problems. All said it had been hard to overcome the difficulties and face the setbacks but that in doing so they had learnt a great deal about the problems and needs of mothers under stress and the difficulties of those trying to work with them. At the same time they had benefitted from the friendships they had formed. Several commended the way in which laity and clergy had worked together, discussed ideas, faced and tackled problems. Several said that the scheme would not have got off the ground without the help and perseverance of the team, but they hoped the work would continue because people felt an increasing obligation to help mothers under stress and had become more confident in their ability to do so.

Subsequent developments

In fact the helpers did have discussions with professional people – the health visitors and the nursing officer for the area. They promised their support and offered them the use of a room in the clinic one morning a week but only after lengthy discussions which assured them that the helpers really wanted to help mothers and not simply to further sectarian, political or religious interests.

And so, in February 1975, the helpers started a club. Health visitors and social workers referred mothers to the club and soon there was a regular attendance of fifteen to twenty mothers of different classes and nationalities.

The helpers continued to promote self-help. Within a short time the mothers organized various social activities and outings, helped lonely immigrants, promoted discussion amongst themselves about their problems, formed a baby sitting circle and arranged for people to talk to them on subjects such as marriage guidance and accidents in the home.

The mothers had an unfortunate experience of church authorities. They applied for permission to hold a Christmas party in a church hall (neither of the ones referred to earlier). The church took a long time to reply and then refused permission. Although another church did allow them the use of their hall, this experience put them off applying to churches for other club room facilities.

The club was greatly valued by the mothers because, one of them said, 'It provides a chance for women to make friends and begin to break through any loneliness and depression they may be feeling'.

Several enquiries were received from mothers who attended other clinics about how to set up such a club. One such enquiry led to a club being formed in the Cranstead community centre in April 1976. The club attracted a lot of local support. One of the members said, 'We want to give ourselves a chance to get out, so we're not tied to the house all the time'.

One of the founding members of the Helping Hand club was actively engaged in setting up the Mother and Baby club at St Patrick's (see p. 90).

YOUNG MOTHERS AND THEIR NEEDS

A young married woman moved into Ronsey and gave up her job on having her first child. Soon she found herself depressed, frustrated, bored and desperate because she did not have sufficient intellectual stimulus, because she was living in an area in which she was unknown and looking after a baby without the help of friends and relatives. Through writing to the local paper she met three other mothers similarly placed. They wanted to set up a centre for mothers and children but did not know how to go about it.

Clarifying the needs

At this point someone from the mothers-under-stress scheme put them in touch with the members of the team. A meeting was arranged and for over an hour the mothers poured out their feelings. They explained what they wanted to do; they talked about their ideas on bringing up children; and they said that they feared their negative reactions to the daily routine of child-minding and housework could have adverse effects on themselves, their children and their marriages.

The outburst released their pent-up feelings and frustrations and enabled the mothers to relax. Then with the aid of a diagram the team members helped them to put the various things they had said into some order. First, they had what they called 'material needs': an acceptable baby-minding service or crêche, and a meeting place where they could share their experiences and find support when they were depressed. Second, they felt a need to extend themselves mentally and emotionally. Third, they wanted to find practical ways of working out their ideas about how children should be brought up. Fourth, they wanted opportunities to become involved in something which would benefit themselves, their children and the community.

The team helped them to clarify their purposes and objectives and the principles upon which they thought child-minding services should be based. Then the team explained that basically there were two approaches by which they could try to put their ideas into practice: the directive and the non-directive. On the one hand, they could set up and run a centre according to their own ideas (directive) or, on the other hand, they could bring in other mothers with similar problems and work out ideas for a centre with them (non-directive). The mothers decided in favour of this second alternative since they felt it would at one and the same time meet all their needs and not least their desperate need of mental stimulation. They were now excited about the possibilities open to them.

Immediately after the meeting one of them wrote an excellent paper as a basis for discussion. It described their needs; it outlined different ways of meeting them and listed the pros and cons of each. It emphasized the importance of the values in a nursery or crêche being consonant with those of the home, and of mothers, and desirably fathers also, being involved in planning, organizing and running crêches and meeting places on a self-help basis.

The team introduced to the group the young wife of a minister who, since she came to Ronsey not long before, had been in much the same plight as themselves, and she quickly became an active member of the group.

Meeting the needs

The group of mothers asked one of the team to work with them because, they said, 'on our own we go round in circles at meetings'. And so, one member of the team attended seven meetings between May and July 1973.

The group members met some of their immediate needs by organizing a crêche in their homes twice a week. This attracted several other mothers some of whom attended regularly. Initially they tried to do their long term planning at the crêche but they found it hard to concentrate because of interruptions by the toddlers and so decided to hold planning meetings in the evenings while the fathers looked after the children. The original group of five did most of the planning since some of the mothers who had joined them did not want to take part but they wanted to keep in touch with developments. This they did at the crêche.

The team member found it difficult to get the mothers to plan as systematically as she would have liked since, not surprisingly in view of what had originally brought them together, they were all most interested in conversation and in swapping anecdotes about their children. However, in spite of this handicap, she was able to help the mothers to work a little more systematically than they would otherwise have done. After a few meetings, the mothers decided to approach the borough authorities to find out if they would provide accommodation for a mother's and children's centre. They thought they would only get what they wanted if they could exert a good deal of pressure, so they talked of 'mounting a campaign', 'getting up a petition', of writing demanding letters to officials and of getting councillors to pressurize officials to act. The team member asked them what they hoped to achieve through contacting the borough officials. They said they wanted to share ideas about the unmet needs of young mothers, to see what the council was prepared to do to help them, and to say what they were prepared to do to help themselves and others. Then, she got them to compare the likely results of making the approach they initially thought of with that of making a reasoned request for help. Finally, she gave them information about the existing provision in the borough for 'under fives' and explained how the council wanted to promote consultations with local residents.

The group members became less aggressive. They began to think of borough officials as human beings and they decided to act in the first instance as though they expected co-operation. They wrote a letter to a borough official briefly describing their ideas and asking for a meeting and, prior to the meeting, they spent two hours with the team member working out just what to say at the meeting and how to say it. They found the borough official sympathetic. In due course he arranged for them to use a vacant social services centre where their children were cared for by play leaders and where they could have sessions of the kind they wanted on 'understanding children's art', 'making music' and 'new maths'. These sessions were provided by the education authority in consultation with the mothers.

Assessment after the team withdrew

One member wrote later: 'The team was helpful in giving time, support and encouragement to a group in its early uncertain stages' and she said that the team had helped them to make effective approaches to the borough official and local day nurseries. Another mother who joined the group in order to arrange for her child to be looked after during the day so that she could return to work, said she had decided not to return to work because she found working on the scheme more satisfying.

One person found the educational programme valuable but she left the group early in 1974 because she preferred a different type of provision and had found it elsewhere. She felt the strength of the group lay in it being 'a grass roots movement' but thought that it would have been more effective if it had been more formally organized, if it had 'hammered out its aims and methods more clearly'. if it had been better informed about 'the working and structure of local government' and if it had 'presented a more professional front to them'.

Subsequent developments

The sessions on understanding children's art and other subjects continued for about a year. They ended because the needs of some of the mothers had changed when their children went to school and because some mothers moved from the area. Two people who met through this scheme developed a handicraft business. One person said, 'I found it tremendous at the time'.

CREATING A MORE CARING COMMUNITY IN A Y.M.C.A. CENTRE

The general secretary of the Ronsey Y.M.C.A. after attending the training sessions for lay people, requested help from the team. Two members worked with the Y.M.C.A. from May 1973 to June 1974. In all there were thirty meetings and three half-day conferences.

The Y.M.C.A. was both a hostel and a community centre. It provided residential accommodation for a hundred and thirty men and was about to build study bedrooms for twenty more. Its extensive premises were used by a considerable number of non-residents for a wide variety of indoor sports, leisure activities and clubs. It had a management council, a general secretary and two full-time assistant secretaries who wanted to extend their work with people of both sexes. In order to do this the general secretary had, amongst other things, recruited four people who said they were concerned to think out how to develop a more caring community in the Y.M.C.A. and its neighbourhood. This group is referred to as the 'Y.M. group'. The staff said they wanted the team to work with the staff and the Y.M. group as one group and that is how they started but later they met the staff to prepare for Y.M. group meetings and to consider how to implement decisions.

Discussions with the staff

The discussions described in this section were triggered off by joint meetings of the staff and the Y.M. group who, over a period of several months, had come to the conclusion that the Y.M.C.A. would be a more caring community if there was better communication between leaders of the various organizations. Subsequently and independently, however, the staff came to a different conclusion and discussed it with the team. They now said the basic problem was caused by changes taking place in the Y.M.C.A. In the past Ronsey Y.M.C.A. has been organized as a 'benevolent autocracy'. The local president had been very much in charge, and he, with the members of his council and the general secretary, had constituted the management whom voluntary leaders and members saw as the 'bosses'. The assistant secretaries were seen as subordinates whom voluntary leaders regarded as colleagues. Now they were trying to do away with this hierarchical system in favour of getting more and more people to work together in partnership and do things for themselves. Their problem, they said, was how to get people in the Y.M.C.A. to understand what the staff were now trying to do and how to get them more involved in doing things for themselves. In effect they said many of them now behaved as if the staff were their servants and directly answerable to them, whereas, in fact, they were employees directly answerable to the management council. The staff said they could not possibly work for more than one master and, anyway, the members were represented on the management council.

How to get people in the Y.M.C.A. to understand what the staff were now trying to do?

The team thought that the staff themselves were unclear about their role and after discussions with them prepared the initial draft of the chart reproduced on page 118. At the next meeting the staff pored over the chart, agreed that they had not previously got each other's roles clear, edited it with great care and worked out precisely each of their roles when all three were on duty, when only one or two were on duty, and in emergencies.

They now saw that the source of some of their unease had been continual role switching: 'one moment we are giving orders to domestic staff and the next trying to help non-residents to help themselves'.

They also considered how best to deal with complaints: two felt it best to listen without any intention of doing anything about it and then to forget what had been said, 'to let it go in one ear and out the other'; while one felt that it was important to take seriously what people were saying. Eventually they agreed that to be heard goes more than half-way to overcoming many problems and decided that they would take their members' problems more seriously in future and that they would try to get others to do the same.

How to get people to do things for themselves?

The staff said the only way they could guaranteee not to get involved in doing things for people was by not being present when they had to be done; 'If you get involved people will drop everything in your lap and not do their own job'. This made the team realize that the staff were thinking solely in terms of *either* doing things for people *or* leaving people to cope entirely on their own. The team asked the staff to consider the third alternative of helping people to do things for themselves and they gave examples to clarify what they meant.

Discussions with the Y.M. group

At a meeting with the Y.M. group the staff used the chart to explain how they saw their role and function. The Y.M. group pored over the chart in much the same way as the staff had done and thanked the staff for being so open with them. They said that they were now better equipped to explain the staff's role and function to others. They also felt that the Y.M.C.A. would function better as a caring community if the leaders of organizations also understood the staff's role and function and suggested that the leaders of the various organizations should meet regularly. The staff felt that a meeting of this kind would be unduly dominated by sectional interests and suggested setting up a Y.M. team of people, whether leaders or members, who felt really committed to making the Y.M.C.A. a more caring communtiy. The Y.M. group agreed to this suggestions and it was decided to convene a half-day consultation to consider it.

Setting up the consultation

When the staff and the Y.M. group discussed how to select people for the consultation a deep difference of opinion quickly became apparent. Two members of the staff thought the staff ought to select, otherwise the 'wrong people might be nominated' and the consultation degenerate into a 'grouse session'. The others, including one staff member, thought that the organizations should select. The views of members would then be better represented and the risk of faction minimized.

The members of the team worked to get this difference of opinion resolved by promoting discussion of four key questions.

RESPONSIBILITIES & FUNCTIONS PERFORMED BY THE STAFF IN RELATION TO ALL MEMBERS OF THE Y.M.C.A.

to stimulate people and give them ideas (for example, the secretary performs this function in relation to managers and fund raising);

to get all the different groups of people to see the situation realistically;

to manage (that is, to co-ordinate different activites, to act as a go-between to different groups of people using Y.M.C.A.: managers, leaders, members);

to help people to make decisions;

to be resource people;

to tell people what is permissible

ROLES, RESPONSIBILITIES AND FUNCTIONS OF Y.M.C.A. STAFF IN RELATION TO THE DIFFERENT PEOPLE WITH WHOM THEY WORK

People with whom Y.M.C.A. staff work	Functions of Y.M.C.A. staff in relation to these people	Roles of Y.M.C.A. staff in relation to these people
Managers	to advise to give relevant information	partners, colleagues, friends, advisers, co-professionals, employees
Paid leaders	to see they do what they are paid for, are competent to get on with job to see they don't do anything against Y.M.C.A. to supervize	employers supervizors
Voluntary leaders	to help them do their job, and encourage them to train them to see they don't do anything against Y.M.C.A. to help them to get to know each other, to care for and consider others	trainers
Members of Y.M.C.A. a) residents or potential residents	to let rooms to supervise accommodation to ensure rules are kept to deal with personal and accommodation problems	landlord estate agent manager counsellor
b) non-residents	to promote self-help to 'push from behind'	leader
Office & domestic staff	to allocate and supervize work	boss, employer, works manager

STAFF ROLES, FUNCTIONS AND RESPONSIBILITIES AS THEY SAW THEM

1. How to get people to respond positively?
The staff and the Y.M. group decided that people would be most likely to put the overall interests of the Y.M.C.A. first and their own personal or sectional interests second if the staff were open with people about the Y.M.C.A. and asked for their help. And this they did.

2. How to avoid conflict and criticism having a negative effect on the consultation?
The staff was afraid that the consultation would become a 'grouse session' like other meetings in the past and said that the only way to avoid this was to ban the habitual grousers and to rule emotionally-loaded topics such as hostel meals out of order.

The team members said that denying people opportunities of discussing things about which they felt strongly can engender resentment and faction which will then be expressed in other ways. They too wished to avoid grouse sessions, but conflict can nevertheless be creative if it is dealt with objectively with a view to seeing just what can best be done to resolve it. They illustrated this from the way in which they were now helping the staff and the Y.M. group to deal with their opposing views about the best way to convene the consultation.

The staff and the Y.M. group then asked the team to put these ideas into practice by acting as workers to the consultation.

3. What kind of people should desirably be selected?
Eventually it was agreed that the people selected should have the desire and ability to work together with the staff for the development of the local Y.M.C.A. and its neighbourhood. This prepared the way for the fourth question.

4. How to select people for the consultation?
The staff and the Y.M. group decided to describe to the organizations what the consultation was about and the kind of people they hoped would attend and then to ask them to suggest whom they would like to be invited. Practical involvement, however, of the organizations in any selection process was in all but two or three cases not possible because there were many fewer such organizations than the Y.M. group and the staff had led the team to believe.

After very lengthy discussions the Y.M. group also decided to allow the staff to invite people whom they thought were suitable.

The consultation

In the event, the staff, the Y.M. group and eleven people representative of the Y.M.C.A.'s work attended the consultation. Some Y.M.C.A. people met for the first time. By common consent it was a success.

They felt that a Y.M. team could help leaders and people in the Y.M.C.A. to get to know and help each other, to co-ordinate activities and to discover just what the Y.M.C.A. could do to help people in trouble.

But, they said, most people will attend meetings only if they are of value to them and to their organizations as well as to the Y.M.C.A. as a whole.

They considered three ways in which a Y.M. team could function: as an informal social meeting with a master of ceremonies; as a committee with a chairman and secretary and following normal committee procedure; and as a working group structured in the same way as the consultation, with a worker and a recorder. In the end they decided that a Y.M. team should be a working group committed to work for the Y.M.C.A. as a whole and they decided unanimously that they would constitute themselves as the first Y.M. team.

Inaugurating the Y.M. team

Before the Y.M. team met, the project team members got the staff to talk about the part they were going to play and found them very uncertain. On the one hand, they felt that in the initial stages they should play a dominant role to ensure that the Y.M. team made a really good start. On the other hand, what they really wanted was to leave the Y.M. team members to work on their own. (In spite of the earlier discussions about 'how to get people to do things for themselves' [p. 117] the staff did not think they could successfully act as non-directive workers to the Y.M. team.) Eventually they decided to start by working out their roles and functions with the Y.M. team using the chart on p. 118 as a basis.

The project team found this outcome unsatisfactory since the staff continued to oscillate between the two mutually contradictory approaches and they could not see how the staff could work out their role and function with the Y.M. team until they had resolved their dilemma.

Meetings of the Y.M. team

At their first meeting the staff and the Y.M. team listed the jobs they were going to tackle and appointed a sub-group to consider the respective roles and functions of the staff and the Y.M. team. The staff took an active part in this sub-group which produced a chart, the final version of which is presented on page 121.

At the next meeting of the staff and the Y.M. team there was lively discussion of this chart. The Y.M. team feared that a 'them/us' relationship might develop between the staff and themselves and generate unproductive conflict. Also they said, the staff could experience conflict between their various roles, functions and responsibilities. However, they concluded that these problems were now less likely to occur because they had identified them and agreed to take them into account in organizing their work. They all shared the same purpose in relation to the Y.M.C.A. and its neighbourhood and this they thought would be a great source of strength.

In order to achieve their PURPOSE — more caring communities in the Y.M.C.A. and its neighbourhood — team members:							
PERFORM FUNCTIONS		**ACCEPT RESPONSIBILITIES**		**ADOPT ROLES AND ESTABLISH RELATIONSHIPS**		**PERFORM THEIR FUNCTIONS BY:**
STAFF	TEAM	STAFF	TEAM	STAFF	TEAM	
provide information	acts as a working group, ginger group and clearing house	for their function in relation to the team	for decisions and their consequences	They are co-workers (i.e. the staff is not 'over' the team; the team is not the staff's boss) who have different positions in the Y.M.C.A.		meeting in one group and in sub-groups
share experience	helps co-ordinate work & activities of Y.M.C.A. and promotes co-operation between groups and between leaders		for work they undertake or ask others to do			circulating information before meeting
check all issues considered	helps facilitate co-operation between people in Y.M.C.A. and people outside		for keeping team members informed			adopting decision-making and problem-solving procedures
help make decisions	tries to discover ways of meeting special needs of neighbourhood	*Staff and team are responsible for:*		full-time paid officers	part-time voluntary or part-time paid workers	establishing criteria for selection of people to do jobs
	overviews work of Y.M.C.A. as a whole	ensuring team acts within Y.M.C.A. constitution				delegating team-meeting jobs:
put their professional expertise at service of the team	*In order to do this work effectively the team:*	assessing team's work in relation to its purposes		professional answerable to management	amateur	*worker* (to help open honest, realistic and systematic discussion
	critically appraises & apportions its work: what should be done	tackling problems preventing team achieving its purposes		advisors to team	advisors to staff	*recorder* (to make and circulate records)
	how should it be done					*convener*
	who should do it					
	makes an appraisal of the finances necessary for work undertaken					
	establishes means of dealing with its business					
	keeps staff, absent team members and others informed					
	decides whether to work 'with' or 'for' people					
	shares expertise					

STAFF AND NON-STAFF TEAM MEMBERS: FUNCTIONS, RESPONSIBILITIES, ROLES AND RELATIONSHIPS

This meeting also considered carefully how the Y.M. team could best function as a working group. It appointed a worker (trained in non-directive group work), a co-worker, a recorder and a convenor. The team members met these people and two members of the staff to discuss how they were going to do the work they had undertaken. The staff said that they would be represented on the Y.M. team and that they were prepared to meet separately with the Y.M. team workers to prepare for meetings in much the same way as they had done with the project team members. Everyone was enthusiastic and the project team, feeling that there was now every possibility of the Y.M. team working effectively, withdrew by agreement in June 1974.

The subsequent course of events

The staff withdrew from the Y.M. team in September 1974 because, they said, its members were turning to them for ideas and suggestions instead of putting up their own ideas. The staff then became closely identified with building up a community centre committee which the Y.M. team members saw to have similar functions to themselves, while the staff felt the Y.M. team members were taking on jobs that should be performed only by the staff. These events caused tensions which led to the eventual disintegration of the Y.M. team in the first quarter of 1975 although up to that time it did very useful work.

Assessment after the team withdrew

Only four questionnaires were returned and they were inconclusive. Clearly, it was necessary to hold an evaluation meeting and since the staff felt that it would be unwise to reconvene the Y.M. team, a meeting with the staff and the Y.M. group was held in November 1975. (Originally this meeting was planned for the Spring of 1975 but was postponed by the staff because of unresolved problems betwen the groups.)

At this meeting the staff and the Y.M. group said that the Y.M. team would have been more likely to succeed if the staff and the project team members had continued to work with it. One member of the staff said, 'I think we were wrong to withdraw from the Y.M. team as early as we did. We should have acted as workers to the Y.M. team. They were just not capable of thinking and acting for themselves at that stage'. They also thought 'the transition from the Y.M. group to the Y.M. team had not been thought out carefully enough'. However, they said that the Y.M.C.A. had become a more caring community because of the work done by the project team. Leaders who had first got to know each other through the Y.M. group, the consultation and the Y.M. team were now helping and supporting each other. Organizations were less inward-looking and more people now felt part of the Y.M.C.A. as a whole. Communications had been improved through a newsletter, a 'surgery' and a communications committee. Some people had become active in community care for the first time, and the members of two new Y.M.C.A. committees which were run as working groups like the Y.M. group and the Y.M. team both cared for each other and promoted the care of others.

They attributed these changes to the way in which the project team had helped them to get a clear picture of their situation; sort out under-lying ideas; clarify the staff's role and function (they said that this was no longer a problem); 'finish off conversations', that is, prolong dis-cussion until people had reached an agreed conclusion; and produce useful working documents such as diagrams and charts.

Difficulties encounted by the project team

For their part the project team members were conscious of several difficulties which had prevented them from helping the staff to establish really effective working relationships with the Y.M. group and the Y.M. team. First, the staff had seemed ambivalent in their attitude towards the Y.M. group and team. For example, sometimes they said they were ordinary members of the Y.M. group, but at other times they said their jobs precluded them from being so. Sometimes they spoke of 'our group', but at other times they addressed both the group and the team as 'you' or referred to them as 'they'. Second, the staff frequently made decisions with the Y.M. group and the Y.M. team which the staff subsequently revoked. This led to another round of decision making which tended to be more reliable but not entirely so. Third, the staff seemed unwilling or unable to adopt a non-directive approach them-selves although they saw the need to do so if the Y.M.C.A. was to change from an 'hierarchical system' to an organization in which people did things for themselves.

During the time they were working with the Y.M.C.A. the project team became progressively aware of the accumulative adverse effect these difficulties had on the scheme and they did all they could to overcome them. But it is only in retrospect that they have been able to clarify the exact nature of the problems and they are still unclear about their underlying causes.

4 Working with the council and the fraternal

The team worked with the Council of Churches, the executive and the fraternal on schemes variously related to *church, church-community* and *community* work. Concurrently, through the council, the executive and the fraternal, members of the team stimulated a wide constituency of people who were not engaged on schemes to consider what implications the project work might have for them. In this way they extended the effect of their work beyond the individual schemes and promoted overall development. The team also helped to establish effective working relationships between the borough community development unit and the council, the executive, the fraternal and the churches.

The council and the executive usually met eight or nine times a year and the fraternal monthly. The average attendance at council meetings was forty, at executive meetings twelve and at the fraternal eleven. Generally speaking these groups worked amicably. The clergy, however, did not take as active a part in the council as the lay-people wanted them to. Also, the relationships between the council, the executive and the fraternal remained ill-defined and there were serious organizational gaps (cf. p. 29). Generally speaking the council and the executive were formally structured and task oriented while the fraternal was valued by the clergy principally as an informal fellowship group and it rarely responded to requests for help from the council and the executive. The team acted as a 'bridge' between the executive and the council on the one hand and the fraternal on the other, and was able to establish a slightly better working relationship between them in relation to community development work.

In June 1974, just before the team withdrew from Ronsey the council implemented a new structure proposed by the executive. The council continued to determine overall policy but responsibility for implementing it now rested with sub-committees, each of which had responsibility for one of six areas of work: worship and prayer; house groups and Christian education; community work, community development, social responsibility, community relations and the good neighbour scheme; Christian Aid and world development; work with children and young people; publicity and information. Members of the team were not involved in working out or implementing the scheme. They did, however, help the chairman of the community work sub-committee to consider how to work with his committee and the borough community development unit. They attended two meetings of the council under the new scheme but no meetings of the sub-committees.

RE-MODELLING A GOOD NEIGHBOUR SCHEME

The good neighbour scheme had been started by the Council of Churches in 1968 to serve the local community and to foster a sense of community and shared responsibility by encouraging people, especially members of the church, to care for the community in which they live, to accept some responsibility for its problems and needs and to work with statutory and voluntary agencies to meet some of those needs.

The scheme was modelled on a standard design used by churches in different parts of the country. The neighbourhood was divided into areas and each area into roads. The areas were staffed voluntarily by area organizers, road stewards and helpers. The helpers, mainly church members, acted as good neighbours in giving assistance to people in trouble. The road stewards were responsible for the road in which they lived and provided the link between people in trouble, the area organizers and the helpers. The area organizers co-ordinated the work done in their roads, helped sort out problems, convened occasional meetings of road stewards and helpers and liaised with other care agencies. Road stewards and area organizers had to be church members – an arrangement referred to as the 'church membership rule'. Overall policy was determined by the council, and the scheme was administered by the executive, a co-ordinating committee and a voluntary secretary.

Problems of staffing and the church membership rule

For a few years the scheme did valuable work in two areas but was not very successful in a third, and it became increasingly difficult to find church members to staff it. Some members of the executive, the council and the co-ordinating committee felt this difficulty could be overcome if non-church people were allowed to become road stewards and area organizers, but others were adamant that the church membership rule must be maintained to safeguard opportunities for Christians to witness to their faith by talking to their neighbours about it as they served them.

Then early in 1973 a member of the team intervened in a particularly divisive discussion on this subject between members of the executive. He suggested they might make more progress if, rather than arguing for or against the church membership rule, they reconsidered it in relation to their purposes for the scheme and the most effective way of achieving them. This idea appealed to people on both sides. The executive asked the team member to prepare a report.

In his report he summarized what the scheme had done since 1968; objectively considered the conflict about the church membership rule in relation to the scheme's purposes; showed how the church membership rule prevented them from fostering a sense of shared responsibility

125

in the community which was one of their stated aims; and suggested that they should further clarify their purposes and then use them as a touchstone when deciding on what action they needed to take. They could then remodel their scheme to fit *their* purpose, *their* situation and the kind of working relationships *they* wanted to have with others.

Reviewing and re-modelling the scheme

On the basis of this report the executive and the council asked the co-ordinating committee and the team to undertake a thorough review of the scheme. This review started in March 1973 and concluded in July 1974. It involved ten meetings of the co-ordinating committee, two meetings of all those engaged in the scheme, and private meetings with the area organizers and the secretary and chairman of the co-ordinating committee. At all of these meetings the chairman acted as worker. He made a crucial contribution to what followed. A team member helped the chairman by acting as co-worker but at no time did he take over as chairman. The conclusions reached were embodied in reports prepared by the co-ordinating committee for the executive and council. These reports made recommendations that involved remodelling the scheme to fit both the beliefs and purposes of the organizers *and* the working situation.

Fitting the scheme to the beliefs and purposes of the organizers

At the team's suggestion the co-ordinating committee started the review by trying to define just *what* they wanted to achieve through the scheme, but they were not able to do this until they had decided *why* they desired to help others. In other words, they were unable to clarify their *purposes* until they had defined the *beliefs* that motivated them. Eventually they agreed on the following statements about their underlying beliefs after three long and intensive meetings at which every word and phrase was thoroughly discussed:

'This scheme is organized by people because of the beliefs they share. They believe in God, in Jesus Christ and in the Church. They believe that:

— God wishes people to help, care, support and love each other regardless of class, colour or creed;
— God is concerned about everyone and about all their needs;
— Jesus showed the love and care of God by giving of himself freely and helping people;
— Christians are called to live for others as Jesus did, to love, care for and serve them;
— Christians have responsibilities both in the Church and through the Church to the local community;

— Christians should be actively engaged in fostering a quality of life based upon love and mutual respect — in the church and in the neighbourhood;
— the ways in which people are served and helped should aim to satisfy their deeper needs for friendship and love, and should help them to become and feel better people;
— Christians should in the name of the Church co-operate with others similarly concerned, but who may have different beliefs, to help people achieve more satisfying lives.'

This done they had little difficulty in defining their purposes. These were:

'1. to help people to live more satisfying lives through the development of a sense of community;
2. to enable Christians, as an expression of their faith, to care, and to help others to care, for people in the area;
3. to show that people in the churches care for others and are prepared to help them regardless of their attitudes to the Church;
4. to fulfil one of the Ronsey Council of Churches objectives, that is, to give service to the local community.'

They then agreed to work to achieve their purposes by:

'1. helping people to care about each other, help each other and help themselves;
2. helping people to obtain the support and care they require without depriving them of dignity, self respect or independence;
3. providing opportunities for members of different churches and people who are not church members to serve their neighbours;
4. working with other organizations and services.'

These statements were acceptable to all those who had been engaged in the argument about the church membership rule and enabled them to resolve the conflict. Those who previously had thought that only church people could witness to Christianity came to see that others could often do so even more effectively if, for instance, they said, 'I don't go to church myself but I find church people good to work with on a scheme like this'. Eventually it was agreed by the co-ordinating committee, the executive and the council that area organizers should be people 'who can represent the interests of the Church' and that road stewards and helpers should be people who 'act in ways consonant with Christian teaching and practice as set out in the statement of belief' whether or not they were members of the Church.

Fitting the scheme to the working situation

Some members of the co-ordinarting committee engaged in the field work became impatient with what they described as 'the theory': they wanted to get to grips with 'practical problems' about which they were most concerned. At the suggestion of the team the co-ordinating committee arranged meetings at which the area organizers, the road stewards and the helpers could discuss the difficulties they were facing.

Amongst other things these discussions showed that the formal structure of the scheme frustrated rather than promoted neighbourly care in several ways: for instance many people who would accept help from a private individual refused to do so from someone belonging to a formal organization; some who wished to act as good neighbours would not join 'the scheme'; and few would take organizational responsibility because they wanted to spend what time they had with people in need. An area organizer actually said 'would-be helpers run away from the good neighbour scheme because it is too formal'.

The discussions also showed that the scheme did not fit into existing informal systems of neighbourly care: for instance in middle class neighbourhoods it was not too difficult to recruit road stewards but their services were not used. The stewards and helpers said: 'People don't want someone in their road to know their business'. On the other hand, in working class areas it was difficult to recruit road stewards but there were many requests for help. Road stewards and helpers found that they got into helping relationships with people in need through personal contacts and introductions: few people in need made direct approaches to them.

All valued the support they got from each other and from the co-ordinating committee but they felt:

– that the organization ought to be flexible and unobtrusive;
– that those working in an area ought to work as a team. (This, they said, would enable them to support each other and to learn how to make contact with people and to tackle their problems.)

In spite of all this a few people – those not involved in the field work – said that the scheme as it was *should* work and that it would do so if administered properly. However, eventually they, the co-ordinating committee, the executive and the council, agreed that the 'scheme should be allowed to develop with a greater degree of flexibility' and that in each area the members should be free to work in the way that seemed most appropriate to them.

The re-modelled scheme

The decision to re-model the scheme led to exciting and rapid changes from January to September 1974. First, the co-ordinating committee defined just what its functions would now be: to find finance; to review work done in the light of agreed purposes; to stimulate new work; to recruit and train workers; to organize inter-area meetings; to negotiate with borough authorities and other organizations; and to report to the council. The members re-organized themselves to do these things and recruited clergy and lay people to help. Second, at the request of the co-ordinating committee the team helped to establish the new pattern of work in each of three areas. Third, the clergy became much more actively engaged in the scheme.

The Furzedown area

The work in this area had been allowed to run down although seven people still continued their regular visits to old people. They formed themselves into a team and arranged to meet monthly. (To avoid confusion with the project team this team will be referred to as 'the group'.) A member of the project team started to work with them in January 1974. The area organizer had attended the training sessions for lay people but she needed help to put what she had learnt into practice. The team member helped her to do so by assisting her to clarify her job in the group and to re-organize her work. They discussed what they could do to help the group; they prepared for meetings together; and they acted as co-workers at meetings in such a way that gradually the area organizer took over more of the worker's functions.

Much progress was made during the first five months: the members discussed the problems they were facing in their visiting; they recruited new members (by September they had thirteen); they made contact with more people in need through a local doctor and social workers; they learnt a lot about how best to visit people from a social worker they invited to their group; and they established links with other individuals and groups involved in neighbourly care. The group shared with the area organizer the responsibility for finding ways of helping people referred to them. Together the members and organizer decided who should help whom and together they worked out how best to do so. They also helped and supported each other in the practical problems involved in looking after sick and elderly people. The members enjoyed the meetings which were well attended.

It was at this juncture that the area organizer was unexpectedly transferred to another part of the country. The time spent in building the members into a group paid dividends for the group itself now worked out with the team member just how it could take over the functions previously performed by the area organizer. Thus facing this crisis strengthened the group, and the team member was able to withdraw in September 1974.

The Abbeyfield area

The ten people engaged in this area were dispirited and without an area organizer. Prior to the review they were thinking of giving up the scheme. Two of them, however, were members of the co-ordinating committee which had reviewed the good neighbour scheme, and with the help of the team they set about reviewing the work in their area.

They felt that one of the things that had militated against the scheme was the lack of clergy support, but the local clergy had recently become much more concerned to promote community work and pastoral care (p. 101) and, when the problem was put to them, proved willing to give their support. Two other caring organizations in the area were also contacted, and eventually a meeting was arranged between the members of the good neighbour scheme and representatives of the clergy and the two care organizations, with a team member acting as worker. To their surprise those at this meeting discovered that between them they belonged to no less than fifteen organizations in the neighbourhood which cared for their own members and friends. These included a baby sitting circle, a fruit and vegetable co-operative, a men's club and church fellowship groups for women. They also realized that it was the people not connected with any of these and similar groups who were often in need of extra neighbourly help, and they decided to work together to discover such people and ways of helping them. They decided to arrange a meeting of representatives of all the groups in their area. They asked a clergyman and a laywoman who had attended training sessions in community development work to act as workers. They did so, they said, because through their present meeting they saw the value of someone acting as a worker. Everyone felt that the possibility of promoting neighbourly care was now much more hopeful.

The St Margarets area

The organizer for this area was a full-time parish worker, and at first she had hoped that both jobs would 'grow together' but in fact her work as an area organizer did not fit in at all well with her parish work. As a parish worker she was authorized to work in only one parish, but as an area organizer she was involved in work in other parishes, and this created many difficulties for her. At the request of the co-ordinating committee and the area organizer a team member contributed to the solution of this problem by helping her to present it for consideration by a group of the clergy in her area (p. 101).

Assessment after the team withdrew

In the final evaluation several people said the team arrived at a time when the good neighbour scheme was 'breaking down'. One person summed up the feelings expressed by many: 'Efforts to make the old system work through adapting it, all seemed to fail. We realized there were unmet and undiscovered needs, but workers either got swamped or could not find enough to do; we were failing to tap the manpower resources and we needed time to think the scheme out again from first principles ... we lacked the expertise to tackle this on our own.'

All said that they were pleased by what had now been achieved and several specifically commended the way in which the scheme had been reviewed. They said that the objectivity of the team's initial report on the scheme had provided the basis for subsequent work. In their opinion the scheme had been made far more effective through clarifying aims, priorities and needs; through getting to know just what the less articulate road stewards and helpers felt and the problems they were experiencing; through helping them to discuss their problems 'methodically'; and through asking thought-provoking questions which helped all engaged in the scheme to find their own solutions for themselves and to gain self-confidence. One person said, 'The team's methods brought home to people how they can better help themselves'.

All felt that as the result of the team's work the scheme was more flexible, the co-ordinating committee and area meetings were better prepared and run, and produced a more definite programme of work; people were treated with more respect; and the clergy were now taking more interest in the scheme and seeing it 'as a possible way forward for them and their churches in the field of community care'. One person said that the review had caused him to become actively involved in the work whereas before he was 'only a planner'; that the reorganization of the work to suit each area had engendered 'new life and a revival of enthusiasm' amongst the helpers; that relationships were being established with others engaged in neighbourhood care; that barriers were breaking down between age groups and between church and non-church people; and that there was closer co-operation between members of the scheme, the clergy, the churches and the council.

Subsequent developments

The re-modelled scheme facilitated all round development. Within a very short period of time (September 1974 to February 1976) the original members of the scheme were working more closely than they had ever done before with each other, with the Ronsey Council of Churches, with clergy and churches, with social and community workers and with the local residents on a variety of care schemes: and the co-ordinating committee had co-opted a representative of each area, a senior borough social worker and a local community worker, so there were more effective referrals.

The work in the Furzedown area had been consolidated. The community work clergy task group had become involved in the Abbeyfield and St Margarets areas. Discussions with other care agencies in this area led to the formation of a community care club which met monthly in the Moravian church and the scheme's team was starting to build up a care network to meet unmet needs.

New work was under way. The co-ordinating committee had asked Manor Road to call together people in their part of the St Margarets area to consider forming a community care scheme. The minister of Manor Road was already working closely with a local tenants association in relation to the care of people on their estate. Also, again at the request of the co-ordinating committee, St Saviours, the leader of the parish visiting scheme and representatives of the local social service team had formed a new team to work in central Ronsey. It dealt with referrals from the social services and was caring for the residents of an old peoples home who felt neglected.

Involving local churches as well as ecumenical groups in community care had increased the number of helpers and brought local clergy into the centre of the work of the good neighbour scheme.

THE FRATERNAL AND THE PLANNING OFFICER

Just before the team started work in Ronsey each of the clergy received a questionnaire from the borough planning department asking for detailed information about the seating capacity of his church, the size of ancillary premises, the number of people who used them and for what purposes in 1951, 1961 and 1971. A minority co-operated. They said they were on good terms with the planning department and were pleased that the planners were taking the churches into account.

The majority, however, refused to co-operate. Some saw the questionnaire as an unwarranted interference in church affairs. Others thought the borough was trying to prove that churches were under-used so that they could either acquire them for other purposes or refuse planning permission for new buildings. This was because the borough had already issued a compulsory purchase order in respect of one church and because churches wanting to rebuild were finding it difficult to get planning permission. All these clergy were annoyed and some irate.

The fraternal invited the planning officer to attend their July 1972 meeting at which they asked for the help of the team. At the meeting the clergy said what they felt in a very forcible way. The planning officer explained that the questionnaire had been sent out in his name because he was the convenor of a working party on community development and that it had nothing to do with his job as planning officer. He described how the working party was trying to make arrangements for the borough to become actively engaged in community development. He said he was interested in what the churches in Ronsey were proposing to do in connexion with Project 70-75, that he saw possibilities of co-operation, that he would welcome advice about how best to approach the churches, and that he hoped it was not too late to undo any damage that might have been done. This was followed by a long period of altercation which ended in deadlock. It was at this point that the team member was able to come in. Taking great care not to side with either the clergy or the planning officer he drew diagrams to summarize and illustrate the nature of the conflict. This helped to reduce the tension. Using the diagrams the clergy and the planning officer clarified their positions.

The team member then got the clergy and the planning officer to examine their respective purposes vis-à-vis community development. As they came to see that they had some common objectives they began to talk to each other in a more conciliatory way, and the team member then asked them whether or not they wanted to work together and if they did, what this would imply. For some time they avoided the question, but the team member persisted until they did answer it. They said that they did want to work together and agreed that the planning officer and the secretaries of the fraternal and the executive should meet to discuss informally how they would do so. Now a desire to co-operate was apparent. One of the clergy said he would fill in the questionnaire, others said they would fill in parts of it and another said he would co-operate with the borough in using his ancillary premises for community work. The planning officer undertook to revise the questionnaire and to look into points raised by the clergy about difficulties they were experiencing in applying for planning permission.

Subsequently, and as a direct consequence of this meeting, the clergy did provide the information required but, sadly, without evoking any apparent change of attitude on the part of the planning department. Thus the clergy heard nothing from the planning officer about the points he said he would look into, and difficulties over planning applications continued. The members of the fraternal felt that they had been badly let down and lost all hope of establishing a good working relationship with the planning officer and his department. They saw no point in having informal consultations, and relationships with the planning department did not improve until after the borough community development unit had been established (pp. 149).[1]

[1] Subsequently in 1973 the way in which the borough's working party on community development saw these events was made known in its report: 'The 100 churches in the borough provide a large reservoir of accommodation for community activities. Unfortunately, our knowledge of this accommodation, and its use, is somewhat limited. We carried out a survey in 1972, but many of the clergy were not forthcoming in their response. There appears to be a strong latent fear of the 'Big Brother' of the council becoming over-involved, and attempting to acquire such property which is under-used. The wide ranging questions in the questionnaire might have exaggerated these worries. Attempts at conciliation by the borough planning officer were summarily negatived by the recommendation of the housing committee for compulsory acquisition of St Gabriels Church ... Clearly, a major public relations exercise needs to be carried out with the Church authorities to ensure a sensible co-ordination of the use of their accommodation with that of the council. This is an activity which could well be left to the new community development unit.'

CONCERNS ABOUT CHURCH BUILDINGS

In 1972 there was widespread concern amongst clergy and laity about church buildings. Only St Giles and Cherry Tree Road had modern suites of premises. St Patricks was too small and needed a new centre (pp. 79 ff.) Other church buildings were too large, and congregations were finding it increasingly difficult to heat and maintain them. Six churches wanted to rebuild or modernize their premises but were finding it difficult to raise sufficient money and to get planning permission. Some felt strongly that the churches of all denominations ought to work together to decide just what buildings were required. They said that it was 'sinful for churches to waste money and effort building two churches where one would do'.

It was these feelings that led the Council of Churches in October 1972 to ask its executive to promote inter-church discussions about buildings and relations with the borough planning department and to invite the team to participate. The team agreed. The team and the executive felt that, because the clergy were key figures, the fraternal should also be asked to participate, but the fraternal made no response when approached.

However, several of the clergy did discuss church buildings informally with members of the team and it quickly became obvious that they did not want to get involved in the inter-church discussions suggested by the council. Two of them, whose churches were already involved in complex negotiations about rebuilding programmes, said that neither they nor their churches could face the added complications and delay that would ensue from inter-church discussions. One said, 'It would be like starting all over again and putting the block back five years. We just couldn't face it. It would have a very bad effect on the morale of our people'. Others, who were currently exploring the possibility of establishing team ministries, while agreeing that this might ultimately involve discussion about buildings, felt that the time was not yet ripe. The team therefore decided to drop the subject, but members of the team did later become involved in discussions about buildings through the work they did with individual churches.

In July 1973, whilst reviewing the first year's work (see p. 153) the chairman of the council expressed regret that the team had not been used to help explore this concern systematically and in the final assessment after the team had withdrawn several other people said similar things.

SOME CHURCH CONCERNS

Some churches were concerned because they could not adequately staff their Sunday schools, clubs and uniformed organizations or because they were short of scholars and members. Most said they found it difficult to 'communicate' with young people. All of them had experienced vandalism in their open clubs.

Again some churches were very concerned about immigrants who attended church: 'They don't integrate . . . We don't understand them . . . They are not on our wave length . . . We don't communicate . . . Some children in our Sunday school don't understand English very well and those who do will not translate for those who don't . . . We have to deal with fifteen nationalities in our church.' Some churches were also concerned about immigrants in the community: 'Our over-riding general social problem is one of racial segregation . . . There is great enmity in our area between Turkish and Greek Cypriots'. All churches wanted to see more integration of racial groups both within the churches and in the community.

In October 1972 the council asked the team to pursue these concerns. The members of the team realized that tackling these concerns could involve them and the churches in a lot of work and they did not want to undertake work that they and others could not complete. Therefore they thought long and hard before deciding what action to take. Should they concentrate their effort on working with individual clergy, whose churches felt these concerns? or with their church committees? or with their church members? or should they try to promote one or more ecumenical conferences on specific concerns, for example, Sunday school work, visiting, communications, and immigrants?

From April to June 1973 they discussed these possibilities with the seven clergy and two lay people whose churches had expressed these concerns. At this stage, however, none of them were willing to commit themselves. It was not until after the training sessions for clergy and lay people that they embarked on the schemes already reported in Part Three chapters 2 and 3 and on the conference described below. But none of the schemes related specifically to immigrants. Nonetheless team members now feel that they might have made more progress, and schemes or conferences related to the concerns about immigrants might have emerged, if they had been more persistent.

The assessment made by the local people after the team's withdrawal shows that at least one Sunday school teacher was disappointed because he had not received the help he wanted from the team.

CONCERNS ABOUT MANPOWER SHORTAGE

A conference entitled 'The Servant Church' held in February 1970 had given new impetus to the work of the council. In October 1973 the executive felt the time was right for another council conference and they suggested it could be about community development. They asked the team to consider the idea and report to the next meeting.

On reflection, members of the team felt the conference would best help people in Ronsey to work more effectively *and* to learn about community development and non-directive processes if they considered, within the context of their Christian faith, what they themselves could do about their key work problems. They searched for a suitable conference theme and found it in the manpower shortage every church was facing and in the concept of Christian vocation which motivated church people to serve God and man in church and in community.

Members of the team felt that this theme would attract many of those engaged in church and community work in Ronsey, including some who might be put off by a conference on community development. They also felt that it would consolidate the work done and pave the way for the team's withdrawal by helping people to see how to tackle the problems which had been identified but not tackled during the past two years. The team also decided to offer to undertake the organization of such a conference.

They asked the members of the executive to consider these ideas very critically since they did not want them to be swayed into adopting them by the team's offer to undertake much of the work. The executive thought that the ideas were apposite, accepted the team's offer of help and decided to recommend to the council that a conference entitled 'Situations Vacant?' be held in March 1974. The council accepted this recommendation and commissioned the team to organize the conference.

The conference

The conference was attended by sixty-four lay people and ten clergy on the Friday evening and by fifty lay people and ten clergy on the Saturday. The team's objectives for the conference were to help church people to reconsider their actual manpower problems within the context of the Christian faith; to decide what they themselves could do about them; and to help them to find new hope, enthusiasm and inspiration. Achieving these objectives involved five major problems.

Problem one – How to ensure that the council and the churches accepted the conference as their conference?

From the outset team members realized just how easy it would be for people to see it as the 'team's conference'. They realized that this could adversely affect the way in which people prepared for, participated in, and followed up the conference. They tried to avoid this danger and promote participation during the planning stages by consulting the clergy, the executive and the council about the content of the conference and how it should be run; by getting the executive and council to decide on practical arrangements; by involving as many people as possible in providing information, thinking about and preparing for the conference; and by ensuring that it was described and advertised as the Ronsey Council of Churches' conference. In fact, some twenty of the eighty people who attended the conference as well as some who did not attend helped to plan and prepare for it. Consequently the conference was based on what local people felt and thought and what they knew would 'work'. It became 'their' conference.

The team also reduced the danger by getting the chairman of the council to preside. He had overall control and consequently the conference was seen to be the council's conference. He described the overall purpose and explained that the council had arranged that the team members would act as 'workers' to the conference. He introduced each session and invited the team to conduct it, and he brought each session and the conference to a conclusion. This arrangement worked admirably and throughout he worked closely with the team member acting as principal worker.

Problem two – How to base the conference on an accurate picture of jobs and vacancies?

Members of the team felt that getting an accurate picture of the jobs and the vacancies in each church was essential for the success of the conference, but they realized the size of the task was daunting and that they were on sensitive ground because they remembered how difficult the clergy had found it to be open with each other about their working situations during the training sessions.

They therefore set themselves the task of making it as easy as possible for the churches to provide the information. They devised charts on which the jobs and vacancies in *church, church-community* and *community* work could be listed – a classification with which Ronsey people were now familiar. But they knew just how difficult it could be to get people to complete charts and questionnaires especially when, as in this case, it involves a lot of work. Eventually they decided that they would be most likely to get them filled in if they asked two people rather than one to undertake the task; and if they convened a 'briefing' meeting of the people from each church at which they could explain why the information was required, introduce them to the charts, discuss how they could be completed and sort out any problems.

Also, before putting this plan into action, they cleared it with each clergyman individually. Each responded very positively and three of them decided to fill in the charts themselves because they did not want to ask their lay people to undertake so much work. The executive and the council were also approached and agreed to co-operate. With this backing the team put the plan into effect.

Representatives from fourteen churches attended the briefing meeting held in February, and those unable to attend were contacted later. A member of the team explained the background and purpose of the conference and how they and the council wanted it to be based on the specific manpower problems the churches were facing. Those at the meeting saw the need for collating information about jobs and vacancies in each church, and said they were willing to co-operate in getting it. Then a member of the team demonstrated the charts they had prepared and these were found acceptable. Finally, and somewhat hesitantly, the team asked if the charts could be completed and returned within two weeks. This request met with an immediate response. Without hesitation people volunteered to do the job in the time and said, 'This is important, it will be the first time that our churches have had a picture of what they are doing'.

Completed charts were received from fifteen churches and from the council. Only one church did not fill in a chart. Generally speaking the charts were filled in with great care and with information that must have taken a lot of work to collect. A sample chart appears on p. 139.

The charts showed that in addition to *church work* all were engaged in *church-community work*, some of them heavily so. This work involved running a wide variety of clubs and uniformed organizations. Members of thirteen churches were also engaged, some on behalf of the church and others privately, in a wide range of *community work*, for example, tenants associations; clubs for the blind, the deaf and the mentally handicapped; a car service; Samaritans. The council was involved in *church work*, for example, organizing lent groups and united services; and *community work*, for example, Christian Aid and the community relations council.

The charts also showed that to maintain their current work fourteen of the fifteen churches required people to fill the following vacancies.

Church work vacancies: Sunday school teachers (seven churches); pianist (one church); choristers (four churches); people to read lessons (one church); servers (two churches); sidesmen (three churches); parish visitors (two churches); church flower rota secretary (one church); Bible reading fellowship secretary (two churches); sisterhood leaders (one church); coffee bar helper (one church); study group organizer (Council of Churches); Legion of Mary visitors (two churches); and St. Vincent-de-Paul workers (one church).

Church-community work vacancies: cub and scout leaders (six churches); guide leader (three churches); brownie leader (three churches); youth club leader (three churches); Girls Brigade officers (one church); and Boys Brigade officers (two churches).

Community work vacancies: Christian Aid secretary (one church); people to help start tenants association (one church); good neighbour scheme helpers (Council of Churches and one church); social responsibility secretary (one church).

CHART SHOWING THE WORK, THE WORKERS AND THE SITUATIONS VACANT OF EACH CHURCH

Area of work:	CHURCH-COMMUNITY WORK: groups and activities, clubs and organizations meeting on church premises which cater equally for people who do, and those who do not, attend church, for example, scouts, old peoples' luncheon clubs, youth clubs, etc.			
Work	Workers	To whom responsible	Situations vacant	Comments
Brownies	—		Leader	In abeyance since leader resigned
Guides	Leader & helper	Vicar	Assistant leader	
Cubs	Two leaders			
Scouts	Leader		Two leaders	Situation desperate
Young wives	Leader & small committee	Vicar		
Mothers club	Leader & two mothers	P.C.C.		Only the leader is a church member
'Over 60's Club'	Leader & three helpers & four drivers	P.C.C.	More drivers to transport elderly to club	Problem to ensure successors to leader & helpers when they retire
Hall lettings	—	Vicar	Hall caretaker	
Youth club 14+	Leader & two assistants	Vicar local youth council	Could expand if had more staff	Meets Thurs. eve. & Sunday eve. Club leader also a church warden
Welfare	two representatives	Ecumenical committee		
Old people's whist drive	two leaders	Autonomous	—	three times weekly, not connected with the church
Play group	Supervisor & two assistants	Management committee which includes Vicar & two church members		every morning

Note: This is an example of p.1 of a three-page chart. The other pages were headed:
p. 1 CHURCH WORK: the work involved in organizing and conducting worship, Sunday schools, confirmation classes, devotional meetings, bible discussions groups for church members, pastoral work, and so on.
p. 3 (a) COMMUNITY WORK: work done by a church with individuals or groups or organizations not connected with a church or its buildings, for example helping to run clubs, play groups, car service good neighbour scheme, and so on.
(b) COMMUNITY WORK undertaken by members of the church personally.

General vacancies: people to duplicate, assemble and distribute magazines (three churches); caretake (one church); people to look after
lawn and premises (one church); church 'letting secretary' (two churches); members of principal church committee, for example, P.C.C.
(four churches); chauffeurs with cars (three churches); and secretarial
help (Council of Churches and one minister).

Also one church said it wanted to attract more members to its
Sunday school, one to its sisterhood and one to its social club.

Generally speaking these charts showed that most of the vacancies
realted to work with people and to practical and administrative work.
Although people continually complained about attending committees,
there were only a few vacancies for committee members.

Notes on the forms indicated that the manpower shortage was far
more acute than this extensive list of vacancies indicated: each church
said that many workers had too many jobs; some churches foresaw
acute difficulties in filling vacancies caused by retirement or death and
this was a source of great concern where most of the people holding
key jobs were elderly. It was also felt that church development and
expansion would put an even greater strain upon manpower resources:
and one church which had developed youth clubs and playgroups by
paying leaders was experiencing difficulties with those who were voluntarily engaged in work they felt to be comparable.

The information on the charts amply justified the caution with
which church people in Ronsey regarded any plans likely to involve
them in yet more work. A brief description of the charts and a resumé
of its main points were distributed to all members of the conference.

Problem three — How to set the conference in a Christian context?

The team felt that the members of the conference would tackle the
manpower problems most vigorously if they saw them in direct relation
to the mission of the Church. A presentation of Christianity was required which would enable people of very different theological perspectives to work together on common problems; would show that each
aspect of the work described on the charts contributed something to
the mission of the Church; would help people to think positively about
the vacancy problems; would be meaningful to people of different
denominations; and would be understood by people whose ability to
conceptualize varied greatly. It was agreed that an introductory talk
which met these points should be given in order to establish the basic
common ground for a down to earth approach to what people in
Ronsey themselves could realistically do to resolve their manpower
problems.

It was also decided that one of the team would describe the Christian context as the team saw it, since it was felt that it was important that members of the conference should realize that the team was as closely identified with the Christian faith as with community development.

Deciding how best to convey this was difficult and led members of the team — themselves representative of the Anglican, Methodist and Roman Catholic traditions — to engage in much theological debate. Eventually they did it in the following way. They laid out objects which would 'speak' about aspects of Christianity to people of different denominations: a bible, a missal, a book of offices, a hymn book, a table (communion table or altar), a chalice, individual communion cups, a cross, a crucifix, hammer and nails, a basin and towel, a basket of loaves and fishes, candlesticks and a collection plate! Pointing to these a member of the team said:

'These are symbols of our faith and belief. They say to us that we are members of God's church and that we live in God's world. We in this conference start with them because the life, work and mission of the Church have their origins in God, Jesus and the Holy Spirit. Our beliefs motivate and enable us. They are the source and context of our mission. They give us purpose and direction.

They are also symbols of Jesus' work and that of his Church. Vacant situations indicate that the Church is still in business with a work programme which requires a limitless number of helpers. They indicate that the Church has a manpower shortage but not that it is redundant or obsolete.

These symbols also represent the practical and religious aspects of our Christian lives. They are about life and death, sin and forgiveness, salvation and service, faith and works, prayer and love, God and man, man and man, and the Church and the world. Therefore, they direct us to the theory and the practice of Christianity'.

On the wall above the symbols there was a map of Ronsey showing all the churches and a copy of Salvador Dali's painting 'The Last Supper'. The team member pointed out that the figure of Christ was painted in such a way that the landscape behind him could be clearly seen. In fact, by concentrating on the figure of Christ in this picture one found oneself concentrating on an aspect of the world. The team member said, 'At the beginning of this conference we are concentrating on Christ in order that together we may examine church manpower problems in Ronsey in the context of his life and ministry. Therefore both map and picture are closely related'.

This introduction concluded with a period of silent meditation and a brief prayer.

This session achieved its objective. It was supplemented by two devotional sessions taken later by local clergy.

Problem four — How to help members of the conference, the churches and the council to tackle their problems and feel more optimistic about finding solutions?

The team introduced members of the conference to four ways of getting people to realize what they themselves could do to solve their own problems.

1. Using drama to get problems considered

In this approach three sketches were used to promote discussion about manpower shortage problems. The team wrote scripts which local people adapted to fit their experience before performing them at the conference.

The first sketch, entitled 'It's leaders we want!' was a conversation between Mr James, a church official, and Mr Graham, a friend, who had once been a keen scouter. Mr James took the opportunity of a chance meeting in a local bus to try to persuade Mr Graham to become the leader of a scout troop. Mr Graham showed interest but said that he did not regard himself as a leader and he did not think he could deal with discipline problems. He also felt he would need training but doubted whether he could spare the time to go on courses. He would help, but not as a leader. However, Mr James did not take up Mr Graham's offer of help. He wanted him as a leader and tried to force the issue by reminding him of what the troop had done for him when he was a boy.

The idea for this sketch came from discussions with the clergy which had shown that people in Ronsey tended to think of 'leaders' as charismatic people who inspired others to follow them. Few people felt they had these qualities. Consequently when asked to become leaders they declined. But the same people responded positively if asked to teach scouts first aid, to befriend them or to go camping with them.

The second sketch entitled, 'It's all or nothing' was a conversation between two loyal church workers, Mr Joyce and Mr Sharman. Mr Joyce was worried because he knew the vicar was lining up another job for him. He was already over worked and this was causing trouble between his wife and himself. He could not face the consequence of taking on additional work and he did not know how to get out of it, so he reluctantly decided to join another church where he would refuse to take on any work at all because 'once you start they pile one job after another upon you. The willing horse gets lumbered'. Try as they might neither of them could think of a way in which Mr Joyce would be able to get out of the job and stay at the church, 'The vicar just will not take "No" for an answer' nor could they think of ways in which he could reduce his work load, 'People just won't take jobs on'. Sadly, Mr Sharman agreed that Mr Joyce had no option but to leave if he was to save his marriage.

The third sketch entitled 'I would if I could' was a conversation between Mrs Groom and Miss Holden after a church service. Mrs Groom detained Miss Holden to ask her to join a parish visiting scheme. Miss Holden wanted to help but genuinely felt that she needed training for the job. Mrs Groom said Miss Holden didn't need training because she was so 'good with people'. She would 'know just what to do in any situation'. Miss Holden disagreed and said 'flattery won't get you anywhere'. Mrs Groom then tried to get her to join the choir but Miss Holden said she could not attend the practices regularly unless they were on another night. Again Mrs Groom tried by flattery, 'You will be able to sing without practice', but without success.

A team member summarized each sketch before asking members of the conference to answer the questions listed on their 'work-sheet': that is, what were the basic problems? are they common? have you experienced them? why do you think they occur? how can they be resolved? The questions were considered in groups of ten. Each group had a worker, concentrated on one sketch and reported to a plenary session. Later their findings were collated in a report of the conference.

Each sketch provoked much laughter but also stimulated intensive discussion. The members of the conference quickly listed why they thought the three people declined the jobs and why the approaches of the would-be recruiters were ineffective. For example they said that both Mr James and Mrs Groom were so insensitive and inflexible that they did not even consider looking at possible ways of overcoming the difficulties which prevented Mr Graham and Miss Holden from offering to do the jobs.

The members of the conference said that such problems occurred, *inter alia*, because churches tend to persist with outmoded kinds of work also taking on new kinds of work — 'We feel guilty if any job of work has to stop . . .'; because churches plunge into ventures too big for them; because church leaders feel that people *should* fit in with them rather than the other way round; because churches do not give sufficient thought to ways of overcoming recruiting and training problems; because many lay leaders find church services do not meet their needs as they cannot attend them without being involved in work and/ or thinking about it; because some take on jobs which they do not want to do to avoid feeling guilty; and because clergy allow committees to overload people.

They identified several ways in which they thought these problems could be overcome.

First, clergy and church leaders need to consider the problems of their church workers and potential recruits and maybe even to discuss with their families the effect of church work on family life and relationships. One group said that the way the church dealt with its workers demonstrated 'a lack of concern about Christian family life'.

Second, they thought that the churches ought to adopt a more business-like approach. Thus, before attempting to fill a vacancy they ought to define the job and consider whether or not it still needed to be done. If it did, then they ought to consider whether a person needed training for it or support whilst doing it. Then they ought to plan carefully just how they could recruit the right person for the right job, they said there were 'too many square pegs in round holes in churches'. They felt they would be most likely to do this if they:

(a) asked people to do specific jobs rather than asked them to become 'leaders' or 'helpers';

(b) considered carefully whom to approach and how to do so with tact and sensitivity, (churches are inclined to ask established workers to take on more and more work rather than search for people, possibly on the periphery, who have no church job; many people, they said, would help if they knew what was to be done and/or were asked but they would never 'push themselves forward');

(c) helped people to see the work in the kind of Christian context described in this conference.

Third, they thought that clergy should make it their business to ensure that people were not 'pressurized' into taking on church jobs. Members said, 'the church has a responsibility to help people to assess their responsibilities to their family, themselves, their employers and to the church'. They also said, 'People must know and cherish one another before they use one another'.

Fourth, they felt that ways should be found of encouraging and supporting people who are engaged in church work.

Fifth, they felt that churches could reduce the work load on various people and build up labour reserves by rotating jobs and by encouraging workers to recruit and train assistants and successors.

2. Considering 'solutions'

This was designed to get members of the conference to think critically about 'solutions'.

Three people were asked to prepare to explain how they would solve some of the problems revealed by the charts if they were given a free hand.[2] They put forward three ideas. *First*, that a properly equipped 'central office' be established to serve all the churches. The conference thought this idea would work and wanted it implemented. *Second*, that the churches should set up a centralized delivery service for circulars and magazines to avoid having several people from different churches delivering in the same road. The conference felt this service could be

---

[2] The team got this idea from a series of Programmes entitled 'The Very Idea' which was currently being shown on B.B.C. 2. The series was about problem solving and was conceived and introduced by Professor Edward de Bono.

very useful but foresaw difficulties in organizing it and in keeping distribution lists up to date. *Third*, a churches magazine or inset should be published to promote inter-church understanding and cut production costs. The conference thought this idea had many possibilities but that much would depend on finding a really capable organizer. They asked the executive to consider each idea with a view to taking appropriate action.

3. A problem solving sequence
The team described to the conference in the following way a problem solving sequence that many people in Ronsey had found useful:

Problem identified and defined	→	Possible causes of problem considered	→	Possible solutions considered	→	'Best' solution selected	→	Put into practice	→	Results assessed

The team members decided not to get people to try it out during the conference because not enough time could be spared to do it properly and they wanted to avoid the danger of involving people in superficial discussions.

4. 'Problem solving tools'
During the training sessions the clergy had found diagrams or charts which set out step by step what they could do to tackle their problems useful. This gave the team the idea of producing charts as tools for helping to solve manpower shortage problems.

These charts plotted what some would call a critical path a group could take in working towards a solution. The team produced eight of these tools, four of which drew heavily upon the work already done in the clergy training sessions on recruiting, training and deploying voluntary leaders. They were about the following problems:

– *how to find leaders and helpers to replace those who will or should retire in the next year or two?*
– *how to teach children Christianity in areas where most of them don't attend Sunday school?*
– *how to recruit leaders and Sunday school teachers?*
– *how to reduce the work load on those who have too many jobs?*

The team produced one tool to show people how to identify underlying causes:

– *how to discover why people will not or cannot take on jobs?*

The team also produced tools related to three key underlying causes of the manpower shortage that they had identified. One of these causes is a sequence of events only too familiar to the Ronsey people and already illustrated in the second sketch: an able individual highly committed to church and community work, takes on more and more work to ease the manpower shortage – has inadequate leisure and does less preparation and training – becomes grossly overworked – experiences tension between family, work and church – experiences a personal crisis finally gives up – leaves many jobs vacant.

Another cause is also a commonplace sequence of events: overworked individuals and groups make decisions without thoroughly considering the implications – ill-considered action causes avoidable difficulties which take time to sort out – other work is held up – in clearing the backlog more ill-considered decisions are made – people feel grossly overworked and dissatisfied with what they have done. ('We feel we are on a treadmill', they frequently said.)

A third underlying cause is that some people decline jobs because they feel unable to do them without help, and no help is offered.

The following tools were designed to get people thinking about these three underlying causes and ways of tackling them:

– *how to reduce excessive pressure of work by establishing purposes and priorities and ways of keeping to them?*
– *how to make decisions more systematically?*
– *how to help and support workers?*

One of these tools is reproduced on pp. 158-59 to illustrate what they were like.

The conference members worked in eight groups to consider one or other of the problem solving tools. They were asked to examine each step of the proposed approaches *to see just what it involved and to decide if it would work in their church, and, if it would not, to work out an approach that would.* This avoided the danger of the tools being accepted uncritically as blue prints. The conference members were most excited about these tools. They decided that they needed only minor modification to be effective in their situations; that they would be helpful in solving the problems they had already discussed (see pp. 143 ff); and that copies of all the tools and the groups' comments should be supplied to all conference members and all the clergy in Ronsey.

Problem five – How to help people to meditate?

The team members wanted to help members of the conference to meditate about what they themselves needed by way of inner resources from God and the Church to be able to carry on with the work in which they were engaged. They entitled the session, 'From whence cometh my help?' The symbols, the picture and the map used in the session describing the Christian context were used again.

A member of the team introduced the session by saying that Christians are helped to do their work through their natural gifts and graces, through their experience and training, through the support they receive from others, through their belief in God, through Christian worship and prayer and through their own determination. He drew their attention to the symbols of faith and suggested that they might meditate on just what it was that they required from God, from the Church and from each other in order to continue their work in the church and the community. He said that after a period of silent meditation they would have opportunities to talk to their neighbours. Later, those who wished would also have opportunities to share their thoughts with the conference as a whole.

Members of the conference, apart from a small minority, responded very positively to this exercise and were soon in a deeply meditative mood and a prayerful atmosphere developed. Most people talked in twos and were obviously deeply engaged in conversation about things which were very important to them. After this a few people did share their thoughts with the whole conference. They said that they were greatly helped by the knowledge of God's forgiveness, by the experience of being accepted by others for what they were and by the Bible. The whole experience was very moving because of its sincerity and the depth of sharing. It ended in prayer.

Some fifty people found this exercise so helpful that they asked the executive to make arrangements for a monthly or quarterly meeting at which people of different denominations could meditate together in this way: and fifteen of these asked for a weekend retreat.

Assessment after the team withdrew

The final evaluation shows that most people felt the conference opened their eyes to new and effective ways in which they could tackle their problems. As a consequence they became more sanguine and experienced a boost in morale. They said what they had learnt had a wide application and that it had already promoted change and would continue to do so. The following quotations illustrate what was generally felt.

'The main change effected by the team is the encouragement to look at problems constructively and to think through them logically. This has led to effective action'.

'Approaches and methods used and demonstrated at the conference could be invaluable in tackling any schemes in the overall work of the churches in Ronsey.'

'Members of different churches could together try to find answers to the declining attendance at Sunday school using these approaches.'

'I think some of the methods used will be tried again.'

'Changes will continue because people have learned how to think out their problems in a logical and detailed way.'

Members of the executive said that for them and for most of those who attended, the conference struck the right balance between the various aspects of *church, church-community* and *community work.*

The preparation and the conference itself, they said, led to improved ecumenical relationships: 'I don't think we'll ever feel isolated in our own parishes again'. 'You helped the ecumenical process by involving people other than appointed representatives'.

And, they said, it was enjoyable and satisfying as well as productive.

Subsequent developments

The information on the charts showing the work, the workers and the situations vacant of each church proved to be useful to the council in thinking out policies and programmes of work.

Arrangements were made to enable people to meditate together In October 1975 eighteen people from nine different churches in Ronsey shared in a residential weekend retreat on 'Prayer and the spiritual life'. Talks were followed by periods of discussion. In March 1976 twenty-five people from eleven different churches in Ronsey and six different denominations and whose ages ranged from the early twenties to the early seventies spent a residential weekend discussing aspects of their faith. Those present decided to hold a monthly ecumenical prayer meeting; a silent retreat weekend in September 1976; and a weekend conference in the Spring of 1977 on 'The healing mission of the Church'.

A CHURCHES' OFFICE AND MAGAZINE SERVICE

Soon after the conference the chairman of the council's publicity committee undertook to consider the suggestion about a churches' office and magazine service and asked for the team's help. He said he intended to ask his committee to recruit helpers and to equip a room as an office as soon as possible 'so that people can see that something is being done'.

The team said that this took for granted that such a service was needed, and suggested that it might be wise to find out from the clergy and their churches what additional help, if any, they required with office work and with the publication and circulation of magazines so that the most relevant kind of service could be planned.

The chairman was quick to see the advantages of doing this: it would lead to a more relevant service; it would avoid conflict with those organizing the existing services; it would help them to see it as 'their service' and therefore they would be more likely to use it. Together the chairman and team worked out the way in which it could be done.

The team members began to work out the steps in a diagrammatic form similar to that used in the problem solving tools (pp. 158 ff.) The chairman asked them to write it up and so the team prepared a draft which they discussed thoroughly with him before producing the final copy as on pp. 160-61.

A team member worked out with the chairman how he was going to use the diagram. He decided to construct the overall sequence on a blackboard at a committee meeting because he had 'found the sight of nine steps a bit daunting'. If the committee adopted the approach he could then plot out the first two or three steps. After these steps had been taken he said he would give them copies of the diagram.

This was the only help the chairman and his committee required from the team. They followed the steps. They interviewed key figures in all the churches and ecumenical organizations using questions which they prepared together. The information they got revealed that although several people needed additional secretarial services, a central churches office would not be generally used, and that there was no enthusiasm for a centralized delivery service. It also revealed a real demand for a magazine inset giving information about the churches in Ronsey. Such an inset was introduced in 1974. It was widely appreciated and was still in monthly production in 1976.

Assessment after the team withdrew

During the final assessment the chairman said, 'I looked at the directive and non-directive way of doing the task I was set. I saved myself a great deal of trouble and eliminated two of the tasks which could not have been successful because of lack of support by approaching them non-directively'. The executive commended the way in which the need for a magazine service and central office had been explored and assessed before action was taken. This led them to reassert the importance to their work generally of finding out what precisely is needed before providing it.

THE BOROUGH COMMUNITY DEVELOPMENT UNIT

Prior to the team starting work in Ronsey the borough had set up a working party on community development (p. 133). The team were told of this when they met the borough officials in 1972. The working party produced a report in 1973. It recommended setting up a borough community development unit staffed by a principal community development officer and five community development workers who would each be responsible for a section of the borough and a particular subject such as education or youth work. The report also referred to the churches. It said, 'the church provides the main range of "voluntary" community activities in the borough, and the clergy could be termed

149

the largest group of community workers . . . Different clergy have adopted differing attitudes to community work. In Ronsey the Council of Churches has established a church and community development project'.

The report was accepted and the unit set up. The community development officer started work in November 1973; and the borough community development worker with responsibility for Ronsey in March 1974. Their job was to co-ordinate statutory and voluntary social and community services; to receive and report suggestions and criticisms of community services; and to encourage people to form autonomous community groups and to support those that already existed.

The team set out to help the churches and the unit to decide whether or not they wanted to work together and if they did, to help them to establish effective working relationships.

With the executive's agreement the two full-time members of the team met the community development officer in January 1974. He described the unit and his approach to community development work. The team described Project 70-75 and the *church, church-community* and *community* work in which they were engaged in Ronsey. He said that the team had opened his eyes to a new area of work as he had not previously thought of the churches as organizations through which to promote community development. He now saw that a non-church person could act as a catalyst to church people just as church people could act as workers to non-church people.

The community development officer and the team felt that much could be gained from co-operation between the unit, the council and the churches. The unit could benefit from the experience of the churches and the team; the unit could help the churches especially after the team had withdrawn; and the churches and the unit could be more effective if they worked together in some situations than if they worked independently. The team agreed to report the discussion to the executive.

The executive responded very positively to the team's report of their discussion with the officer. A meeting of representatives of the executive, the team, the community development officer and the newly appointed community development worker took place in March 1974.

The following points emerged from their discussion:

1. The officer and worker offered to service schemes on which the council and churches were engaged. The members of the executive were delighted and said they would make the offer known to the churches.
2. The members of the executive asked if the borough worker would consider an invitation to attend the council's sub-committee on comm-

unity work *either* to liaise between the unit and the council *or* to act as a worker to the committee. The worker said he would be pleased to attend in either or both capacities. The chairman of the community committee said he would ask his committee and the council to consider issuing an invitation.

3. The officer said the unit and the adult education department would be organizing various courses for voluntary workers on such subjects as committee procedures and how to run organizations. The officer and the worker said they could see the need for training sessions like those arranged by the team but they had no experience of them and had no idea where to find people to run them. The team suggested it might be possible to draw on the experience that the clergy and laity in Ronsey now had of this kind of training. It was agreed that this was a potential area for co-operation.

4. The members of the executive said they would like one of the unit's workers to take an especial interest in church and community development work. The officer said he would bear this in mind.

As a result of this meeting the executive and council decided that they wanted to co-operate with the unit and they asked the team to help them to inform the churches how to obtain help from it. They also said that the members of the team could share with the unit anything they had learned from working in Ronsey. The council's sub-committee on community work invited the borough community development worker to attend their meetings, in order that he could liaise between the council and the unit.

In March and April the two full-time members of the team discussed their work with the borough community development worker. He said that in addition to the contacts he had with the council he had been invited to co-operate with the community work clergy task group (p. 105) and he was helping clergy with two other schemes, but he wanted to get in touch with as many churches as possible. The team said that they were letting the churches know about the unit and would put those which were interested in touch with him. They described to the worker how and why they made their first contact with the churches through the fraternal. The worker decided to adopt a similar approach and visited the fraternal in May. At that meeting he described the unit and, in answer to questions, said that its services were available to individual clergy and churches and that he wanted 'to carry on from where the team leave off'. The clergy asked him to help overcome problems they were facing from gangs of youths.

Good working relationships between the churches and the community development worker developed quickly and within a few months he was involved in no less than eight church and community development schemes, five of which had resulted from project work. He was pleased to be working with the churches and wished to continue developing his working relationships with them.

PROMOTING OVERALL DEVELOPMENT

Some people in Ronsey were engaged in one scheme but had no knowledge of others. Some were helping to organize the local area work and had a general idea of what was being done but were not involved in training sessions or in schemes. Some were interested only in a superficial way; and some were simply not interested. The team worked to promote overall development by getting as many people as possible to learn as much as they could from the work programme as it evolved.

Promoting overall development through formal and informal contacts

Team members kept in touch with as many people as possible in addition to those with whom they were working. They attended council meetings, ecumenical services, meetings and other special church functions. At least one of the three clerical members attended fraternal meetings, and the two full-time workers attended executive meetings. They made themselves available during set periods each week in a room put at their disposal by a church in the centre of Ronsey. They gave talks about their work to various church and community groups, for example, guilds, women's meetings, the Young Conservatives and a local Anglican deanery. One member of the team conducted no less than six services a quarter in the Ronsey area. Two members often stayed overnight in a convent and another in the Y.M.C.A. The team met people informally in their homes and around the town.

These formal and informal contacts provided members of the team with many opportunities to get to know people better, to understand what they really felt and thought about church and community devement work and to talk about the work in which they were engaged.

Promoting overall development through reports and articles

Members of the team presented verbal reports at meetings of the council, the executive and the fraternal. They produced serveral pamphlets about their work for circulation within the churches and at the invitation of clergy wrote articles for church magazines.

At first, all the team's contacts with the borough had been through the churches. However, in the second year, without in any way compromising their decision to work through the churches and with the backing of the executive and the fraternal, team members were able to report directly to twelve borough officials with interests in community development. Their report was well received and helped to establish good working relationships with the borough community development unit (p. 41).

Promoting overall development through reviewing the work with the chairman, and secretary to the council

In July 1973 the two full-time members of the team and the chairman and secretary of the council met to review the work of the project. The team members described the work that had been concluded during the first year and the work on which the team was currently engaged. They also described the pattern of working relationships they had built up and the way they had now adopted of classifying the work.

The chairman and secretary said that the work the team had described helped them to see more clearly than ever before just what community development was all about. They now saw its relevance to *church, church-community* and *community work*. They were excited by what they saw and said, 'We had no idea of the extensive amount of work in which you are engaged'. They felt that it was vitally important to get over to as many people as possible the picture they now had of church and community development work in Romsey because it would help to overcome the misunderstandings some people still had about the project — misunderstandings such as people still thinking that community development was only about 'getting already over-busy people to work outside the church in the community', or about why the team was not working through a task force, or that the team was 'not doing very much'. They felt that the next step was to arrange for the council to review the work in the way in which they themselves had done. The team said that there were at least three other ways of getting the work and the project more deeply understood. One was an evaluation of the project by the fraternal. This the fraternal had agreed to undertake. Another was to implement the council's decision to arrange meetings for people interested in church and community development work (see pp. 155-157). The third was for the team members to visit church committees. Five committees had invited them to do so.

Promoting overall development through reviewing the work with the council

The review with the council took place in November 1973. For this review the team prepared two visual aids: the diagram illustrating *church, church-community* and *community work* shown on p. 61 and a simplified form of the work chart on p. 60. Members of the council approved the way in which the work was developing and decided to hold an evening meeting on church and community development work to Ronsey in February 1974 which they asked the team to organize on their behalf. They said it would be helpful if some of those with whom the team had worked were 'to give an account of the team's work from the receiving angle'.

Promoting overall development through evaluating the work with the fraternal in October 1973

Members of the team asked the clergy to think about the effects of the initial discussions about locating the project in Ronsey upon them and their work. Similarly they asked them to consider how they felt about the initial work programme, the training sessions for clergy and the resulting schemes. The clergy said that the overall effect was positive and that this can best be seen from their assessment of the training sessions (pp. 57-58). Apart from that the discussion was mainly about two problems.

First, the clergy and the laity had found it difficult in the early stages to understand the community development approach sufficiently well to be able to explain it to others, and to see how it could be applied to their work (cf. p. 28). Generally speaking, they said, they began to understand when they experienced it for themselves in a training group or on a scheme or when they saw it being worked out locally by others.

Second, two or three of the clergy with whom the team had not worked maintained that it was very difficult if not impossible to get some people to think effectively together either because they are not used to doing so, or because they are not very intelligent, or because 'they are "doers" and not "discussers" and do not take to an approach which calls for verbalization'. One clergyman said that members of the team had been working in his church on a scheme with people whom he would at one time have classified in this way, but that they had, in fact, succeeded in helping them to 'think, plan and work realistically and systematically and had, therefore, shown that the approach is relevant to working with such people'.

From discussing these two problems it emerged that *the clergy felt that it would be more helpful if discussion about concepts and approaches followed rather than preceded work on schemes because the people with whom they worked were most effective and happy when 'doing and thinking went together'. In fact, once they had established themselves in Ronsey the team members did work in this way.*

A member of one of the consultative groups commenting on the point made in the previous paragraph said; 'The non-directive approach seems to me to need a certain amount of working experience in a parish (or wherever) to provide enough material to reflect on. I doubt whether you can cope with the community development approach until you have "lived" a little, and have had the chance to reflect on how individuals and groups have reacted to your initiatives. Case studies are useful but there is no substitute for your own experience duly reflected on'.

Promoting overall development through re-visting church committees

Between January and March 1974 the team members visited five church committee, and in each case they were well received. One of the clergymen asked to meet the team members beforehand to work out their respective roles and at the meeting he acted as worker in a most competent way. The team members explained the work in which they were engaged in much the same way as they had at the review. Two committees were sorry that the team members would not be working in the area longer because they were only just beginning to see how they could use them. Two of them discussed the relationship between development work and the mission of the Church.

Promoting overall development through sharing work experiences

The evening meeting in February which the team had agreed to organize for the council was entitled 'An evening to share experiences'.

Up to now members of the team had taken the leading part in describing and reporting on the work. Now, however, they thought that the idea of getting people to describe their experiences could promote deeper understanding of the project work and stimulate people to think about their experiences and ways of telling others about them. It would also open up lines of communication between friends who respected each other's judgement and who knew that they were working in similar situations.

But there was a practical problem. Team members expected eighty people to attend the meeting and that was the number that did attend in spite of a heavy fall of snow during the day. There were nine schemes and only two hours in which to describe and discuss them, that is, roughly ten minutes a scheme. They overcame this problem in the following ways.

Nine stalls were erected around the church hall in which the meeting took place. Each stall was about a scheme and was manned by two or three people who could speak from experience — for example one stall was for the training sessions for lay people and another for the Anglican parish visiting scheme. There was also a stall about the project as a whole. The stalls displayed posters, charts and diagrams and any leaflets or records available for general circulation.

As they arrived people were welcomed by the chairman and secretary of the council and by the team. They were each given a sheet which listed the stalls, described the programme for the evening and provided space for notes, and they were asked to visit the stalls at their leisure and to discuss the schemes with the people engaged on them. The team acted as guides and stewards. Later, in eight groups people formulated their questions about the schemes. Then for about an hour in a plenary session they put their questions to a panel consisting of the team and people with experience of the nine schemes.

People began to see the overall pattern of the work in a way they had not seen it before. They were surprised at its scope and were especially interested in ecumenical schemes. Many people said that they now saw new ways in which churches could profitably co-operate on schemes and problem solving.

They plied the panel with questions. They wanted to know just how the work had been done in the schemes, exactly what the in-service training sessions for lay people had entailed and how useful they had been to the participants. The short answer given by the participants was, 'The team helped us to think for ourselves'. A layman said, 'The course was a way by which people think things through together . . . subsequently I found myself trying to help a men's committee to do the same'. A lay woman said, 'I learned that you should not push people around and decide what is best for them because what you think is best for someone may not be. You have to be very humble and accept the need to go slowly and let people think for themselves'. Several explained how the team had helped them to think and work through schemes.

There were many questions related to the practical difficulties of contacting and helping people in the community who 'really need help'. These questions were answered by the people engaged in the Anglican parish visiting scheme, the mothers under stress scheme and the good neighbour scheme. Surprisingly many of the people present knew nothing about this scheme.

By common consent the meeting was interesting, enjoyable and productive. Throughout there was a sense of 'togetherness' and sharing. People were both serious and lively. The meeting ended with an epilogue conducted by a team member.

Someone, not connected with any of the schemes, wrote an article on the meeting for her church magazine, she concluded with this paragraph: 'I, personally, was much impressed by the enthusiasm with which the churches in Ronsey seem to be tackling their problems, sharing experiences and discussing progress, not with any competitive feeling against each other but with a common love of Christ and a desire to share this love with each other and among the community'.

Working on schemes promoted development in various parts of the local area. Encouraging people to learn from the work programme as a whole in the ways described above promoted development throughout the local area by helping people to see their work in a wider context. It also played a critical part in helping the local people to understand more thoroughly the relevance and applicability of the non-directive approach to their work in the church and their neighbourhood.

PROBLEM: OVERWORKED CHURCH WORKERS AND DECISION MAKING

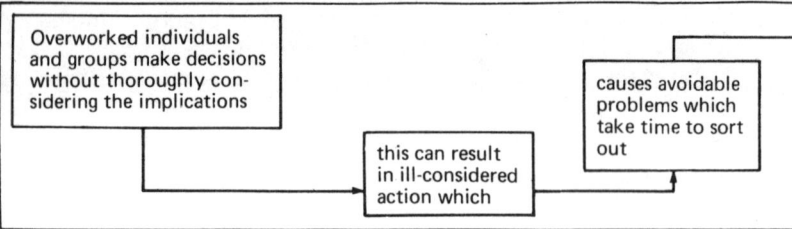

Overworked individuals and groups make decisions without thoroughly considering the implications

this can result in ill-considered action which

causes avoidable problems which take time to sort out

TOWARDS A SOLUTION

STEP A

STOP! It is not as difficult as it may seem (things go on when we are ill) to reduce business to a minimum for a time so that people can

THINK! especially about

PURPOSES

OBJECTIVES

POLICY

FREEDOM AND RESPONSIBILITY OF OFFICER

in order that more and more EXECUTIVE ACTION can be taken which is in line with purposes, policy, and so on

STEP B

Devise committee procedures for making decisions

They could be:

to ask WHAT must be decided?
WHEN must it be decided?
WHO must decide?

consider all RELEVANT INFORMATION

list CHOICES

Choice 1 pros and cons
Choice 2 pros and cons
and so on

MAKE DECISION

DECIDE ON ACTION

It is surprising how these approaches can become 'part of people'; how they help people to make better informed decisions; to feel in control; and save time and energy.

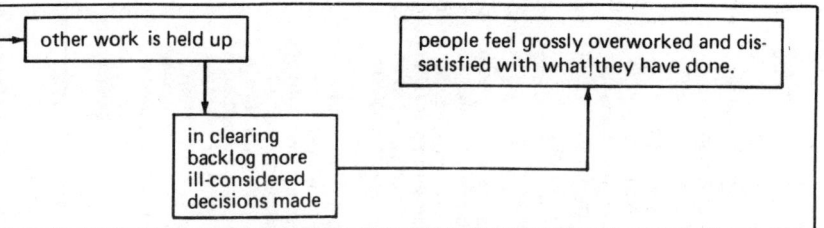

| other work is held up | people feel grossly overworked and dissatisfied with what they have done. |

in clearing backlog more ill-considered decisions made

STEP C

Devise ways of reducing length of agendas and time taken on agendas, possibly by:

Officers and/or members asking themselves the following questions about agenda items for which they are responsible:

> *Questions 1, 2 & 3*
> Why am I bringing this matter to the committee?
>
> What do I want them to do or to decide?
>
> Am I clear enough about the 'why' and 'what' and the 'choices' to be made?

Questions 4, 5 & 6
Have I got enough information?

Have I done all the work I can/must do beforehand?

Is this the best time to raise the subject?

> *Questions 7 & 8*
> Can this committee deal with the subject in this time?
>
> How can I save their time?

Working through these solutions involves Christians in prayer, thought and action.

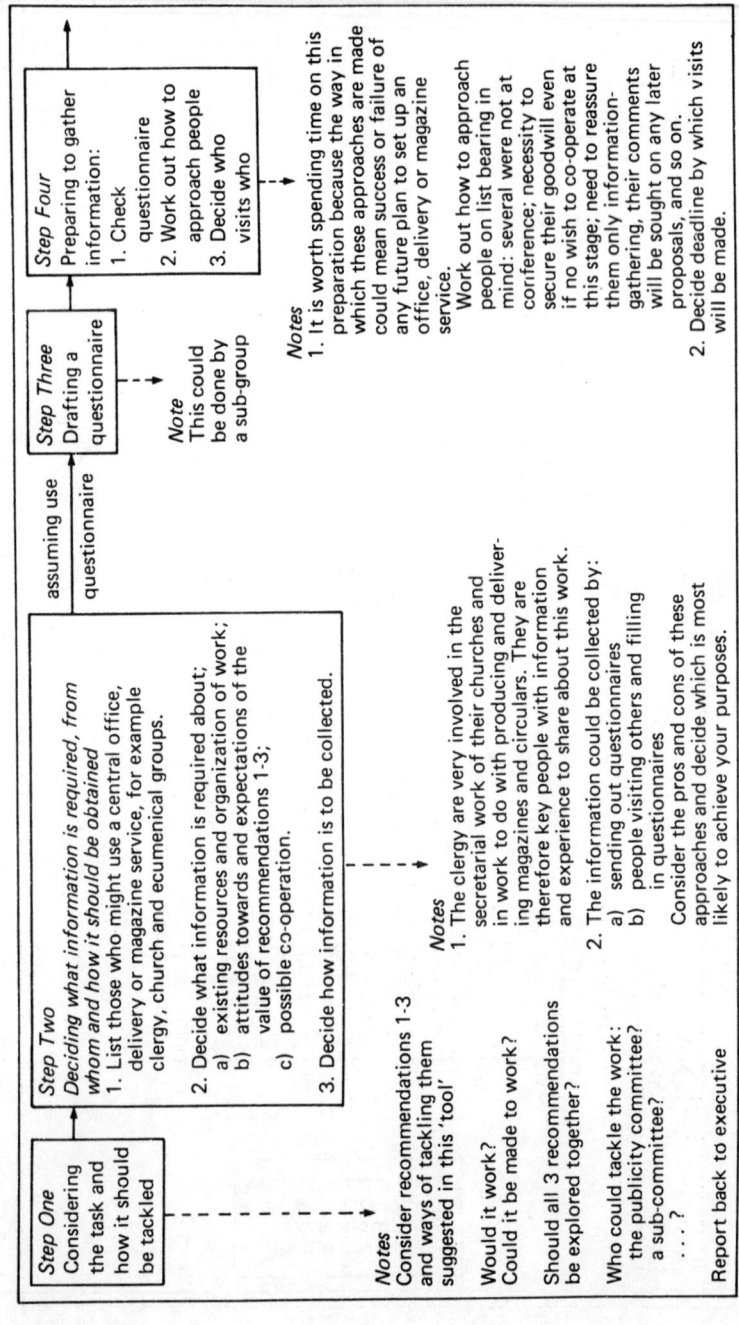

Step One
Considering the task and how it should be tackled

Notes
Consider recommendations 1-3 and ways of tackling them suggested in this 'tool'

Would it work?
Could it be made to work?

Should all 3 recommendations be explored together?

Who could tackle the work: the publicity committee? a sub-committee? ...?

Report back to executive

Step Two
Deciding what information is required, from whom and how it should be obtained
1. List those who might use a central office, delivery or magazine service, for example clergy, church and ecumenical groups.

2. Decide what information is required about;
a) existing resources and organization of work;
b) attitudes towards and expectations of the value of recommendations 1-3;
c) possible co-operation.

3. Decide how information is to be collected.

Notes
1. The clergy are very involved in the secretarial work of their churches and in work to do with producing and delivering magazines and circulars. They are therefore key people with information and experience to share about this work.

2. The information could be collected by:
a) sending out questionnaires
b) people visiting others and filling in questionnaires
Consider the pros and cons of these approaches and decide which is most likely to achieve your purposes.

assuming use questionnaire

Step Three
Drafting a questionnaire

Note
This could be done by a sub-group

Step Four
Preparing to gather information:
1. Check questionnaire
2. Work out how to approach people
3. Decide who visits who

Notes
1. It is worth spending time on this preparation because the way in which these approaches are made could mean success or failure of any future plan to set up an office, delivery or magazine service.
Work out how to approach people on list bearing in mind: several were not at conference; necessity to secure their goodwill even if no wish to co-operate at this stage; need to reassure them only information-gathering, their comments will be sought on any later proposals, and so on.

2. Decide deadline by which visits will be made.

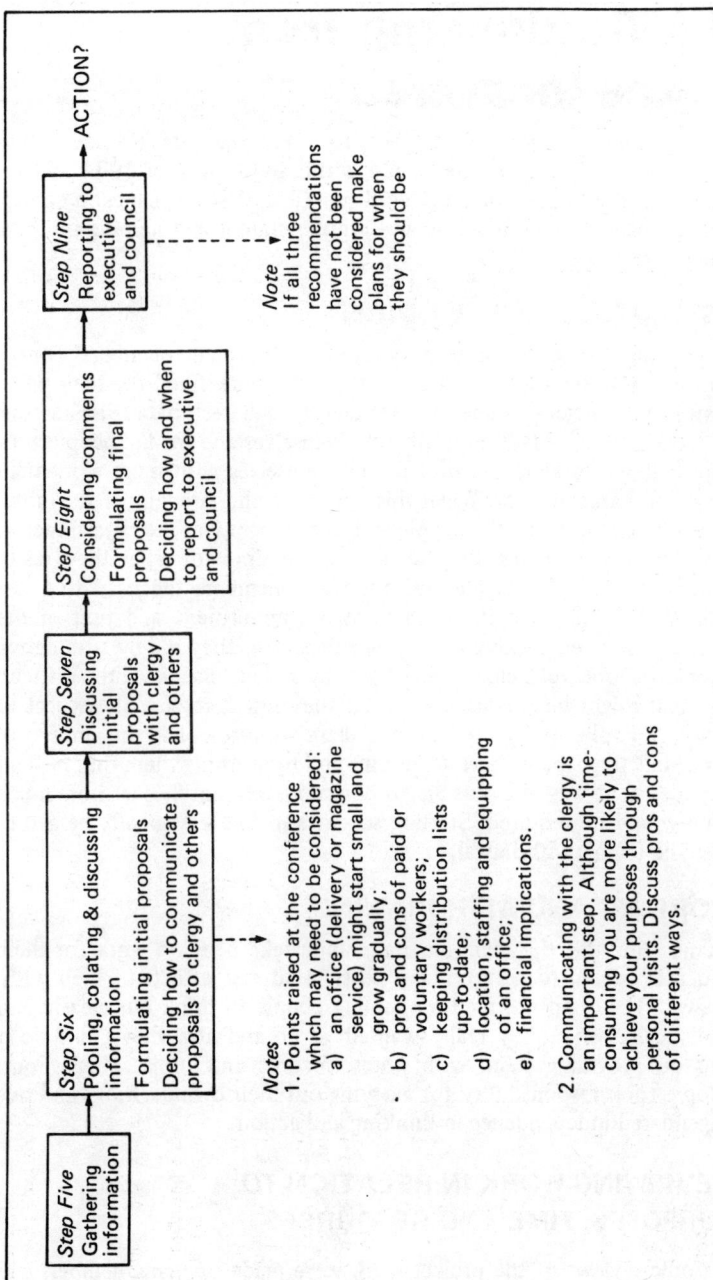

Step Five
Gathering information

Step Six
Pooling, collating & discussing information

Formulating initial proposals

Deciding how to communicate proposals to clergy and others

Step Seven
Discussing initial proposals with clergy and others

Step Eight
Considering comments

Formulating final proposals

Deciding how and when to report to executive and council

Step Nine
Reporting to executive and council

→ ACTION?

Notes
1. Points raised at the conference which may need to be considered:
   a) an office (delivery or magazine service) might start small and grow gradually;
   b) pros and cons of paid or voluntary workers;
   c) keeping distribution lists up-to-date;
   d) location, staffing and equipping of an office;
   e) financial implications.

2. Communicating with the clergy is an important step. Although time-consuming you are more likely to achieve your purposes through personal visits. Discuss pros and cons of different ways.

Note
If all three recommendations have not been considered make plans for when they should be

AN OUTLINE OF A WAY OF WORKING ON THE CONFERENCE RECOMMENDATIONS 1-3

5 Withdrawing from the local area

During the discussions about locating the project in Ronsey it was agreed that team members would withdraw in August 1974 and by that date they had completed work on all but two schemes: a community centre scheme in a Roman Catholic church and helping mothers under stress

ESTIMATING TIME REQUIRED

Organizing the work programme so that the team members' contributions to schemes would be made by the date fixed for their withdrawal was difficult, since they frequently underestimated the amount of work actually involved, both for themselves and for the people with whom they worked, and thus found themselves with more work than they had bargained for. When this happened the strength of the initial commitment both of the people and of the team was the crucial factor, for generally speaking they always found time for what they really wanted to do. This highlighted for team members the need to assess realistically the strength of their own commitment and that of the people *before* embarking on any schemes. This they did by stimulating people to look very closely at what they aimed to achieve, the difficulties that might be encountered, what they might reasonably expect to have accomplished by the time the team withdrew, and the amount of time that they might have to put in: and by warning them that in their experience it was not possible to determine accurately just how much time would be required. Starting schemes in this way greatly helped to ease the team's withdrawal.

WORKING AND WITHDRAWING

At no time did the team members undertake people's work for them and this helped to reduce many possible adverse effects of their withdrawal. They concentrated on helping people to think out clearly and realistically what they really wanted to do and how they could do it and on providing them with notes, records and tools. Throughout, people took responsibility for carrying out their own decisions and this engendered independence in thinking and action.

REVIEWING WORK IN RELATION TO PURPOSES, TIME AND RESOURCES

Periodic reviews of the project work were made by team members and their consultant, by the executive, by the council, by the fraternal and by those engaged on schemes. Basically these reviews involved evaluating the developments that had occurred; considering their implications for future work; and deciding what action to take. These periodic reviews helped both the team and the people to see more clearly the overall pattern. It enabled them to identify the key areas of work and to concentrate upon them. It also helped them to establish goals which could be achieved in the time available.

ARRANGING A MUTUALLY ACCEPTABLE WITHDRAWAL

In May 1974 the two full-time members of the team met the executive to make arrangements for their withdrawal. During the first part of the meeting the team members described the project work which they expected to complete by August 1974 and that which they did not expect to complete. They said that from September 1974 they would be preparing a final report and involving people in Ronsey in evaluating the project work.

The team and the executive were equally concerned that the withdrawal should have minimal adverse effects on the schemes and the members of the executive were anxious to ensure that the arrangements gave the team the objectivity and the continuing links with Ronsey which they considered essential during the evaluation and the preparation of this report.

Thus after a long discussion it was agreed that from August 1974 the team would not be expected to attend executive or council meetings but would be kept in touch with developments, and that either the executive, the council, people engaged on schemes or the team could request a meeting. It was also agreed that the team members would arrange to withdraw from schemes with those concerned, but continue after August 1974 to do all they could to promote effective working relationships between the churches and the borough community development unit; submit suggestions to the executive in the autumn for ways in which the people in Ronsey could help to evaluate the project work; and write a report for the council about the principal things they had learnt through working in Ronsey and about any discussions they may have had with the borough community development unit. These arrangements were confirmed by the council and the fraternal.

Members of the executive were thorough and worked hard and systematically. They were warm towards the team and most appreciative of the work done. They said that they considered the next phase of the team's work 'to be vitally important as it will enable the maximum benefit to be gained from a project which we have found of value'.

They also said that they were willing to continue to help in any way they could.

PROMOTING LOCAL INTERDEPENDENCE

Throughout, members of the team did all they could to enable people in the churches and in the community to make arrangements to work together for common objectives. This involved linking people on one scheme with those on another, and helping to establish effective working relationships between the churches, the council and the fraternal on the one hand and the borough community development unit on the other. Then in September 1974 the two full-time team members met the community development officer and worker to review work done on the project. They considered each scheme in relation to the help the unit was already giving and might give in the future.

The officer and worker said that the Ronsey Council of Churches and the local churches were far more involved in community work than those in other parts of the borough. The worker thought that this resulted from the work of the team. The officer thought that whilst his judgment was probably correct there might be other explanations and that the evaluation of the project work might help to determine the part played by the team. Both said that they had far more links with the churches in Ronsey than they or their colleagues had with churches in other parts of the borough. These developments, they said, generated self-help but they created more need for support services and training and more work for the unit!

The team members realized that the churches were making heavy demands upon the officer and the worker and asked if this concerned them. They said that they were pleased to be developing their working relationship with the churches and that the team must not tell the churches to 'cool off'. 'If we cannot cope with the work then we will have to see what can be done to find other workers'.

6 Working with consultative groups and advisers

An integral part of the action-research process was the exchange of information and ideas between the team, the consultative groups and the advisers about the project as it proceeded. This was done through seven interim reports and four newsletters, and by correspondence and discussions. In response to the reports the team received a hundred letters containing many carefully considered comments and criticisms. The two full-time workers discussed the project at meetings (thirty in all) arranged by six of the consultative groups. Members of the team also met advisers to discuss various aspects of the project. These exchanges had several effects.

First, preparing the interim reports helped team members to see the essence of the local area work and this helped them to work more effectively.

Second, the reports enabled the advisers and consultative groups to follow the project stage by stage; to see just what using the non-directive approach implies in terms of actual work; and to critically appraise the project work and the ideas upon which it was based (see, for example, the criticisms about working with the institutional church in Part Two chapter 1). They found 'the form of reporting was helpful, clear and easy to read'. One wrote, 'The reports are really very impressive in their professional presentation, models I should think for such an exercise. I have found them rather "dense" reading but I'm just about familiar enough with the approach to find them very rewarding'. The team learnt much from the response of the advisers and consultative groups to the reports and especially from the points at which they disagreed with the team.

Third, the team learnt just how difficult it is for people who have no experience of the community development process to understand it from reports alone. Many advisers and some consultative groups could not grasp what team members were doing or picture how they were doing it because for them the reports 'did not bring the working situation to life'. Discussing these difficulties led to the conclusion that case studies could help and to the decision to provide such studies in this report.

Fourth, there was evidence of a growing awareness of the value of the non-directive approach to church and community work. Quotations from two advisers illustrate this:

'I have just finished reading your report No. 7. I have been following the project carefully by reading the reports, but I haven't felt that I had anything useful to contribute and so have been silent. But perhaps I can say, as you are moving into the final stage, how much I have admired it all from afar. In the reports you have given me there is so much that illustrates a properly professional way of going about ministry'.

'I have been glad to read the reports of the project. It is particularly fascinating to notice at this stage the accumulating evidence that the work of the team has enabled much greater structural strength to emerge in a number of the local schemes. I would assume from this that a much higher level of individual satisfaction prevails in the various working groups. I think this lends considerable support to the view of a previous correspondent who said that the team have carried out a significant piece of organization development work which has enabled the organizations concerned to work effectively as agents of community development at various levels . . . I like very much the sense of coherence which seems to be marking the phase of incipient withdrawal.'

Fifth, a less tangible but nonetheless real result of the work done with the consultative groups and advisers, is the better climate of opinion towards church and community development work: many people in the churches are now better informed about it and more sympathetic towards it and this paves the way for future discussion about the implications of this report.

DIARY OF EVENTS

July 1970	Project team formed and Dr T.R. Batten agreed to act as consultant.
January 1971	Working paper produced Mr R. Press agreed to act as honorary accountant.
January to December 1971	Consultations with people in churches or with specialist knowledge of community work.
April 1971	The Methodist church agreed to George Lovell being a full-time worker to the project.
May 1971 to December 1972	Negotiations for funds.
June 1971	Panels of advisers and consultative groups formed.
November 1971 to June 1972	Looking for a suitable local area.
July 1972 to July 1974	Working in Ronsey, producing seven interim reports and four newsletters and discussing this work with Advisers and consultative groups.
August 1974	'Withdrawing' from the local area.
September 1974 to August 1976	Carrying out local assessment of work done, evaluating the project, working out its implications and preparing the final report.

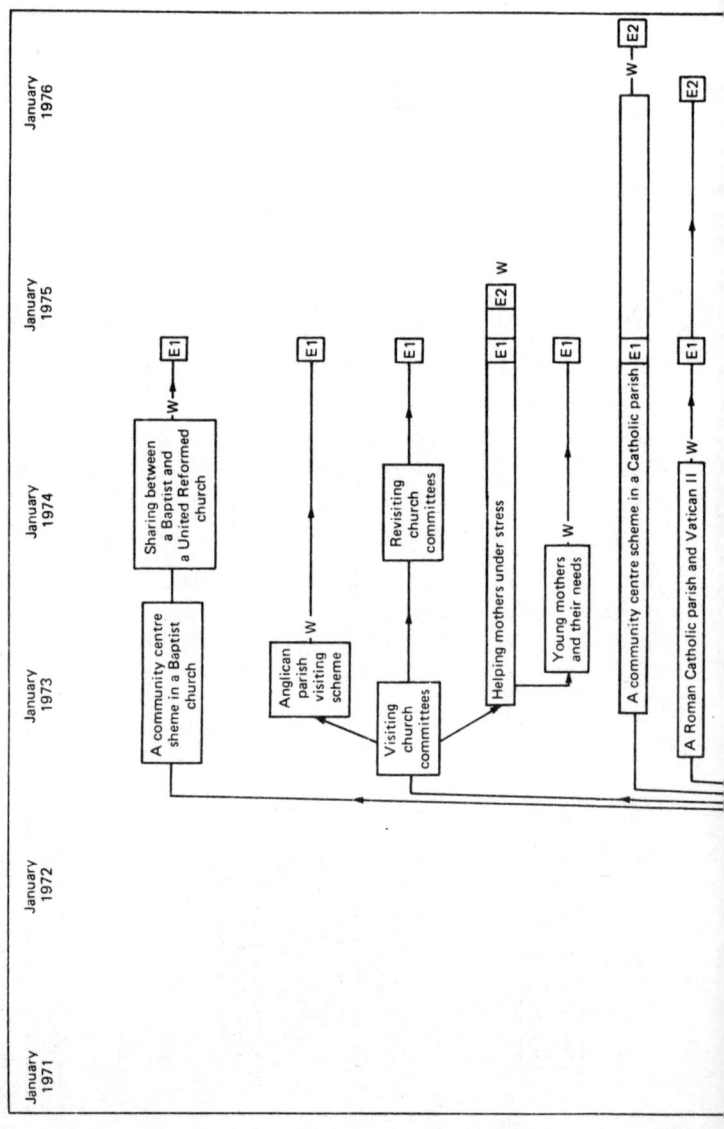

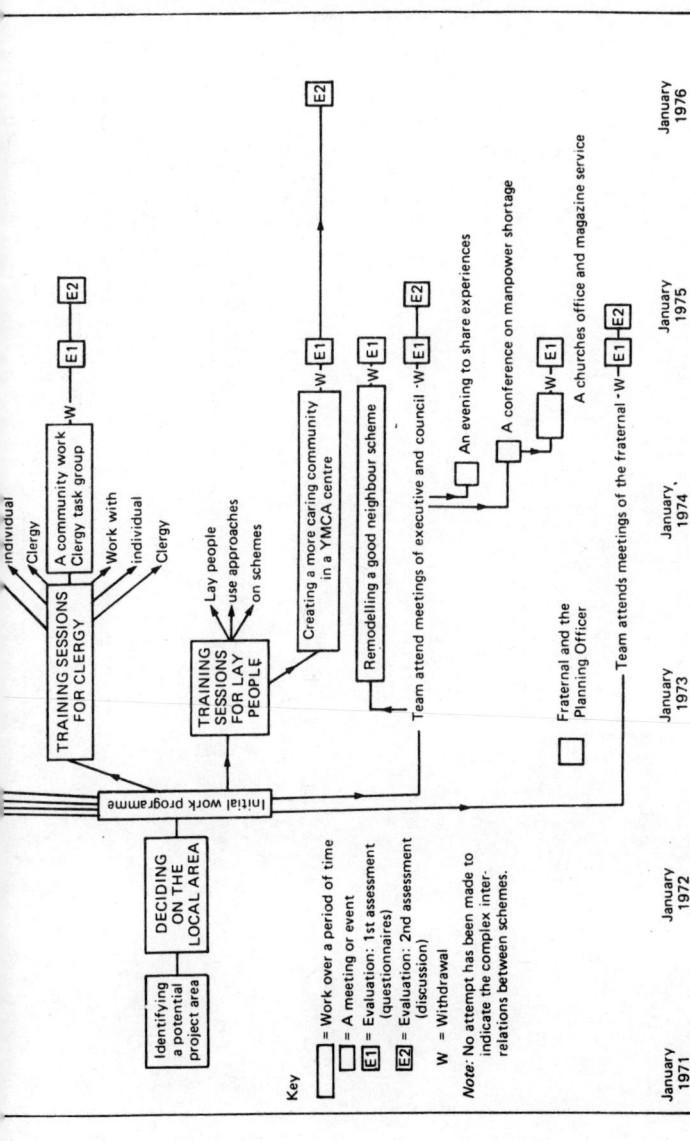

Key

▮ = Work over a period of time

| = A meeting or event

E1 = Evaluation: 1st assessment (questionnaires)

E2 = Evaluation: 2nd assessment (discussion)

W = Withdrawal

Note: No attempt has been made to indicate the complex inter-relations between schemes.

PROJECT 70-75: DEVELOPMENT OF LOCAL AREA WORK

169

PART FOUR: LOCAL ASSESSMENTS OF WORK DONE

Introduction

The team members' records of what they did, why and how they did it, with what results and with what implications for future action enabled them to make their own assessment of the project work. However, they realized that it was not enough for them to make their own assessment, however honest and objective they aimed to be. They also needed the views of the people with whom they had worked to supplement and amend or correct their own observations. Thus they would have two sides of the story: the team's and the people's.

As the local people had become involved in the project they had also agreed to assess the work done, and as the work proceeded team members had regularly invited comment and criticism from the people with whom they worked, and recorded what they said: and now that the field work had been completed and the team had withdrawn, they invited the local people to evaluate what they had done. How they did this and with what response is described in Part Four chapter 1. What the people said about the local area work as a whole is described in Part Four chapter 2. What they said about each scheme is described *in loco* in Part Three chapters 2 and 4 and Part 3 chapters 1, 4 and 5. Some of the major issues are considered in Part Five.

Although this is the final assessment as far as the set term of the project is concerned, it cannot of course be regarded as the ultimate evaluation in any real sense: there is always the possibility of future developments radically altering the significance of past events. Therefore, whatever the local people felt about the project at the time the team withdrew, their real assessment will only become apparent through what they do in the years to come. Meanwhile, their interim assessments are by no means without value provided they are used as internal evaluations and not as though they are (or should be) objective and final measurements of change.

1 What to assess and how

WHAT TO ASSESS?

The team members wanted to determine what effect their work had had on people with whom they had worked, and whether or not the development they had initiated was likely to continue after their withdrawal. They also wanted to know what people really felt about the relevance of the community development approach as a means by which they themselves could promote future development in Ronsey. In order to do this members of the team needed to get the people with whom they had worked to assess the value of the team's work in relation to what they themselves aimed to achieve.

HOW TO ASSESS?

The first step the team members and their consultant decided on was to prepare suitable questionnaires and to invite people to fill them in anonymously. The answers thus obtained would give an overall picture of what people thought individually. However, they knew from experience that answers obtained in this way, though useful, do not always reflect the *considered* view of those who give them. They therefore decided wherever possible, to invite the respondents to meetings to discuss the results and their apparent implications. What people said at these meetings would constitute a second assessment which would amplify and elucidate the results of the first. Although it was not practicable to get all the respondents to engage in a second stage assessment – because many would have felt that this was asking too much of them – a significant number of such meetings was held and they proved helpful.

TESTING IDEAS FOR ACCEPTABILITY

Before acting on these ideas team members sent a letter explaining what they proposed to do and why to each clergyman, each local church secretary and to each member of the executive. Later, through telephone conversations, they found the ideas were acceptable to these people and that they were willing to co-operate.

MAKING THE FIRST ASSESSMENT

The team members decided to send a questionnaire to each person who had attended meetings about church and community development work in Ronsey or with whom they had worked on schemes. Each questionnaire contained the following questions:

1. Have there been any changes, good or bad, in your work, organization or people which you feel are attributable in whole or part, to members of the team and the work they have done?

2. Do you feel that any of these changes, good or bad, are likely to continue after the withdrawal of the team?

3. Do you attribute any of these changes to particular approaches or methods used by the team?

4. In general, do you feel the approaches and methods used by members of the team have any application to your work? If so what approaches and methods, and in what areas of work?

5. Have you any suggestions as to how the team might have contributed more?

6. Please say what led you to become involved or not to become involved in church and community development work with the team.

7. Any other comments.

These questions were framed with great care to try to make them unloaded. They did not suggest answers, for the aim was to get people to think out their own answers for themselves. They asked people to describe changes rather than effects for two reasons: first, because, while people can describe and illustrate changes, some would find it very much more difficult to describe effects; and second, because once certain changes are identified as the results of the work done, the team members (and others) could assess them in relation to their own aims.

The questionnaires

Implementing the decision to send questionnaires to all those with whom the team had been in contact involved preparing thirteen questionnaires, each of which was addressed to a particular grouping of people and invited them to answer the questions from a different perspective. In fact they prepared a separate questionnaire for:

1. the clergy (they were asked to answer only one questionnaire which dealt with all aspects of the work);

2. members of church committees between 1972-4 (amongst other things this questionnaire covered the schemes undertaken by individual churches);

3. church committees, that is, a questionnaire completed by the committee *after* individual members had completed theirs;

4. members of the executive between 1972-4;

5. members of the Council of Churches between 1972-4;

6. non-council members known to have attended open council meetings about the project, task force, 'an evening to share experiences' and the conference 'Situations vacant?';

7. those who had attended the training sessions for lay people;
8. those who had taken part in one or more of the following schemes:
   (a) An Anglican parish visiting scheme;
   (b) Helping mothers under stress;
   (c) Young mothers and their needs;
   (d) Creating a more caring community in a Y.M.C.A. centre;
   (e) Remodelling a good neighbour scheme (one questionnaire for members of the co-ordinating committee and one for members of the area teams).

This arrangement minimized the number of questionnaires any one person received: most people received only one although some received three and a very few people four.

Generally speaking questionnaires 1 to 5 were to do with the project work as a whole, whereas 6 to 8 were to do with specific aspects of it. Each questionnaire had an introduction describing what it was about and inviting people to say just what they felt about the work undertaken from one of five perspectives: that of a clergyman with primary responsibility for a local church but variously involved with other clergy, churches and ecumenical and community organizations; that of a layman primarily concerned with his own local church; that of a layman involved in an ecumenical organization; that of a layman deeply involved in a particular scheme; and that of a layman who attended training sessions or meetings on church and community development work. Then followed in various combinations the seven questions listed on p. 175.

In order to establish the experience of the project upon which the answers were based, questionnaires 1 to 6 asked about the person's involvement in the project work. Each of these questionnaires also contained the question: 'Is there anything you wish to say about the discussions which led to the team working in Ronsey?'

The space allowed for answers indicated that the team were hoping for full and carefully thought out answers and one of three pages of the questionnaire addressed to clergy was given up to 'other comments'. Also each questionnaire stated, 'If . . . there is inadequate space on this form use a separate sheet'.

Before finalizing the questionnaires the team submitted samples to two people who were, and two people who were not, from Ronsey. This led to important modifications to the wording of some questions and the order in which they were asked. A sample questionnaire is reproduced on pp. 190-192.

Getting the questionnaires completed

The team members realized that the assessment would seem less important to the people in Ronsey than it did to the team, and that it could be difficult to get them to fill them in carefully and frankly and return them. To enhance the chances of their doing so, they explained the purpose and importance of evaluating the project, stressed the factor of anonymity and appealed to people to co-operate. They also kept key people informed of what was happening and asked them to use their influence to get the questionnaires completed and returned. They despatched all the questionnaires at the same time so that, hopefully, people would reinforce each other in the task of completing them. They enclosed stamped addressed envelopes and asked for the questionnaires to be returned by a certain date. They posted as many questionnaires as possible directly to the people concerned. (In fact they sent three hundred and ninety-nine direct by post and the remaining one hundred and eighty-one via clergy or church secretaries.)

The response

The following table gives an overall picture of the number of questionnaires sent out and returned.

Those to whom questionnaires were sent	Total number sent	questionnaires returned		The % of returned questionnaires which were carefully and fully answered
		number	%	
The clergy	17	15	88.2	80
Members of church committees	304	95	31.9	45.2
Church committees	16	5	31.2	80
Members of executive	10	9	90	77.8
Members of council	48	20	41.7	55
Non-council members known to have attended open council meetings	106	50	47.1	76.1
Those who attended training sessions for lay people	9	4	44.4	100
Schemes	76	40	52.7	82.5
Totals	586	238	40.6	59.6

Questionnaires were completed by clergy and people from all the churches with whom the team worked, and the answers therefore represent a wide range of denominational views. One of the most striking things about the returned questionnaires is that they were *either* filled in carefully and fully *or* the questions were not answered and what the person felt was expressed in a few words under 'any comments'.

With a few exceptions, and not surprisingly, those who filled in the questionnaires carefully and fully had been actively engaged in church and community development work in Ronsey. Many of those who did not answer the questions said they had not been sufficiently involved to be able to do so and some said that regrettably they had not had the time. Another reason for the unanswered questionnaires was revealed during the second assessment. Many people just could not answer them: one clergyman said that 'his people had been flummoxed by the question papers' and two other clergymen who had been amongst the keenest supporters of the project told the team that they had not returned their questionnaires because they had been unable to complete them to their satisfaction (had they done so the return would have been 100%).

All the returned questionnaires except five indicated that people were pleased that the team had worked in Ronsey and thought that they had 'done a good job of work'. Only one person said that he did not see any point in having the team in Ronsey.

The overall response of 40.6% gives an unrepresentative picture because of the poor response from the church committees and their members. There are several reasons which help to explain why only ninety-five of the three hundred and four papers sent to members of church committees were returned. The team had little contact with most of the church committees: the response from those churches with whom the team worked was high and it was low from those churches which had not involved themselves in schemes of their own. Many members of church committees appear to have experienced difficulty in completing the questionnaires and others, according to the executive and fraternal, reacted negatively to the questionnaires because they thought the team was wasting paper at a time when everyone was being urged to save it! Lastly, of the three hundred and four papers sent to members of church committees, one hundred and fifty-nine were sent indirectly through clergy and church secretaries and it is not known whether all were in fact distributed. Apart from the church committees the overall response was 50.8%.

MAKING THE SECOND ASSESSMENT

The team members listed both the positive and the negative points made by each category of person to whom a questionnaire had been sent. This enabled them to pick out the key points for discussion at the second stage of assessment and the key categories of people with whom they needed to discuss them. The choice of whom they decided to try to meet and the objectives were as follows.

The fraternal: to confirm or correct what the questionnaires said about 'changes'; to discuss difficulties experienced in introducing people to community development concepts; to consider differences of opinion about the ways in which the team could have contributed more; and to clarify what they thought about the approach the team had adopted to the clergy and the churches in the light of the criticisms made by some advisers and consultative groups.

The executive: to confirm or correct what the questionnaires said about 'changes'; to discuss whether or not, as a minority had claimed, the project caused the council to be overworked; and to clarify the meaning of some of the answers to the question about the applicability of the team's approach to the work of the council.

The community work clergy task group: to consider whether or not as some had suggested on the questionnaire, the team should have spent more time meeting and working with church members.

Those engaged on the Y.M.C.A. scheme and those engaged on the parish visiting scheme: to consider divergent views about the changes that had occurred.

Those engaged on the mothers under stress scheme: to make a group evaluation of the work done and the problems encountered.

A clergyman who was involved in the Roman Catholic parish and Vatican II scheme and who had left the area: to discuss with him the applicability of the community development approach to work in a Roman Catholic church.

The team had satisfactory discussions with all the people they decided to try to see except the parish visitors, whose organizer provided further information but said the he thought a meeting was unnecessary.

2 What the local people said

This chapter describes what clergy and laity in Ronsey considered to be the overall effects locally of the project work and the applicability of the approaches and methods used by the team to them and their work. (What people said in the first and second assessments about the discussions which led to the project being located in Ronsey and about the schemes is summarized in Parts Two to Four. What they said about the team's emphasis on working with the churches as institutions is reported in Part Five.)

WHAT PROMOTED AND WHAT PREVENTED INVOLVEMENT

Clergy, members of the executive and church committees who had become involved said that they had done so because *either* they were already convinced that community development work was a part of the Church's mission *or* they were looking for more effective ways of meeting the needs of church and non-church people; *or* to promote greater unity between the churches. A clergyman wrote, 'I became involved . . . because I was . . . acutely aware of unmet needs in the community, that church premises are underused . . . and because it seemed to offer a way of hope for our dispirited church people who felt the church did not seem to be needed any more and was too weak to make any impact'.

Most of the laity who had not become involved said it was because *either* they already had too many other commitments *or* they were elderly. Two people only said they did not become involved because they were out of sympathy with the team.

CHANGES ATTRIBUTED TO THE TEAM

There was widespread general agreement amongst the clergy and the laity of all denominations that changes for the better had occurred which were attributable in whole or in part to the team and the work they had done.

First, they said there had been an all round improvement in personal and working relationships between the clergy, the laity and their neighbours.

A few quotations will illustrate:

'There is a greater genuine interest in each other's affairs and a deeper understanding and appreciation of each other.'

180

'The links which existed between the individual churches and the team have brought about what I can only describe as a family feeling among all churches.'

'Some people are more aware and sensitive to the needs of the community around them and of the necessity for full involvement and participation of people – not just to organize something and then expect people to come.'

'In two churches there has been a warming towards the people of the immediate neighbourhood, their efforts and their needs . . . One of them is quite happy now with a club run by a tenants' association on church premises and eager to further the working/friendship/advisory relationship with its leader.'

Second, they felt they were working more effectively with church and non-church people because more people were now thinking for themselves and with a greater sense of purpose. They referred to the schemes to illustrate these points. They also said that people were now more open 'to consider new ways of working' and that 'some members of the council including clergy are more aware of ways in which community development type projects can be successfully launched and undertaken'. One clergyman wrote, 'I, personally, understand how better to cope with committee work' and another, 'My ministry is more organized and more under control'.

A layman said he had learnt 'how important it is to begin from the real needs of people'. In the first assessment a working class member of the executive said that there had been 'an overweighted middle class approach to most things within the church' and that this had frequently silenced the 'less articulate who have so much . . . to offer but remain quiet because of the sense of class and education which is so unnerving'; and he claimed that the team had 'temporarily, at least, overcome this class difference by coming to our churches to talk to, and most important of all, to listen to ordinary people in uninhibited surroundings'.

Third, they said that there had been an increase in the number of people actively and responsibly participating in the work sponsored by the council and in that of some churches. Again they illustrated this from the schemes. The executive said that the members of the council had become 'more active and less passive' and that more 'non-council members now take part in events organized by the council', and one clergyman said of his church: 'There is a greater involvement of people in parish affairs, a more responsible attitude of church workers towards large projects, a greater understanding by other parishioners about the problems facing both clergy and workers in church and community and parish development and more responsible comment'.

Fourth, they said the churches and the council were helping to provide more and better amenities for people. Again, they illustrated this with reference to the schemes and especially to the re-modelled good neighbour scheme, the facilities provided for mothers under stress and the extended use of church premises for community activities.

Fifth, they said they had much greater job satisfaction. In the first assessment some people said that a bad effect of the project and the team's approach was to increase the work load of an already over-worked council. In the second assessment, the executive said that the increase in work was no more than they bargained for when they agreed to the project being located in Ronsey and that the important thing was that their productivity and job satisfaction had increased out of all proportion to the extra effort they had put in.

Sixth, they said that their morale was much higher. One clergyman wrote, 'One's feeling of inadequacy in facing present day problems in London gave way to the hopeful possibility of achieving far more through the methods proposed'. A member of a church committee wrote, 'One now felt one could do something positive about an idea'. Another person wrote, 'Those engaged in our scheme . . . were delighted to find things were working out'. And yet another said, 'The conference on manpower shortage was wonderful, a terrific uplift'.

WILL THE CHANGES CONTINUE?

Most people felt that the changes that had been effected and the schemes that had been inaugurated would continue in the foreseeable future amongst those with whom the team had worked because some local people:

— *had changed:* (some actually spoke of 'permanent change'; one said that 'a permanent mark has been left on the council' and another that 'permanent good in the life of both the churches working together and the life of the individual churches has been achieved');

— *had learnt new skills rather than receiving 'advice and ready-made solutions';* (they said that they themselves had learnt 'how to build up community, think through problems and co-ordinate ideas');

— *had learnt how to help each other more effectively;*

— *had adopted new attitudes towards working with people;* (they said this in various ways: 'The attitudes will not revert . . . now that confidence that other people can run things is building up'; 'The change in attitude by some is something that has been deeply rooted and will grow');

— *have records of training sessions;* (many people used the records of training sessions and meetings; one clergyman said he intended to use his when training leaders for his new centre).

Some said that the process of development would continue only if people continued to practise the community development approach and took trouble and care to introduce and train others in it.

A minority, however, doubted whether the changes would continue *either* because an 'overall co-ordinator/worker' had not been appointed to succeed the team *or* because 'too much thought and energy' was having to be put into making the restructured council work effectively'.

One person said that her high hopes of the changes continuing in her parish had been dashed because a clergyman who had adopted the community development approach had been replaced by one who had no interest in that way of working.

APPROACHES AND METHODS TO WHICH CHANGES WERE ATTRIBUTED

Without exception people said that changes occurred because the members of the team really did act non-directively, that is, they consistently helped people to decide and to do what they themselves wanted to do. The particular approaches and methods to which they attributed the changes are best described in their own words as attempts to summarize them have resulted in lifeless lists of points. The following quotations are typical.

'The team helped people to think through systematically their own approach to community work'. (A clergyman)

'In particular the team's patient non-coercive ways have been helpful as they have given people time to think and adapt without feeling threatened.' (A clergyman)

'The non-directive method; the discipline of sitting back and analysing a situation, the use of diagrams to clarify this and communicate it to others . . . the need, before taking action, to consider and consult all who are involved in a given situation or would be affected by any change'. (A clergyman)

'The advantage-disadvantage method of discussion has helped us to discuss more fruitfully'. (A lay person)

'The listening to people, the taking note of everything which is said, the careful weighing of the points, careful analysis, the care with which priorities are selected, the "step by step" follow up, ensuring that action is taken, the careful notes or minutes, the patient plodding through difficulties'. (A member of a church committee)

'The method by which the team set out on a blackboard in short concise sentences the various views was most useful and we could generally come to a wide measure of agreement as a consequence.' (A clergyman)

'I was unable to attend the training sessions . . . I realise nevertheless that the approaches the team employs — full consultation with as many people as possible, gathering together the various views with simple direct propositions, clarification of opinions, setting out the course to follow by diagram — is the best way to get a common consensus of all those concerned.' (A clergyman)

'Bringing people together to discuss their possible purpose, to gather and consider information and work out ways of achieving their shared purpose in the light of the information.' (A clergyman)

'I have been . . . impressed as much by personalities as by the technique, but perhaps they go together; clarity of mind, seriousness, respect of people combined with hard headed facing of realities.' (A member of a church committee)

APPLICABILITY OF THE APPROACH TO THEIR WORK

Almost all those who took part in the first and second assessments said that the community development approach to working with people is applicable to all the work in which they are engaged. One person only dissented from this view. He said, 'I never felt happy with the non-directive approach adopted by the team. Our church people need leadership, they prefer action to talk and look to a leader for decisions'.

The lay people emphasized the relevance of the non-directive approach to 'working systematically through problems with people so that they find their own solutions rather than adopting ready-made solutions'. One person said that its use results in 'more satisfactory . . . consultations between clergy and laity, lessening the traditional arbitrary approach of the clergy'. Another said that 'the Church will cease to have any relevance to a society which will not accept the paternalistic or authoritarian approach if it does not adopt the community development approach'. It was generally agreed that the effective use of this approach in local churches 'depends upon the vicar's backing'.

The executive said that they could use the approach in schemes and conferences of the kind in which the team had been engaged, but that they could not see how to use it in the work of the council as a whole. The thought of changing from their traditional democratic approach to a non-directive approach in such a complex organization at a time when the team's withdrawal was imminent, overwhelmed them because of the difficulties and the work involved in doing so. And that, they said, is why they did not use the team or their methods in re-structuring the council. (It was obviously right for the executive not to undertake a task of which they did not feel capable. They had made a sound assessment of the difficulty of the task. The council is a difficult area of work because it is inclusive of people and organizations who hold very different convictions and views about Christianity, the church and the world. In such a situation it is easier to promote faction than development. All of this adds up to the fact that some aspects of ecumenical development will occur only as more people become capable of taking effective non-directive action in inter-church work.)

The clergy and the fraternal said that the team's approach was applicable to work with people in the whole area of church and community work and especially to 'dealing with people who have complaints'; to counselling; to discussions with church leaders; to enlisting workers; to acting as leader of a group; to 'enabling people to meet and discuss their own needs and problems and share information so that they can reach sensible and realistic decisions'; to 'large gatherings of parishioners such as the annual general meeting (of the church), parish council meetings and with classes of children'; to helping people to consider their beliefs; to the work in which the laity are engaged; and to inter-church work. They illustrated what they said with examples of how with some success they had in fact applied the approach.

A clergyman who moved into the area during the second year the team was in Ronsey wrote, 'My own work has been considerably helped by the team's systematic and diagrammatic methods of thought. I am impressed by the far-reaching effects of a short and simple introduction to these methods. Church meetings would become twice as effective if their members were helped to think in this way. I'm trying to teach mine! Can the gospel be spread without it becoming complex and thus losing its effectiveness?'

HOW THE TEAM COULD HAVE CONTRIBUTED MORE

Most people said that within the 'given terms of reference the team could not possibly have given more time, energy, concern and interest or achieved more'. But both the first and second assessments showed that some people thought that members of the team could have contributed more if they had used the non-directive approach more skilfully and applied it more widely. (Of itself this is an assessment of the value the local people attached to the approach.)

Some felt that the team members could have contributed more if they had conducted training sessions especially for the council and the executive and group leaders and if they had helped more groups to work systematically at their problems.

For the most part, people felt that the team 'showed the right restraint, coming in where and when help was asked for'. But many felt that the team members would have contributed more if one some occasions they had been more forceful in explaining how they and the non-directive approach could be used and in offering their services. The clergy said, 'Our relationship allowed you to be more positive' and one person wrote 'I think the team were at times far too cautious in sharing their methods and approach with the churches unless asked to. Admittedly the team members were not out to "sell" community development, but at times I felt they held back too much and could have acted as 'catalysts" in a situation more. Grace and tact (which the team had!) are not necessarily expressed by holding back'.

A small minority thought that team members would have contributed more when working with those people who wanted 'to do things rather than talk about them' had they initially taken less time over the planning stages. One person said, 'I think one becomes reconciled to the slowness and wordiness and the patient search for accuracy of language in drawing out the key questions, testing possible answers and defining roles and functions, *if* a group has been drawn together by a common purpose and are willing to plan ahead and reserve longish chunks of time solely for working in this way.'

One clergyman said that members of the team could have contributed more had they stimulated more continuous evaluation. The fraternal thought this would not have been feasible but that it might have been helpful to ask from time to time, 'How do you think things are going?'

Records and reports were appreciated but many people thought that reports should have been 'simpler, less condensed and less technical in language'. Others thought they were too long!

Some felt that the team members should have publicized their work more, got more people involved and made themselves known to more church members. Two quotations illustrate what they felt: 'We should have liked more information, better public relations, more hand out material'. 'It might have been helpful if more had been known about the different schemes, and if ministers had been more aware of help the team could give, and had been more willing to ask for that 'expertise'.

Many people appreciated the services of worship and the devotional sessions conducted by the team and some wished there had been more opportunities for the team to do this. A clergyman said, and the fraternal agreed with him, 'The atmosphere, the prevailing spirit of the team came across well in the working sessions, but the brief opportunities for devotions make me wish a little more time for them had been possible. I realize, of course, that the main work was not devotional but there was obviously a grounding, individual and/or corporate, which gave the team its atmosphere. By just a little extension of the time . . . there might have been further inspiration and strength for overworked clergy and laity alike.'

Several people though that the team members could have contributed more if some of them had lived in Ronsey for all or part of the time and worked there over a longer period. Typical comments on this subject were: 'By one or more of the team staying in the area for part of the time continuously, or for periods, or for some days per week and, by joining in the life of each congregation or parish in turn, they would have been seen around by ordinary church members.' 'I think more churches might have become involved with the team if the period of stay had been longer . . .' (In fact, members of the team did stay in Ronsey for part of the time and they were frequently there from 9 a.m. until 11 p.m.) But some thought the team would not have achieved more by living in the area and might have achieved less by becoming involved in the life of each parish. The team members agree with this judgment although the question is an academic one because they had no choice in the matter.

NOTE: Had team members been able to apply their approach more skilfully they might have stimulated responses in the local people which could have created more openings and therefore widened the field of work, but without more resources the team could not have taken up these opportunities.

SUBSEQUENT DEVELOPMENTS

Immediately after the team's withdrawal, officers of the Ronsey Council of Churches felt the need for a full-time churches community development worker to follow up the work done by the team. They discussed this amongst themselves and then with the two full-time members of the team. The team got them to consider two ways in which a community development worker could help the churches. The *first way* was to concentrate on working with clergy and leaders in the way the team had done. The *second way* was to work with church members and their neighbours on projects. These two ways were expressed diagrammatically by the team and this greatly helped the people to compare them (p. 189). They saw that the second way could lead to the demand for more and more full-time church and community development neighbourhood workers — a demand which simply could not be met even were it desirable. On the other hand they saw that the first way would lead to clergy and lay workers, as part of their work, becoming more effective in promoting development. Ideally, they said, they wanted someone capable of working in the first way but they realized that, even if they could get the necessary funds, it would be difficult to find a suitably qualified worker. They, therefore, also considered the possibility of employing George Lovell and Catherine Widdicombe on a part-time basis *either* to train and support the best qualified person they could find *or* to perform some of the functions previously undertaken by the team.

They discussed these alternatives with the council, the clergy, the churches and the borough community development unit. It was decided to go for a full-time worker for an initial period of three years; to include a sum of money in the budget to cover consultancy help; *and* when an appointment had been made to decide what consultancy help, if any, the person appointed required.

The council and the churches said that they themselves could not afford to pay the salary of a full-time worker but they could afford the office costs. Two sources of financial support which originally seemed promising did not materialize. The council is now approaching charitable trusts in attempts to obtain the necessary funds but to date (June 1976) they have been unsuccessful.

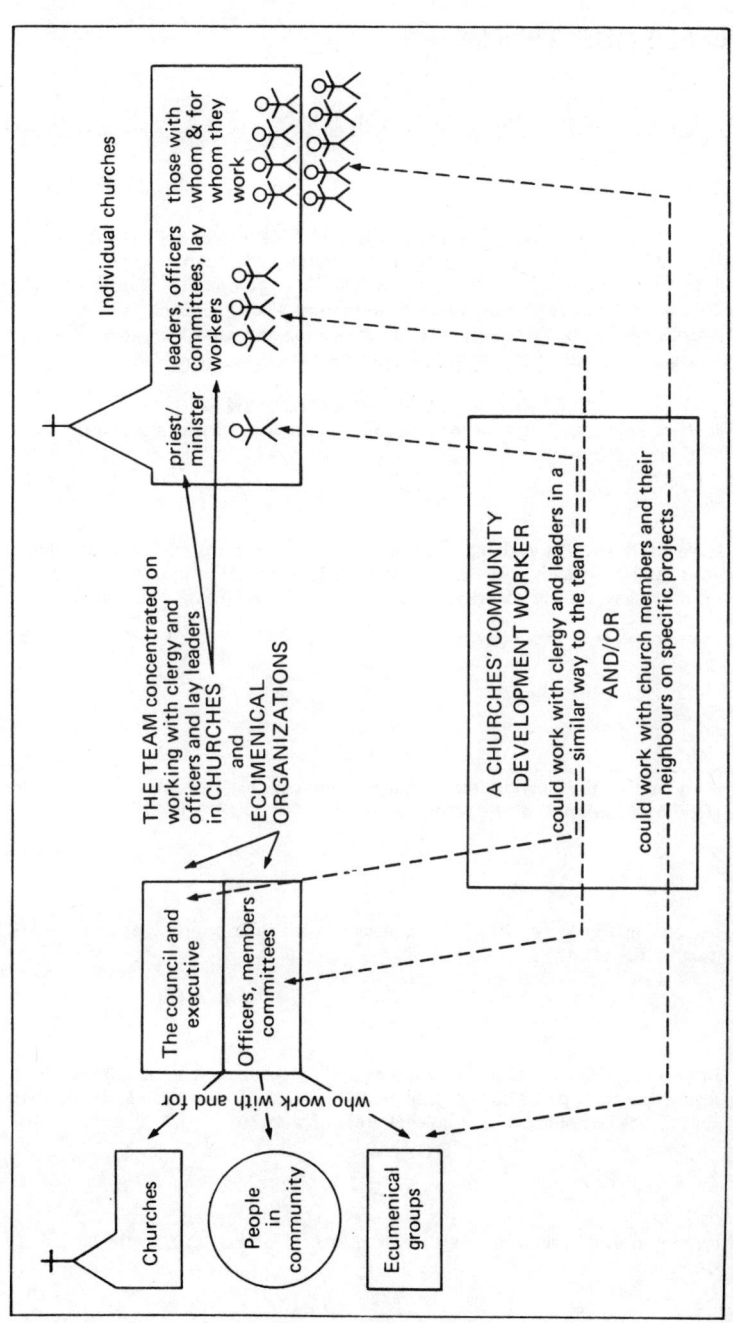

Individual churches

those with whom & for whom they work

leaders, officers committees, lay workers

priest/ minister

THE TEAM concentrated on working with clergy and officers and lay leaders in CHURCHES and ECUMENICAL ORGANIZATIONS

A CHURCHES' COMMUNITY DEVELOPMENT WORKER

could work with clergy and leaders in a similar way to the team

AND/OR

could work with church members and their neighbours on specific projects

The council and executive

Officers, members committees

who work with and for

Churches

People in community

Ecumenical groups

A CHURCH AND COMMUNITY DEVELOPMENT WORKER IN RONSEY AND THOSE WITH WHOM HE COULD WORK

SAMPLE QUESTIONNAIRE

Please return this paper within ten days.
We need it by 25 November if possible. THANK YOU!

To the clergy

CHURCH AND COMMUNITY DEVELOPMENT WORK IN RONSEY

This paper is about different aspects of the church and community development work in which the clergy and the project team have co-operated during the past three years. It gives you an opportunity to say just what you think and feel about the work undertaken by the team. If, in answering any questions, there is inadequate space on this form please use a separate sheet.

SECTION ONE: YOU AND YOUR CHURCH

1. Is there anything you wish to say about the discussions which led to the team working in Ronsey?

2. Have there been any changes, good or bad, in your church, your people or your ministry which you feel are attributable, in whole or in part, to members of the team and the work they have done? If so, please give illustrations.

3. Do you feel that any of these changes, good or bad, are likely to continue after the withdrawal of the team?

4. Do you attribute any of these changes to particular approaches or methods used by the team?

5. In general, do you feel the approaches and methods used by members of the team have any application to your work and that of your church? If so, what approaches and methods and in what areas of work?

6. Have you any suggestions as to how members of the team might have contributed more?

7. Did you attend the 'Clergy Course' (October – December 1972); Yes/No*
   Did you attend the 'Clergy-Team Meetings' that followed the course (January
   – June 1973)?   Yes/No
   Have you subsequently found them helpful? If so, in what ways?

8. Can you suggest any ways in which they might have been improved?

9. Please say what led you and/or your church to become involved or not to
   become involved in church and community development work with the team.

* Cross out whichever does not apply.

SECTION TWO: INTER-CHURCH RELATIONSHIPS AND ACTIVITIES

1. Did you take part in:

Fraternal meetings attended by the team?	Yes/No
Executive meetings?	Yes/No
Ordinary meetings of the Council of Churches?	Yes/No
The Open Council Meeting 'Sharing Experiences' in February 1974 at St Saviours Hall?	Yes/No
The Council Conference 'Situations Vacant?' in March 1974 at the Y.M.C.A?	Yes/No
Any inter-church projects in which the team participated (eg. G.N.S., Open Youth Work in the Victoria Park Area, 'Mothers under Stress)?	Yes/No

2. Have there been any changes, good or bad, in inter-church relationships which
   you feel are attributable, in whole or in part, to members of the team and the
   work they have done?
   If so, please give illustrations.

3. Do you feel that any of these changes are likely to continue after the withdrawal of the team?

4. Do you attribute any of these changes to particular approaches and methods used by the team?

5. In general, do you feel that the approaches and methods used by members of the team have any application to inter-church relationships? If so, what approaches and methods and in what ways?

6. Have you any suggestions as to how members of the team might have contributed more to inter-church work?

SECTION THREE: OTHER COMMENTS

Thank you!

Please return to Miss C Widdicombe, 125 Waxwell Lane, Pinner, HA5 3ER

PART FIVE: CONCLUSIONS AND IMPLICATIONS

1 Development in Ronsey

The team attributes the changes that occurred in Ronsey to six principal and interrelated factors:

— good local ecumenical co-operation;
— the conviction that community development is consonant with Christianity and relevant to the mission of the Church;
— working in the local community without intent to proselytize;
— the use of the non-directive approach;
— the emphasis on working with clergy and lay leaders;
— the emphasis on working through the local institutional churches.

GOOD LOCAL ECUMENICAL CO-OPERATION

The fraternal, the council and the executive made a crucial contribution towards getting church and community development ideas considered thoroughly and critically before Project 70-75 was located in Ronsey and throughout the time the team worked in the area: they promoted training programmes; they played a major part in establishing, co-ordinating and extending a programme of work which promoted development in individual churches and enabled ecumenical groups to undertake tasks that churches could not do separately; they took initiatives in establishing working relationships with the borough community development unit; and they provided a network of communication. In short they proved to be extremely effective groups through which to promote overall development and to introduce people to new ideas.

THE CONVICTION THAT COMMUNITY DEVELOPMENT IS CONSONANT WITH CHRISTIANITY AND RELEVANT TO THE MISSION OF THE CHURCH

The clergy and laity in Ronsey agreed to Project 70-75 being located in their area but only after they had satisfied themselves that what they understood of church and community development work was consonant with Christianity and relevant to the mission of the Church. Theological reflection — an integral part of the training sessions and schemes — was better informed and therefore more rewarding when clergy, laity and team were thinking about their own experiences of the non-directive approach to community development. Gradually several things became clearer.

First, that the emphasis on the non-directive approach to church and community development work does not deny the need and efficacy of those things which Christians believe God alone has done and continues to do for their salvation through Jesus Christ, the Holy Spirit and the ministry of the Church. It complements what God does for us by helping us to do those things which each of us must do to work out our own salvation.

Second, that the non-directive approach was the most effective way of helping Christians and non-Christians to do those things which no one else can do for them: to think, decide and choose responsibly for themselves; to form their own attitudes; to formulate their own beliefs about God and man, life and death; to decide what of themselves they will share with others; to live their own lives; to endure their own pain and to die their own deaths.

Third, that, although we all depend on the vast range of personal, medical, social, scientific, technical, industrial and economic services which create and maintain the environment in which we live, such services and environment, no matter how excellent they are, do not of themselves make better people, because people grow from within. And the distinctive value of the non-directive approach is its unique power to promote that growth from within. And this is consistent with Christian belief about the relationship between man and his environment.

Fourth, that the non-directive approach helped the team and those with whom they worked to love themselves and each other, to love their neighbours as themselves, to love God with their mind and strength as well as with their heart and soul and to strive for that 'mature manhood measured by nothing less than the full stature of Christ'.

As people became sure that this approach was theologically valid so they became more confident and effective in using it.

WORKING IN THE LOCAL COMMUNITY
WITHOUT INTENT TO PROSELYTIZE

Clergy and laity expressed their ultimate Christian aim for individuals and society differently according to their theological persuasion and denominational background but each church was doing something to achieve three principal objectives:

1. to initiate people into the Christian faith and the Church;
2. to assist Christians to mature and develop by helping them to understand Christianity, to live Christian lives and to build Christian communities;
3. to help non-Christians to develop by helping them to meet their personal and social needs and to build up the neighbourhood community.

All three objectives can be pursued concurrently and effectively in church work and the second and third in church-community and community work. It is, however, counter productive to use church-community and community work solely as a means of bringing people into the church especially if overtly altruistic activities are used as a cover for attempts to proselytize. Most church people in Ronsey realized this. The more genuinely altruistic they were, the more effective they were in the work they did with non-church people and not surprisingly, people came to trust the Church more, to believe it was really interested in them and to be more positive towards it, the clergy and the church workers. In fact, churches and clergy were taken more seriously by the community when they were working in the community without intent to proselytize.

THE USE OF THE NON-DIRECTIVE APPROACH

Throughout, the team adopted a non-directive approach towards the local people and amongst other things this meant that local clergy and lay people planned and directed their own work programmes; got used to more systematic ways of working and problem-solving; and began to learn how they themselves could apply the non-directive concept to their work.

Local people planned and directed their own work programmes

The clergy, and then their churches and the Council of Churches, decided whether or not they wanted the project located in Ronsey, and the team took great care to ensure that those who had local responsibility, power and authority were not by-passed. Similarly the local people decided what the initial work programme should be; that the emphasis should change from the task force idea to action by the local institutional churches; and what direction the subsequent work programme should take.

Great dividends accrued from working in this way: the people felt really committed to the decisions they themselves had made; accepted responsibility for them; did all they could to work them out; and never went back on them. They were in control and knew that they were.

Local people got used to more systematic ways of working and problem solving

Local people, in one way or another, found it helpful in relation to their work:
– *to clarify just what they wanted to achieve in the lives of those with whom they worked and why*
(Two outstanding examples of this are the good neighbour scheme and the community work clergy task group. Both groups found it difficult to arrive at a clear statement of overall purpose because it involved them considering the beliefs, attitudes and philosophy by which they were motivated – it was, therefore, amongst other things a theological

exercise. It led them to distinguish between beliefs, purposes and objectives and this was something which they did not normally do. Beliefs were the assumptions about God and man underlying their purposes. Purposes were the ends people wished to achieve, and objectives were the stages by which they achieved them. So if, for example, a person's purpose is to love and care for the sick in underdeveloped countries in the name of Jesus Christ, his first objective is likely to be to qualify as a doctor and the second, to become a medical missionary. The fact that the clergy and laity clarified their beliefs, their purposes, and their objectives and stated them in their own words helped them to make critical choices, assess progress and consciously direct their efforts towards their self-chosen goals.);

– *to decide exactly what they could do to promote overall development and how they would do it*

(Had they decided to emphasize church work to the exclusion of other work they would have lost contact with the local community and failed to help them meet their non-religious needs; if, on the other hand, they had emphasized church-community or community work to the exclusion of church work they might have lost their Christian identity and failed to meet their own religious needs and those of others.);

– *to decide in what situations they would work to promote their purposes and through what specific objectives*

– *to decide which approaches they were going to adopt towards working with people in specific situations*

(Generally speaking they chose to work *directively* if they felt they must be the ultimate judge for people of what was good for them, and *non-directively* if they felt they ought to help others judge for themselves what was good for them.[1] Making this choice was both a theological and pragmatic exercise: it involved deciding which approach best fitted the worker's beliefs, attitudes and purposes *and* the people *and* the practicalities of the situation.);

– *to get as clear a picture as possible of each of their work situations*

– *to assess and evaluate how effectively they were promoting their purposes through pursuing their chosen objectives*

(This helped to give purposeful direction to the people's work, schemes and enterprises).

The order in which people worked out these steps varied: what was important was that they themselves clarified their beliefs and purposes, chose their objectives, approaches and activities and evaluated their work and its results. Doing these things led them to work far more sytematically than they normally did. They are set out diagramatically on p. 199.

---

[1] cf. T.R. Batten, *The Non-Directive Approach to Group and Community Work* (London, 1967), p. 3.

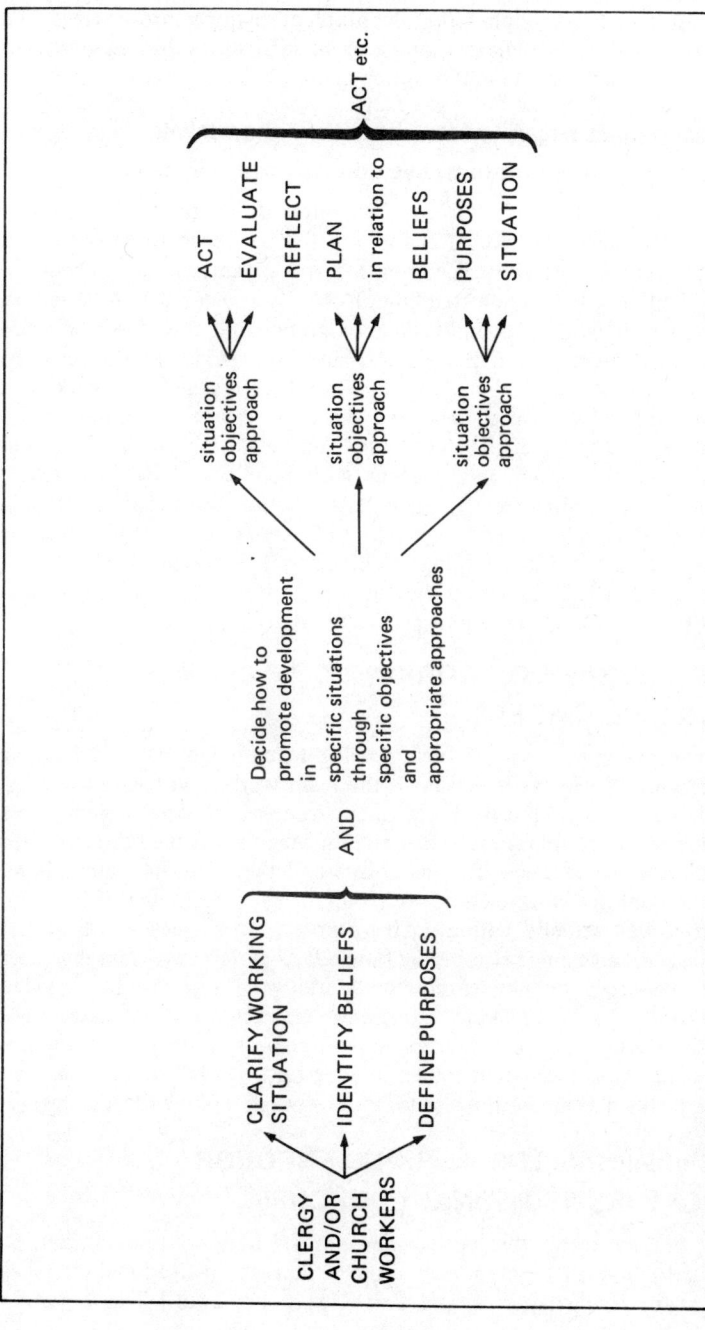

CLERGY AND/OR CHURCH WORKERS

CLARIFY WORKING SITUATION

IDENTIFY BELIEFS

DEFINE PURPOSES

AND

Decide how to promote development in specific situations through specific objectives and appropriate approaches

situation
objectives
approach

situation
objectives
approach

situation
objectives
approach

ACT
EVALUATE
REFLECT
PLAN   in relation to
BELIEFS
PURPOSES
SITUATION

ACT etc.

CHURCH, CHURCH COMMUNITY AND COMMUNITY WORK: BASIC ELEMENTS IN A SYSTEMATIC WAY OF WORKING

Also, the local people found the problem solving approach described on p. 46 very helpful in relation to all the difficulties they encountered in working with people in the church and in the community.

Local people began to learn how they themselves could apply the non-directive concept to their work

When the team entered Ronsey it found that although clergy and church workers were skilled in the directive approach to working with people and in the normal committee and organizational procedures, they had very little understanding of or skill in using the non-directive approach in work with individuals or groups and therefore the team gave high priority to training clergy and lay workers in it. However, the team members had no power over the clergy and lay workers — even if they had wanted it — and the only way in which they could hope to achieve their objective was through establishing and maintaining good working relationships with people *and* by consistently using the non-directive approach itself in the hope that the people they worked with would come to understand it and appreciate its relevance as a way of working for themselves. While in the short term this demanded discipline on the part of the team and was fraught with frustration, in the long term it produced satisfying results.

THE EMPHASIS ON WORKING WITH CLERGY AND LAY LEADERS

Implementing the decision to work with the churches involved deciding with whom to work. In the main the team worked with clergy and lay leaders but during the final assessment some people said that members of the team would have achieved more if they had worked directly with more church members. The team discussed this with the fraternal and the community work clergy task group. They thought that if the team had worked directly with church members, the clergy could have felt by-passed and could have been offended. They felt that team members had been right to concentrate on working with clergy and key lay workers while also making themselves generally known through their participation in services of worship, conferences and meetings. In fact, some of them thought members of the team might in the long term have achieved much more had they worked only with the clergy.

THE EMPHASIS ON WORKING THROUGH LOCAL INSTITUTIONAL CHURCHES

The project team, the local clergy and the laity were committed to work for overall development through the local institutional churches (cf. Part Two chapter 1 and Part Three chapter 6.) This common commitment combined with the team's ecumenical outlook meant that the team was acceptable to the vast majority of clergy and laity engaged in local church work in Ronsey, and that the work programme that evolved emphasized involving local churches in promoting development amongst their own members and neighbours.

None of the twelve consultative groups and only two of the thirty-eight advisers made any adverse comments about this approach. Most of them commended it because they too were committed to work through the institutional church and because they realized the enormous latent potential it has for overall development. They felt this approach to development had been neglected because of its difficulties. One consultative group said, 'Many church people have become involved in community projects outside the church because of their frustrating experience of working with and through the institutional church for community development.'

Two advisers, on the other hand, were highly critical of what one of them described as 'the total church-centredness of the approach'. They saw in the team's approach 'a grave danger that the church was attempting to put itself back in the centre of community life rather than as a partner in the general community dialogue'. They felt that it encouraged 'the dependence of the church on the clergy, and the neighbourhood on the church'. They said the team should have worked from the outset with people from all sections of the community, that is, 'with a structure which expressed their wish to work for the inter-related development of the church and the world'. They thought that the team ought to have urged the churches 'to enter the political arena, criticizing policies and helping to shape them because many of the problems of the area result from political decisions or neglect or bureaucratic structures'. They felt that the first concern should have been the felt needs of all those in the area. And they were convinced that the church-centred approach would not meet the needs of the underprivileged majority of the inner city which require urgent action.

Although these comments reflected the views of only two of the advisers and none of the consultative groups, they may nevertheless be representative of the views of many other people and the team took them very seriously.

The effects of the 'church-centred' approach

The local people's response to the church-centred approach and their assessment of its effect in Ronsey appears to demonstrate conclusively that the right choice was made. It proved to have all the advantages the team had hoped for[2] and this is not surprising because the Church is the organization of which the team members and those with whom they were engaged were members and workers. Thus it was within the Church and its associated ecumenical organizations that the team and the local people could discuss all the questions about beliefs, purposes and approaches to development in the light of the Christian faith, their own needs and those of their neighbours. Consequently for the local people and the team the Church was the natural point at which to start on an action research project designed to discover the implications for the *churches* of promoting the inter-related development of Christian and secular communities.

The description of the schemes and the assessment of the work done by the local people show that the approach did not produce the bad effects the two advisers feared it would. In fact it had the opposite effect. First, better working relationships were established between clergy and laity, between church and non-church people and between the clergy, the churches and the borough. Second, the church people did become more effective in meeting the needs of people in the community including some of the underprivileged. Third, some who had not previously been involved in local politics did get the Council to reverse a decision about outline planning permission for a community centre. One of the advisers having read a full account of this action and as a part of a review of the local area work as a whole, wrote: 'Perhaps most significant of all is the way in which some churches have begun to see the rewards of a longer-term, systematic approach to their community thinking and acting. This is particularly high-lighted by describing the way in which those engaged in "A community centre scheme in a Roman Catholic parish" obtained planning permission. An experience of apparent defeat appears to have been a creative learning experience for the immediate neighbourhood by inviting genuine dialogue, and a considerable process of liberation and co-operation for the local authority through the way in which stereotyped bureaucratic responses and departmental rigidities have been broken through. The spaciousness of this piece of work is delightful'.

In all this there is room for hope because it shows that churches can promote human betterment when they apply themselves seriously to

---

[2] The advantages were that 'each church would be free to evolve its own development programme tailored to its own needs and those of its immediate neighbourhood. It would give clergy and church workers experience of adopting the community development approach in their own churches before trying to use them in the community; and it would give them greater freedom to decide what they wanted to do. Therefore, through this option, the clergy and churches would be more likely to become initiators of community development processes. And this in turn would make it more likely that the work would continue after the team had withdrawn.' (cf. p. 38)

just what is involved. However, the needs are great and therefore there is no room for complacency or for action which masks the enormity of promoting overall human betterment or for depreciating any contribution because it is small in relation to the total.

During the final assessment the fraternal said that if the team had adopted the approach suggested by the two advisers very few of them and their churches would have participated in new initiatives to help the under-privileged because of their internal problems and manpower shortage, and that none of them would have taken political action. They thought that the approach adopted was the better for several reasons. It 'took seriously the fact that the theology of some Christians is church-centred whilst that of others is world-centred and it started where the churches were and worked with them until they were ready to go out into the community rather than saying that the churches should start work outside right away'. It also avoided the risk of the social work agencies and borough authorities pressurizing Christians to take on more work than they could manage. It treated clergy, they said, as what they were and wished to be, *church and community workers*, whereas the alternative treated them as *community workers* and that they did not want to be. Consequently they said, the clergy and churches were now more capable than ever before of working in the community and they 'expected to become more involved in meeting community needs and in political action in the future'. That is, those who previously would not have taken political action and who only reluctantly would have taken on new work to help the underprivileged were now prepared for the sake of others to become involved in community and in political action. This of itself is an enormous change charged with promise and hope, not least because it was self-induced and not imposed *and* because it was set within an understanding of what really contributes to human betterment and how it is achieved. Such change verges on 'conversion to the world'. Bishop Stephen Neill at the World Council of Churches Assembly at Evanston in 1954 said that the true Christian is one who has experienced three conversions: to Christ, to the Church and to the world.

The borough community development officer and worker, without any knowledge of this discussion said that the churches in Ronsey were far more involved in community work than those in other parts of the borough *and* that in their opinion every other organization in Ronsey would be more effective with their own members and would be better able to work for development with others if someone did for each of them what the team had done for the churches in Ronsey.

All this shows that it is essential to centre on the church in order that the church, in turn, can centre on others and, in partnership with other organizations and agencies, make its own distinctive contribution towards the religious, personal and community needs of its members and its neighbours. The team became more and more convinced of this as the project proceeded. Therefore, because they desperately wanted to promote the well-being of people and more especially of under-privileged people and because they are convinced that local churches have a unique contribution to make to human betterment, they worked with and through the churches for overall development.

Political action and community development

There is in what the two advisers said the assumption that political action can promote overall development as described in this report. Clearly, effective political action is essential to the well-being of any society, as are many social and community services. It can improve the amenities of the underprivileged and the poor, raise their standard of living, redistribute power and provide opportunities for more people to participate in civic affairs. It is, however, unrealistic to think that any of these changes of themselves — necessary as they may be — will generate human betterment, that is, change for the better in people as well as in their environment. It is relatively simple, given the will and the resources, to change people's environment for the better. It is an entirely different matter to stimulate real growth in people, for this is a slow and complex process in which there are no short cuts. It is the product of a long process of working *with* rather than *for* people which is potentially applicable to the work that any agency or political party does with people and should be part of their professionalism.[3] Real progress is necessarily slow.

THESE FACTORS INTER-RELATED

Clearly the factors described above are closely inter-related. The team and the local people were able to work with each other because of their commitment to work for overall development through the local institutional church without intent to proselytize and because of their non-directive approach to church and community development work. The team members' non-directive approach meant they started with the clergy and churches where they were and worked on their schemes at their pace. They helped the clergy and laity to put into practice what they believed; to clarify their purposes in relation to their beliefs and their situation; to introduce structure into their thinking and planning; and to discover how they themselves could practise the non-directive approach. All this meant that the schemes were tailor-made to fit the local people, their needs and their situation.

[3]   cf. T.R. Batten, 'The Major Issues and Future Direction of Community Development', *Community Development Journal*, vol. 9, no 2 (April 1974).

2 General conclusions and implications

The conclusions which follow are firmly based on the team's experiences in Ronsey. They are about clergy and laity and the work they do in their local churches, their ecumenical organizations and in their neighbourhoods. Because Ronsey has so much in common with other areas the team feels that the conclusions may be generally valid for them also.

CHURCH AND COMMUNITY WORK: THE GENERAL SITUATION

Conclusion 1.   That many clergy and lay workers miss opportunities of promoting betterment — both within and outside their churches — because they do not think out precisely and systematically enough just what they really want to do and how best to do it.

Conclusion 2.   That many clergy and lay workers act as though external changes — new buildings, the re-structuring of organizations, the revision of liturgies, the redistribution of power and resources — will of themselves change people for the better.

Conclusion 3.   That most clergy and lay workers tend to rely too much on directive approaches and procedures and that this reduces their effectiveness.

Conclusion 4.   That while most churches undertake *church-community work* as well as *church work*, relatively few also engage in *community work* except on an ecumenical basis.

Conclusion 5.   That many individual local churches really do want to help people in their neighbourhoods and more especially the underprivileged but are afraid that working on projects would overtax their limited manpower resources.

Conclusion 6.   That nevertheless such churches either singly or together have considerable potential in manpower and buildings for promoting betterment among church and non-church people in their neighbourhoods.

CLERGY AND LAITY: THEIR REACTION TO THE NON-DIRECTIVE APPROACH TO COMMUNITY DEVELOPMENT

Conclusion 7. That only a few clergy and lay workers are skilled in the non-directive approach and that most of them use it in counselling rather than in working with groups and communities.

Conclusion 8. That most clergy and lay workers initially either do not understand the non-directive approach or they are sceptical about its effectiveness or they are prejudiced against it or they are exasperated by the time that people require to think and decide for themselves.

Conclusion 9. That clergy and laity will not readily adopt the non-directive way of working with people until they have satisfied themselves:
— that the non-directive approach helps people to complement God's saving work by making that contribution towards their own salvation which they alone can make;
— that its emphasis on encouraging people to think and decide for themselves does not diminish the Christian's ability to respond to divine inspiration and the leading of the Spirit and does not inhibit people from acting spontaneously and intuitively when required to do so;
— that it is part of their mission to work *with* people in the church or in the community.

Conclusion 10. That the more convinced Christians become that the non-directive approach to development is a proper expression of their basic beliefs about God and man, the more effective they become in using it.

Conclusion 11. That clergy and lay workers who 'want to get on with things' come to value the non-directive approach only when they discover for themselves that it can lead to more effective action and can save time and energy.

Conclusion 12. That clergy and lay workers only become convinced through satisfying experiences of the approach in relation to their work and by assessing both the approach and its results for themselves.

Conclusion 13. That most people who experience the approach become convinced of its value to the Church's ministry and mission and that it is as relevant to work within the churches as it is to the work with people outside the churches.

Conclusion 14. That most people – and especially those clergy of whom a 'strong lead' is expected – require a considerable amount of help in making the transition from directive to non-directive ways of working with people.

LOCAL CHURCHES AND DEVELOPEMENT: AN OVERALL CONCLUSION

Conclusion 15. That local clergy and lay workers are most effective in promoting development of their own members and their neighbours when:

    (*a*) they work *with* each other through their local institutional churches;

    (*b*) they co-operate with people of other denominations and organizations without intent to proselytize;

    (*c*) they are convinced that community development is relevant to the mission of the church;

    (*d*) they use the non-directive approach in the church and in the community with skill, understanding and a deep desire to promote human betterment.

SOME IMPLICATIONS FOR CHURCH AUTHORITIES

One major purpose of the project was to enable those at all levels of the Church with authority and influence to think realistically for themselves about the application to their work of the non-directive approach to community development, to determine what implications it might have for them and to decide what action, if any, they would take. Hopefully, this report will help them to do this. Experience gained on Project 70-75 suggests, *inter alia*, that those who wish to promote betterment through local churches are likely to be more effective if:

1. they start with the members of each local church and ecumenical organization where they are and encourage them to develop their own programme by thinking out for themselves what they themselves can do;

2. they recognize that the local minister or priest and his lay workers are the key people in determining what happens in their own local church;

3. they provide training to help their clergy and lay workers to understand, value and use the non-directive approach in church, church-community and community work and in ecumenical work; (sometimes this training will be most effective when separate provision is made for clergy as it enables them to think through things more freely).

4. they provide their clergy and lay workers with subsequent non-

directive consultancy help;

5. they make adequate provision for training and consultancy services when budgetting for church and community development schemes;
6. they encourage and promote an action research element in all church and community development work both for what it can contribute to the work itself and for the information and guidance of workers elsewhere.

POSTSCRIPT

Project 70-75 has deepened the team members' conviction that Christian ministry and mission must at the same time help to meet the material, human and spiritual needs of people *and* that Christians and non-Christians can work together to promote human betterment and thus make a contribution towards realizing God's purpose for mankind. It has also deepened their conviction that the non-directive approach to community development is highly productive in promoting change for the better both within the local churches and within the neighbourhoods which they serve. The final assessment illustrates this: the local clergy and laity were impressed by the changes that occurred in themselves as a result of working together for a better church and a better community; they greatly valued the increase in mutual understanding and the growth of co-operation and friendship between the clergy and laity of churches of different denominations; and they also valued the more profitable discussions and the more meaningful acts of joint worship. All these things were symptoms of changes within the clergy and the laity which in turn helped to make them more effective change agents in the work they did with others.

3 The need for training and consultancy help

This report describes how a team with the assistance of their consultant helped clergy and laity to promote development in their area through training them to use the non-directive approach and supporting them as they did so. Few clergy and laity are trained in this approach. Therefore, if similar developments are to occur in other areas it would seem that training needs to be provided for clergy and lay workers in the theory and practice of the non-directive approach to working with people.

Two distinct but interrelated kinds of training are needed: the one, opportunities for both clergy and lay people at all levels of the Church to study the ideas underlying the non-directive approach and the relevance of these ideas to the work and mission of the Church; and the other, opportunities for them to learn the skills they need in order to apply these ideas in the work they do with people. This report describes two local training programmes, one for clergy and one for laity (cf. Part Two chapters 2 and 3). These training sessions played a crucial role in promoting development in Ronsey. For the future, one can envisage some central training programmes as well as local ones.

Clergy and laity also need consultancy help of the kind described in Part Three chapter 1 and of the kind the team received from Dr T.R. Batten. He acted as consultant to the team through meetings with the full-time workers. He adopted a non-directive approach in this consultancy relationship and full responsibility for the project remained always with the team. These arrangements proved effective. The team members decided when they wanted to consult Dr Batten and what they wished to discuss, and took the initiative in making the necessary arrangements. They prepared carefully for these consultations by making as clear a statement of the relevant issues as they could.

Dr Batten, from his wide experience of community development work, raised any questions he thought relevant. Because he was highly identified with the purposes of the project and acting non-directively, consultant and team members were very open with each other. The team members rarely found themselves becoming defensive or ill at ease no matter how revealing and penetrating the questions raised by the consultant were. He also helped the team members to see the range of possible alternative courses of action open to them and to select those objectives and programmes of work through which they were most likely to achieve their purposes.

This way of working was adopted because it helped Dr Batten to maintain an objective position from which he could best view the project and act as consultant. For similar reasons he did not visit Ronsey. This meant that the full-time workers had to provide the information which enabled him to understand the nature of the situation or the problems about which they were seeking his help. As far as possible Dr Batten made himself available to team members whenever they wanted to see him. In all they had fifty one consultations over the six years.

It is this experience which compels the team to conclude that, *without in-service training and some consultancy help local clergy and laity are unlikely to be able to practice the non-directive approach effectively, for while the approach is deceptively simple to describe, it is surprisingly difficult to practise.* The team certainly could not have put the approaches into practice without the training and consultancy support they have received from Dr and Mrs T.R. Batten and it is significant that when the team withdrew from Ronsey the clergy and Council sought to continue the training and consultancy support provided by the team.

It should be emphasized that the aim of this training is *not* to turn clergy and church workers into community workers, but to enable them to learn how they, as clergy and church workers, can use the non-directive approach in their work in the church and in the community. Consequently this kind of training should include opportunities for clergy and laity to reflect theologically on what they are learning and doing.

Unfortunately there is a shortage of trainers and courses. Thus a Report [1] adopted by the Conference of the Methodist church in 1973 stated:

'A number of Universities and an increasing number of Further Education and Colleges of Technology and Art organize courses in community work and community development . . . Nevertheless, whether training is seen in terms of orientation towards the concepts of community development or in-service or pre-service training, much more needs to be done by the Church if it is to practise more widely this approach to working with people. It appears that there are more opportunities offered through existing courses for people to study the

---

[1] *Terms of Reference:* To consider the implications of the Youth Service Development Council Report, Youth and Community Work in the 70s for the whole Church and not just the Youth Department, and to make recommendations to the Conference of 1973 with special reference to the emerging concepts of Community Development.

Membership of Working Party: The Rev. Douglas S. Hubery (Chairman); The Rev. Deryck Collingwood; The Rev. Alan Davies; Mr Derek Hanson; The Rev. John Hastings; The Rev. George Lovell; The Rev. Dr Fred W. Milson; The Rev. Trevor T. Rowe; The Rev. Harry Salmon; Miss Eileen A.H. Tressidder; The Rev. George W. Cloke (Secretary).

ideas underlying community development than there are for them *(a)* learn the skills they need in order to apply these ideas; *(b)* reflect on the ideas theologically; and *(c)* relate the ideas to practical church-community work situations. Also there remains a severe shortage of those who are capable, qualified and sufficiently experienced to train others in church and community development work. This situation will continue unless those responsible for theological training and those holding senior appointments at Connexional, District and Circuit levels, are able, having considered the ideas underlying community development work, to provide more training opportunities for ministers and lay people.

The key to the situation is an in-service training programme so organized that it will: enable ministers and lay people to practise the community development approach to working with people in their church and community work and to reflect theologically about what they are doing; support those involved in this kind of work; train more trainers; provide information to help determine the most effective forms of orientation, pre-service and in-service training. If this training is effective it will create a climate of opinion in which it will be easier for those trained in these approaches to practise what they have learned.

Organizing such an in-service training programme is feasible and would best be done ecumenically. It would have the flexibility and adaptability to meet the current situation and prepare the way for future developments. It would, however, require the informed support of those in key positions. Without that support the Church may find itself regarded by many as a patronising agency and its own life stultified by out-worn notions of spiritual autocracy'.

In order to make a contribution to these unmet training needs the Division of Ministries of the Methodist church has sponsored several ten-day residential in-service training courses in church and community development work for people from different areas and denominations. Four such courses have been held from 1971 to 1976. And, as a direct follow-through of these courses, the report quoted above and the work of Project 70-75, the Methodist and Roman Catholic churches have recently been instrumental in setting up Avec, a self-supporting ecumenical service agency for church and community work.[2] It is staffed by two full-time itinerant trainers who provide courses, both centrally and locally, in the non-directive approach to working with people for clergy and laity engaged in local church and neighbourhood work. They aim to relate the training directly to the situations in which church clergy and laity work.

[2] Further information can be obtained from Avec a Service Agency for Church and Community Work, 7 Reddons Road, Beckenham, Kent BR3 2LY.

Epilogue

Project 70-75 was an action research project designed to explore on behalf of church people everywhere the relevance and practicability of the non-directive approach to church and community development work. This report describes how the work was done and with what results, and the authors earnestly invite those who read it to let them know:

— whether or not and why or why not they consider the non-directive approach to church and community work as here described consonant with the mission of the Church?
— whether or not they feel that the approaches and methods used have any special relevance for their own particular church, and if so in what areas of its work?

Comments received in reply to these two questions will be of great value in providing more information about the opportunities and the problems awaiting churches entering this relatively new field. [1]

[1] Please address any comments to the authors
c/o Avec, A Service Agency for Church and Community Work, 7 Reddons Road, Beckenham, Kent BR3 2LY.

Appendix I

List of those consulted about the project with the positions they held at the time.

Those consulted from March to December 1971

Revd John Ainsley, Secretary, Youth Committee, Church of England Board of Education; *John Baker*, on the staff of the Institute for Community Studies; *Miss J.C. Barbour*, Secretary, Central Churches Group, National Council of Social Services (N.C.S.S.); *Edwin Barker*, Secretary, Church of England Board of Social Responsibility; *Mgr Joseph C. Buckley*, Roman Catholic parish priest in Westbury on Trym and Chairman, Clergy In-Service Training Committee; *Rt Rev. Christopher Butler*, Auxiliary Bishop of Westminster and President Social Morality Council; *Rev. David B. Clark*, Methodist minister in Blackheath and Secretary of the Methodist Sociological Group. *Rev. David V. Clark*, Presbyterian minister in Stepney; the late *Rev. Dr Leslie Davison*, Secretary, Home Mission Department of the Methodist Church; *Professor David Donniston*, Director, Centre for Environmental Studies; *A.N. Fairbairn*, Director of Education, Leicestershire; *Rt Rev. Launcelot Fleming*, Dean of Windsor; *Brian Frost*, Director, Notting Hill Ecumenical Centre; *George Goetschius*, Lecturer in Social Work Studies, London School of Economics (L.S.E.): *Rev. Dr Kenneth Greet*, Secretary of the Methodist Conference; *Rt Rev. Augustine Harris*, Auxiliary Bishop of Liverpool and Episcopal member of the Commission for Social Welfare; the late *Cardinal John C. Heenan*, Archbishop of Westminster; *David Hobman*, Director of Age Concern; *Rev. Michael Hollings*, Roman Catholic parish priest in Southall; *John E.T. Hough*, Secretary, Social Responsibility Department of the British Council of Churches (B.C.C.).

Keith Jackson, Assistant Director and Head of the Social Studies Division, University of Liverpool; *Very Rev. Eric James*, Canon Precentor of Southwark Cathedral and Chairman of the Advisory Group on Social Sciences to the Greater London Churches' Consultative Group (G.L.C.C.G.); *Rev. R.M.C. Jeffrey*, Secretary, Department of Mission and Unity, B.C.C.; *Rev. John Johannsen-berg*, Minister of the Rock Church Centre, Liverpool; *David Jones*, Principal Designate, National Institute for Social Work Training; *Islwyn Jones*, Principal Training Officer, Social Services Department, Leicester; *Dr R.A.B. Leaper*, Professor of Social Administration, University of Exeter; *Jim Leighton*, Senior Lecturer, Department of Community and Youth Work, Leicester College of Education; *Miss Elizabeth Littlejohn*, Head of the Community Works Division, N.C.S.S.; *Rt Rev. Gerald Mahon*, auxiliary Bishop of Westminster; *Rev. G.A.D. Mann*, General Secretary, Free Church Federal Council; *Earl of March and Kinrara*, Chairman of the Board for Mission and Unity of the General Synod of the Church of England; *Rev. Colin Marchant*, Baptist minister and Warden of Lawrence Hall, Plaistow; *Rev. Charles Meachin*, Secretary for Mission of the Congregational Church; *Rev. Dr Fred Milson*, Head of the Youth and Community Section, Westhill College of Education; *Rev. Harry Morton*, Secretary, Methodist Overseas Mission Department; *Foster Murphy*, Secretary, Youth Department, B.C.C.

Owen Nankivell, Treasurer, Methodist Board of Lay Training and Chairman of the Methodist Sociological Group. *A.W.A. Oliver*, Secretary, London Mission of the Methodist Church; *Edward Oliver*, Secretary, Social Morality Council; *Rev. John Packer*, Deputy Director, Urban Ministry Project; *John Prickett* Secretary, Education Department of the B.C.C.; the late *Rt Rev. Ian Ramsey*, Bishop of Durham; *Rev. Laurence Reading*, Secretary, Adult Committee, Church of England Board of Education; *Rev. Trevor T. Rowe*, Lecturer at the Queen's College, Birmingham and Chairman, Board of Lay Training of the Methodist Church; *Rev. George W. Sails*, Secretary, Home Mission Department of the Methodist Church; *Rev. Denys J. Saunders*, Communications Training Secretary, Conference of British Missionary Societies; *Sir Frederic Seebohm*, Chairman, National Institute for Social Work Training; *Rt Rev. David Sheppard*, Bishop of Woolwich; *Canon Eric Shipman*, Vicar of Plaistow and a member of the Greater London Churches' Consultative Group; *Leslie Smith*, Secretary, Social Responsibility Council of the Religious Society of Friends; *Mrs Muriel Smith*, Home Office Community Development Project; *Rev. Lord Soper*, Superintendent minister of the West London Mission.

Canon Norman Todd on the staff of the William Temple College; *Rev. Leonard Tyler*, Principal, William Temple College; *Rev. Herbert Veal*, Chairman, Archdiocese of Westminster Schools Commission; *Rev. Stephen Verney*, Canon of Windsor; *R.P. Walsh*, Secretary, Social Welfare Commission of the Roman Catholic Church; *Miss Pauline Webb*, Director, Board of Lay Training of the Methodist Church; *Anthony White*, Senior Youth and Community Officer, Greater London Youth and Community Service of the Methodist Church; *Rev. George Whitfield*, General Secretary, Church of England Board of Education; *Miss Barbara Wollaston*, Secretary, Greater London Churches Consultative Group; *Miss Audrey Wood*, Secretary, Social, Economic and Penal Affairs of the Social Responsibility Council of the Religious Society of Friends; *Rt Rev. Derek Worlock*, Bishop of Portsmouth; *Rev. Dr Brian A. Wren*, Congregational minister and Programme Secretary, Churches' Action for World Development; *Dame Eileen Younghusband J.P.*, Chairman of the Study Group on Community Work Training set up by the Calouste Gulbenkien Foundation.

Those consulted from January to May 1972

Raymond T. Clarke, JP, Head of National Organizations Division, N.C.S.S.: *Giles Ecclestone*, Secretary, Church of England Board of Social Responsibility; *David French*, Secretary, Central Churches Group, N.C.S.S.: *Rev. John Hammersley*, Anglican priest in Lincoln City Centre Team Ministry; *Richard Hauser*, International Social Planning Unit, University of Nottingham; *Rev. Cyril Lucraft*, Link Minister in Hackney, United Reformed Church; *Mrs Kit Russell*, Senior Lecturer and Field Work Tutor, LSE; *Miss Eileen Tressider*, Lecturer in Education, Sociology and Youth Work, Christ Church College, Canterbury; *John Ward*, Head of Training and Development, N.C.S.S.

List of Consultative Groups

The Church of England Board of Education
The Church of England Board of Social Responsibility
The Churches Consultative Group, National Council of Social Service, which disbanded in 1974
The Commission for Social Welfare, a Committee of the Roman Catholic Bishops' Conference of England and Wales
The Community Development Group of the Board of Lay Training, since 1974 of the Division of Ministries of the Methodist Church
The Friends' Social Responsibility Council
The Greater London Churches Consultative Group, through the Advisory Group on Social Sciences
The Greater London Youth and Community Service of the Methodist Church
The Mission Committee of the Congregational Church which, in 1973, became part of the Church and Society Committee of the United Reformed Church
The Social Morality Council
The Social Responsibility Department of the British Council of Churches now known as the Division of Community Affairs
The Sociological Group of the Methodist Church

Appendix II
Background notes
on the local area

The early history of the churches in Ronsey, apart from that of the Roman Catholics was closely related to the development of the area from a rural to an urban community. The expansion speeded up dramatically in the 1870's when railways enabled people to live in Ronsey and work in London. Prospectors bought up large estates and built both closely packed terraced houses and large family dwellings – the latter for the middle classes who were moving out from over-crowded central London.

From the 1870's to the early 1900's people continued to move into the area and they built and filled churches. New Anglican parishes were formed. People of other denominatings who had come to live in the area, built churches seating between 600 and 1,000 people (and even some of those soon proved too small). For the next fifty years most churches continued to expand, their services were packed and Sunday schools of 300 scholars were the norm.

During this century Ronsey has continued to change like most other urban areas: many people moved out to the suburbs whilst others moved in from central London and overseas. Consequently in 1971 Ronsey was a very much more 'mixed' housing area than it was at the turn of the century. Its population was also mixed, for it contained many Greeks, Turkish Cypriots, West Indians, Indians, Pakistanis, Irish and some Poles, and the people of each nationality tended to settle in one area and 'take it over'.

Many of the population were unskilled manual workers and clerical workers but some were executive and professional people.

Progressively more church people left the area than moved in and some of those who remained no longer went to church. Consequently congregations declined rapidly. For the most part, however, the churches continued to minister in much the same way as they did during their heyday. They kept up old traditions and tried to recover their past glories but the struggle to do this and maintain their old, large and progressively under-used premises was a losing battle for all but the Catholics whose congregations grew steadily. Gradually pressure of events, ageing congregations, lack of manpower and sheer economics led some churches to reappraise their work.

In 1967 a large number of inter-church groups in Ronsey followed a series of studies conducted by the laity entitled *The People Next Door*. This led to most of the churches in the area inaugurating a Council of Churches. They modelled it on the pattern recommended by the

British Council of Churches. It covered the area known as Ronsey — two and a half square miles with a population of some 55,000 — and part of two Anglican and two Roman Catholic deaneries and two Methodist circuits. It had sixteen member churches of seven different denominations served by eighteen clergy. In 1972 the combined membership of these churches was about 4,500, of these 2,900 were Roman Catholics, 2,000 in one parish and 900 in the other. The number of people on the parish roll in the Anglican churches varied from 220 to 30 but most of them had about 100. The membership of the other churches varied from 190 to 50 but most of them were about 100.

The worship and church activities were typical of their denominations. In addition all of them were variously engaged in meeting the needs of their members and neighbours through social and sports clubs for the young, old and mentally handicapped; playgroups, and uniformed organizations for young people. This meant that church buildings (excluding Anglican and Catholic schools) were used by around 15,000 people in all, that is, some 27% of the population of Ronsey for religious and community activities. This made heavy demands upon church manpower of which there was an increasing shortage.

The information given below is about the churches and their neighbourhoods as they were in 1972.

CENTRAL RONSEY

Central Ronsey was bisected by busy roads. It had a busy shopping centre area and contained an admixture of large Victorian houses, Edwardian terraces and expensive modern property. It had four churches.

Furzedown: Baptist; built 1889; membership 190; had its own minister; liberal tradition; as membership dwindled church turned outwards to meet local community needs; planned to build a modern church and community centre; several members served on local race relations and community committees.

Priory Chapel: Congregational; built 1855; membership 90; without a minister since 1969; extensive but rambling premises; once famous preachers and good music drew large local crowds but now had a small congregation; premises used by many church and community groups including a local amateur operatic society.

St Mark: Church of England; built 1903; parish roll 27; had a priest-in-charge; strong Anglo-Catholic tradition; it was under 'benefice suspension'; vicarage used by many church and community groups; church hall venue for local Asian weddings.

St Saviour: Church of England; built 1862; parish roll 214; had a vicar and two part-time curates; two-thirds of its congregation, including many young people, came from outside the parish; noted for its liberal evangelical tradition and for supporting missionary work; large ancillary premises.

NORTH RONSEY

North Ronsey consisted of parallel roads of Edwardian terraced houses of various sizes, some modern and expensive private blocks of flats and some council blocks populated by 'problem families'. It had two churches.

Cherry Tree Road: Methodist; built 1881; rebuilt 1961; membership 75; prior to 1972 it had had its own minister; since 1972 one minister served it and Manor Road; modern premises in a complex of council flats; one third of the members immigrant; other members concerned to integrate them into the church; workers said they felt 'a tiny number surrounded by a great sea of need'; several young adults from a nearby Christian hostel were helping members to set up tenants associations.

St Patrick: Roman Catholic; built 1894; a parish of 2,000; parish priest and two curates members of a religious order; congregations over-crowded the church at each of the six Sunday masses; parishioners were Irish working class people but there were sizeable minorities of Asians, West Indians, Italians and Poles; a local convent ran an infant and a primary school; schools used for some parish activities.

SOUTH RONSEY

Mostly South Ronsey was a select suburban neighbourhood bordered by parkland. It had some of the best private houses in Ronsey and fewer immigrants than other areas. But it also had pre- and post-war council estates and some parts of the neighbourhood were deteriorating. It had six churches.

Cranstead: Baptist church and community centre; built 1873; membership 79; had its own minister; until 1953 in union with Furzedown Baptist church; premises extensively used for community work.

Holy Trinity: Church of England; built 1877; parish roll 94; had its own vicar; the church divided into a worship centre and a small modern hall; planning to run a day centre for the mentally sick.

Manor Road: Methodist; built 1873; membership 118; prior to 1972 it had its own minister, from 1972 one minister served it and Cherry Tree Road; once a successful and typical suburban Methodist church; now a small and declining congregation worshipping in a church too big for it; modern ancillary premises; excellent Sunday school using experiential methods of Christian education.

Moravian Church: built 1908; membership 116; had its own minister; originally attracted local families; becoming a London worship centre for Moravians; half the congregation and church officers were West

Indian; premises used by a West Indian pentecostal church community group and the L.E.A.

St. Giles: Church of England; built 1910; destroyed by bombing during the Second World War; rebuilt 1960; parish roll 112; had its own vicar; 'moderately Anglo-Catholic'.

St Margarets: Church of England; dated from 13th century; parish roll 118; had its own vicar and parish worker; church demolished in 1969 because it was unsafe; the congregation worshipped in a converted church hall; at one time a fashionable church, it now served local artisans and immigrants; orthodox 'middle of the road'; it had two church schools.

WEST RONSEY

West Ronsey was divided from the remainder of Ronsey by a major railway line. It contained parallel roads of Edwardian houses and far more immigrants than any of the other neighbourhoods. It was generally a 'poorer' area. It had four churches.

Ronsey Free Church: Congregational and Church of Christ, united church formed in 1969; membership 52; served by a full-time and a part-time minister; evangelical; situated on a busy thoroughfare; church modernized.

St Anselm: Roman Catholic; parish formed in 1964; parish of 900; served by a parish priest; most of congregation working class Irish immigrants half of whom remained in the area six months or less but some minority groups of Italians, West Indians, South Africans and English people; church a large ex-Methodist with ancillary premises in a poor state of repair.

St Philip: Church of England; built 1891; parish roll 78; served by a vicar; 'central churchmanship'; local population highly mobile; three-quarters of the congregation immigrants; planning to build with borough help a church youth and community centre; premises used regularly by a West Indian pentecostal group and by community groups.

Wells Road: Methodist; built 1885; membership 127; had its own minister; church, but not ancillary premises, destroyed by fire in 1970; planning to remodel premises; many neighbours were Greek and Turkish Cypriots some of whose children attended the Sunday school.